This book shines a much-needed light on the opaque world of the middle-market business sale process. Every page is packed with insider know-how, informing you on all the twists and turns that might occur, uncovering everything you didn't realize you didn't know.

—**Adrian Cronje,** Ph.D. CFA, CEO, Balentine

A must-read for any owner contemplating the sale of his or her business. You have one chance to get it right. This book will prepare you for what lies ahead. It is well organized, informative, succinct, practical, and easy to read and understand. Thanks to David for sharing his wisdom and experience.

—**Timothy P. Brown,** Founder and CEO, Sageworth

All business owners should read this book. It digests intricate concepts into simple, understandable terms. David's expertise shines through in each chapter, providing practical advice that is both accessible and actionable.

—**Kim Perell,** bestselling author

David delivers a thorough guide to navigating the complexities of selling a mid-market business. Packed with practical advice, actionable tools, and valuable insights, this playbook is a must-read for any business owner exploring an exit. From valuation to negotiation to life post-transition, David explores and explains every step of the process with clarity and confidence. Whether you're preparing to sell now or in the future, this book belongs on your shelf.

—**Eric Levin,** Chairman, Atlantic Tractor

Selling Your Business with Confidence

Selling Your Business with Confidence

A Practical Playbook for Mid-Market Owners

DAVID W. MCCOMBIE III

WILEY

Published by John Wiley & Sons, Inc., Hoboken, New Jersey.
Published simultaneously in Canada.

For general information on our other products and services or for technical support, please
contact our Customer Care Department within the United States at (800) 762-2974, outside
the United States at (317) 572-3993 or fax (317) 572-4002.

Wiley also publishes its books in a variety of electronic formats. Some content that appears in
print may not be available in electronic formats. For more information about Wiley products,
visit our web site at www.wiley.com.

Library of Congress Cataloging-in-Publication Data is Available:

ISBN 9781394213993 (cloth)
ISBN 9781394214006 (epub)
ISBN 9781394214013 (epdf)

Cover Design: Wiley
Cover Image: © Tetiana Garkusha/Getty Images
Author Photo: Courtesy of McCombie Group, LLC

SKY10086143_092624

To my beautiful family,
I love you!

Contents

Introduction

Racing heart. Sleepless nights. A sense of impending failure or doom. These are just a few of the feelings my clients have told me they experienced when selling their mid-sized business. (I remember one guy who got so anxious that he had to step outside and get some fresh air as we discussed the selling price. There are a few more who probably should have!)

I'm sure you can relate if you are an owner who has sold a mid-sized business. If you are an owner, especially on the cusp of retirement, odds are that you will be looking to sell in the next ten years and will soon relate.

The fact is that retiring Baby Boomers are creating a silver tsunami. The oldest boomers are approaching 80, while the youngest members of the generation have already reached their 60s. As this cohort of American entrepreneurs ages, more than 70% of the hundreds of thousands of middle-market businesses in the United States (those with sales between $10 million and $1 billion) are expected to sell in the coming decade. For most owners, this is the first and only time they will ever sell a business. Because the stakes are so high and there are so many "unknown unknowns," the sale process becomes an emotional and psychological roller coaster. Here are just a few of the things you will undoubtedly experience:

- It likely involves a sum of money that's an order of magnitude larger than any other transaction you've been involved with.
- It's physically exhausting. You're working two full-time jobs: running your business while managing the deal and all of its detailed requests and decisions.
- Given the stress, you may not be eating properly or sleeping well, and you may even be drinking more than you should.
- Due diligence focuses on the weakest aspects of your business, causing you to feel defensive.
- You are keeping a secret in front of everyone you encounter.
- Everything is new territory with no reference point, so you are dependent upon the judgment of your professionals.
- You're juggling hundreds of legal details in language you don't fully understand – the purchase agreement, noncompete agreements, etc. –

which have real implications, placing significant restrictions, obligations, and liabilities on you in a *personal* capacity.

- The transaction may require you to personally have uncomfortable negotiations with employees, suppliers, and customers under time constraints.
- You repeatedly perceive the deal to be on the verge of dying and then miraculously being revived.

YOU AREN'T ALONE!

"It was horrible. My wife was like my therapist. I don't drink alcohol and I don't do drugs but if I did I would be drunk the entire time. It is a very emotional period. It was awful." – Sam Parr, founder of The Hustle.

"Nothing can prepare you psychologically for what you're about to experience." – Miles Faulkner, founder of Blended Perspectives.

"I got stressed to a point that I could only compare to when I started the business. And I hoped I'd never feel that level of stress again. And I said to my advisors at the end, I don't know how you do this for a living. . . . We finished and I felt like I needed to sleep for a week. . . . felt like there was so much riding on every email and decision. There were just some really low points and it was purely just the stress level, it was incredible because I felt like if the deal didn't happen it was going to be my fault." – Mark Wright, founder of Climb Online

---

I've closed billions of dollars in middle-market deals as an M&A (mergers & acquisitions) banker. I also know what buyers are looking for because I've been a private equity investor myself. Perhaps most importantly, I'm also an entrepreneur. I've experienced the loneliness, the sleepless nights, and the anxiety associated with making payroll, managing challenging employees, and overcoming hurdles through sheer willpower.

Through trial and error (and some good mentors), I've been involved with hundreds of deals as both a seller and a buyer. Because I've made plenty of mistakes that taught me valuable lessons, I've figured out what makes a successful sale versus a stressful sale. That's why I wrote this book. If you fully understand the process, what to expect, and the implications of the range of options, you can confidently make decisions. Unfortunately, most owners enter this process woefully unprepared, underestimating the time, money, effort, and complexity involved in selling their business.

One of the most important things I've learned is that middle-market deals are unique. It is its own world with different sets of processes, buyers, valuation methodologies, and tactics. At the other end of the spectrum, the smaller mom-and-pop businesses – representing around 80% of all US companies – involve an entirely different universe of buyers, typically individual buyers looking to buy a job. Publicly available transaction data is only available for either large public deals or transactions small enough that the Small Business Administration provides financing (generally deals under a few million). Surprisingly, there is little verifiable deal data for all of those companies in the middle.

For executives of large institutional or publicly traded companies, an M&A decision is just a business decision. But for a founder or entrepreneur, the sale process is a more fraught once-in-a-lifetime event. Your personal identity is inseparable from your business. That means the decision to sell often is emotionally charged. Those emotions can spill out at various points in the sale process. Because of the outsized importance of client education and psychology, success in middle-market investment banking is more of an art than a science.

Middle-market business owners have very high stakes in their businesses, and a successful sale is essential. Estimates indicate that between 80–90% of the average middle-market owner's wealth is tied up in their business. If you're typical, you hold an undiversified investment portfolio dominated by one asset – your company. That means this single transaction will have a dramatic impact on your financial future. Getting it wrong has huge implications. With the stakes so high, the angst is correspondingly intense. Doing it well will deliver a significantly higher financial outcome with greater cash up front and fewer contingencies and strings attached.

Now that you're thinking about selling your company, you need to be fully aware of how the sales process works and – more importantly – what you don't know about this complex undertaking. The phrase "unknown unknowns" is used to describe the dangerous blind spots that accompany uncertain situations. My goal is to prepare you ahead of time for what is likely going to occur during that sale and explain to you the *why* behind it in plain English. No jargon. No legalese. Just straightforward information that will help you through what is probably the biggest business decision of your life.

Here's to a successful sale.

CHAPTER 1

The Art and Science of Selling a Company

Jonathan (not his real name) came to me wanting to sell the business he founded in the early 1970s. I could tell he was nervous by the way he clenched his jaw. He had several people approach him over the years, but he wasn't ready to sell until his wife pointed out they were well past retirement age. Now that he had made the decision, he realized he didn't have any idea how to proceed. He told me he didn't even know how to accurately price his business, much less how to handle all the paperwork that would go along with the sale. "It's basically like selling a house, right?" he asked. I had to tell him that selling a business and selling a home were two very different things. But I assured him that I could help him with every step along the way.

CONGRATULATIONS

Before we get into the nitty-gritty of selling your business, let me first offer you congratulations: You've built a company that's worth selling. As an entrepreneur, you understand how rare a feat that is. Many ventures fail or fizzle out, the victims of intense competition, economic forces, or lack of access to capital. Of course, plenty of business owners manage to build profitable little businesses that support their families and a few employees. What you've accomplished is far more difficult: You've constructed a viable middle-market business with loyal customers and a stable workforce. Over the years, you've refined systems for keeping the books, collecting revenues, training employees, and servicing customers. Perhaps most impressively, you've developed a company that can survive without you – the business won't fall apart the moment you leave. That's how real wealth is created.

If you plan the exit properly, you'll be financially secure and set for whatever you want to do next, whether that's retirement or some other endeavor.

This book will help you understand and gain confidence in navigating the mergers and acquisitions (M&A) process. I'll walk you through both the art and science of selling a middle-market company. Granted, some complex technical skills, such as building financial projections and structuring the deal terms, are important, but success in selling a company is just as much about psychology, relationships, timing, and instincts. You need to market the company in a way that creates excitement without overpromising. You also have to keep your employees in the dark – but do so in a way that maintains their respect and loyalty once the transaction is announced. You need to manage your own roller coaster of emotions throughout the process. And you need to come out of the deal knowing you got the best deal possible. That's what this book is designed to do.

I'M HERE TO HELP

Doing it yourself is tempting, I know. After all, you know the company better than anyone. And you made it this far by relying on your own instincts, hard work, and an ability to figure things out. You're an expert at running your business. However, you're probably not an expert in selling it. The business world is a cutthroat place, and those who are unprepared or overmatched rarely come out on top.

So, why should you devote your scarce time to what I have to say? I began my career at a major Wall Street investment bank, and when I started doing middle-market deals, I quickly realized it's an entirely different world with different sets of deal types, processes, valuation methodologies, and tactics. Given the smaller deal teams and the unique attributes of founder-owned businesses, middle-market transactions have a variety of multidisciplinary challenges. As an M&A advisor (to minimize repetitiveness, I will use the phrases M&A advisor, investment banker, and banker interchangeably), I specialize in selling middle-market businesses. This book focuses on the specific needs and challenges of the founders/owners of these companies.

LET'S LEVEL THE PLAYING FIELD

Do-it-yourself sellers put themselves at a severe disadvantage when transacting with seasoned repeat buyers. You can bet your buyer and their advisors have negotiated many deals. Any number of sports analogies apply – and they're all variations on the theme of the enthusiastic amateur going up against a seasoned professional. If you occasionally play a round of golf, you wouldn't expect to compete with a professional golfer and come out ahead. The pro will almost certainly win. He has top-shelf equipment. He practices his swing obsessively. The elite player employs a coach to analyze his mechanics and follows a strength-training program and flexibility regimen designed to maximize his innate talent. In addition, the professional plays in tournament after tournament, going up against elite competitors and performing well. He has learned to control his nerves at stressful moments and to master his emotions as the pressure mounts. Even if you shoot the round of your life, you're still likely to finish well behind the pro. The pro will dominate you throughout the competition while quietly noting all the gaffes in your strategy and cataloging the many holes in your swing. Your flaws aren't obvious to you, but they're abundantly clear to the expert. The same applies to all sports – an amateur has essentially no chance against a professional, well-coached player.

You can level the playing field by arming yourself with information and surrounding yourself with a team that will give you competent professional advice. In fact, I'll share the factors to prioritize when selecting the best advisors for your business.

So, exactly what will you learn by reading this book?

- Context regarding the *why* behind important elements of the process.
- Framework for selecting the optimal time to sell.
- Respective roles and expectations of the various deal team members, expected fees, and factors to prioritize when selecting them.
- Prioritized questions to ask yourself and your advisors to make informed decisions.
- Understanding your counterparty's (i.e. buyer's) perspective and typical strategies.
- Negotiation tactics and the underlying psychology behind many of them.
- What to expect from yourself psychologically/emotionally and how to best prepare.
- Things that can be done *today* to make your business more valuable/sellable.

Given the emotional excitement and pride that owners have in the businesses they built, many expect buyers to view their business as special and anticipate unrealistically high valuations. In his book *Walk Away Wealthy*, financial planner Mark Tepper aptly summed up the unrealistic hopes of middle-market sellers: "Many business owners stubbornly cling to fantasies about selling their businesses easily and for big money. They're certain that they will (a) find multiple high-quality suitors for their company as soon as they put it on the market, (b) get several quick offers worth many times their company's [earnings], and (c) walk away rich and happy without having done any serious exit planning in advance" (Tepper 2014, p. 3).

If only it were that easy. The truth is that selling a company is exceedingly hard. Most business owners I meet are woefully ignorant of what it's going to take, how long it's going to take, and the likelihood of success. Here are the harsh facts:

- Just 20% of businesses of any size successfully sell to a third party. The success rate is probably more like 50% for middle-market businesses – but a 50% chance of victory doesn't sound very good when your life's work and net worth are on the line.
- Private equity (PE) firms close on approximately 1% of all businesses that they review. Statistically, there's a better chance of getting into any of the Ivy League universities.
- Depending on the reported source, only 25–50% of signed letters of intent (LOIs) result in a closed transaction, with many of those at terms materially lower than the initial agreement (Beshore 2018, p. 92). The absolute highest close rates I've encountered among professional buyers are around 80%.

FORGET WHAT YOU KNOW ABOUT SELLING PROPERTY

Many business owners mistakenly assume selling a business is similar to selling real estate. You've probably sold a few houses in your day and perhaps a commercial property or two. Yes, those are complicated transactions – but they're child's play relative to selling a business. There are a number of key differences:

- While a property transaction can be completed in 30 days or less, the total timeline to sell a business is 5 months at a minimum, and frequently in excess of a year.
- Real-estate sales require little of your time, and the process is all about the property, not about you. In an M&A transaction, seller owners and their staff commit significant time and resources to the process – typically more than 1000 hours.

- Businesses are much more complex, involving processes, organizational structures, and human dynamics.
- When a buyer purchases a business, they are buying its people, with a particular sensitivity to dependencies on you as an individual.
- Given this complexity, the diligence process is more thorough and intense, involving multiple professional advisors reviewing thousands of pages of documents.
- Middle-market business valuation is infinitely more complicated. Determining the value is difficult given the lack of publicly available data, especially involving truly comparable companies.
- Confidentiality is critical in a business sale, given the associated risks. Real estate is intentionally listed as publicly as possible.
- Given these factors, the market for businesses is inefficient. This is reflected in the wider dispersion in outcomes between highly effective versus mediocre advisors. This range is 5–10% in real estate but can be over 100% in business sales.
- Unlike turning over the keys to a property and never returning, you probably won't be able to quickly walk away from a business sale. Most transactions require the seller's cooperation during a post-sale transition period of at least six months but likely for year(s).
- Most middle-market deals delay a material portion of the purchase price, with ongoing financial and legal strings attached. Consequently, offers are frequently incomparable. Each will have a different mix of cash up-front relative to other forms of payment, along with extensive differences in the fine print (important!).
- Transaction structures and documentation are customized and highly negotiated versus the standardized templates in real-estate deals.
- Operating real estate requires nominal involvement and can be easily and efficiently outsourced to competent third-party management companies. A business is a delicate organism that only a few insiders can seamlessly jump in and manage. If you were to die or become incapacitated, the impact on its value would be huge relative to that of your investment property.

THE OLD "DATING GAME"

As odd as it might seem, a useful way to think about the dynamics of selling a business lies in terms of the subtle push and pull of a romantic courtship. Sellers and buyers engage in a unique mating dance when transacting. Here are some of the ways these two seemingly dissimilar processes are actually alike:

- Playing hard to get has its advantages. You can't force a buyer to actively pursue you, and overeagerness can make you look desperate. Generally, the person who cares, but not T-H-A-T much, will have the best outcome. This is best accomplished when you have a strong plan B of continuing to run your business and choosing *not* to sell.
- Exuding confidence is critical. Your actions and nonverbal cues are constantly being analyzed to try and assess the strength of your position. In context, some actions may be perceived by the buyer to mean their offer is significantly higher than others, which causes them to worry about overpaying. Objectively assess your behavior and ensure your actions are consistent with a seller who has multiple strong(er) alternatives. Buyers respect assertive sellers.
- Talk is cheap. You roll out your A-Game when trying to impress a romantic partner. You're careful about what you say while taking pains to seem relaxed and spontaneous. Too much honesty – about your personal shortcomings, about your political beliefs – is risky, so you say what you think the other person wants to hear. The same is true for some buyers who say all the right things until the ink dries.
- Lust can cloud your emotions. Your enthusiasm to do a deal can often create wishful thinking that blinds you to things that are obvious to everyone else around you.
- Call me, maybe? Frequently, investors will not provide a clear no but instead keep things in an indefinite and vague *maybe*. It's frustrating for the seller but great for the buyer – after all, it costs nothing not to commit. The dating scene leads to similarly vague interactions – maybe he or she is scared to say no, or maybe they're interested but not ready to say yes. Who knows?
- Money isn't everything. In romance, money is an inevitable part of the equation, but it should never be the driving force behind a relationship. As Dr. Phil says, "People who marry for money earn every penny." Selling for a great headline number to a jerk who you don't trust to honor your post-deal earnout is likely not worth it. Life is too short, particularly when you're going to reach financial security anyway.

■ Monogamy is expected. In most romantic relationships, both parties expect the other to be faithful to them. In the M&A process, that expectation is legally enforceable. Any LOI you sign will require exclusivity – and if you cheat on your suitor, you can expect to be slapped with a lawsuit.

■ There are no perfect options. Just like no spouse is perfect, no buyer will be perfect. You need to weigh all of the different pros and cons and select the best fit. And you'll need to accept that imperfection is part of the game.

■ You only need to find one spouse. Maybe none of the other possible suitors like you. As long as one buyer does, that's all you need. Of course, that's not ideal in a business sale – multiple interested parties will bid up the price and provide you with greater negotiating leverage. But in the end, all that really matters is that you find a single buyer willing to meet your terms.

BEFORE WE START

First, if any of the words you encounter are unfamiliar, you can find a glossary at the end of the book.

Second, I've disguised the names and details of my past clients; in some cases, several people have been condensed into one to make a clearer point. My goal is to recount their struggles so that you can avoid them, while also changing the details enough that my clients won't feel that I've violated their trust.

Finally, while I know it's tempting to skip ahead and read just the chapters on selling and negotiating, I'd urge you to at least scan the earlier chapters. They help set up the psychology and reasoning behind the practical steps.

CHAPTER 2

What's My Business Worth?

She exuded confidence the moment she entered my office. "I know what my company is worth," she said, carefully placing her designer bag on a chair. "And I expect to get at least that or more." I asked her what she thought the company would sell for and she named a figure over $10 million above what I thought was reasonable. When I told her what similar companies had sold for, she got very huffy. "Mine is far better than any of those. I know it." Needless to say, she was very disappointed when the one offer she got was nowhere near her dream valuation.

Contrary to the hopes of many business owners, your business's value unfortunately has no relationship to your desires, expectations, or retirement needs. Ultimately, the value perceived by prospective buyers and the market is what counts.

JUST GIVE ME THE BOTTOM LINE

Like any business owner, you're curious about what your business is worth. Formal valuation exercises are often necessary for legal and tax planning purposes, but they follow specific rules required by case law, which is informed by academic research, and rarely reflect the true market value that a business will command if it were to sell in the market. Given their subjectivity, formal valuations can easily be manipulated, and the results relative to market value or even between reputable firms can be significantly off for private businesses (as in a 10× difference in value). In fact, a study showed that approximately 60% of valuations are off by more than 15% in the actual sales process (Phillips 2016). In any other industry, this performance would result in getting fired.

Hundreds of academic textbooks cover the various technical valuation methodologies that I won't bore you with. That said, all valuations fundamentally use some form of subjective analogy to determine value – i.e. another asset with slightly lower-quality characteristics recently sold for X; therefore, this is worth X+. For example, used car guides (e.g. Kelly Blue Book) can estimate used automobile values with a high degree of market accuracy given the substantial number of vehicles of the same year and model. Without large sets of accurate, comparable transactions, middle-market business valuations end up being theoretical and highly subjective. Valuation can be way off because the sample size of truly relevant comparative transactions is frequently one or even zero. Instead, the art is inferring based on limited untraditional data points.

LIMITATIONS OF COMPARISONS

Unlike real-estate transactions, where nearly everything is public, private market transaction information is extremely limited. It is difficult to value any private business because the evaluation and eventual sale of a business are significantly more complex than, say, selling a house, across multiple dimensions.

Here are a few reasons your business might sell for a dramatically different value than you might hope and expect.

- Business size. This is likely the most important factor in variability because valuation multiples, which we will discuss later, typically increase as a company increases in size. Looking at public company disclosures is helpful, but only to a point.
- Recency of transactions. Whether you're selling in a good or bad economic environment can impact your sales price. As you know, market sentiment can change rapidly in just a few months, and recent transactions may not reflect current conditions.
- Subindustry variances. Another challenge is selecting the right comparative subindustry. Most businesses operate across multiple verticals, and there is seldom a company with exactly the same customer makeup, business models, etc.
- Business growth potential and profitability. Again, comparing past and expected future performance against other companies and

time periods can be challenging, particularly if synergies are involved.

- Risk measures. Factors such as customer concentration, dependency on a single individual, or ongoing litigation can vary among businesses.
- Qualitative measures. Company culture or employee turnover can have a significant impact on how a prospective buyer views it.
- How purchase price is paid. How much of the stated multiple is paid up front in cash versus contingent (like an earnout) or paid in installments?
- Accounting methodologies. Businesses may track their numbers using different methods, making it difficult to compare EBITDA (earnings before interest, taxes, depreciation, and amortization) figures. Similarly, unadjusted versus aggressively adjusted earnings can result in drastically different outcomes.
- Measurement period. The valuation multiple can be measured against different time periods (based upon last year's, last 12 months', or next year's forecasted earnings).

MULTIPLES FRAMEWORK

In the context of real-world, middle-market transactions, nearly all valuations are discussed and negotiated on the basis of multiples. The industry standard is a multiple of EBITDA. As an example, if a business generates $5 million in EBITDA and it sells for an 8× EBITDA multiple, the total purchase price would be $40 million.

Other metrics, such as price per subscriber or a multiple of revenue, can be used, but EBITDA is the best available metric. That's not to say it's perfect, but EBITDA is the preferred measure for a variety of reasons:

- EBITDA is a simple (albeit imperfect) proxy for cash flow, which is much more complex and time-consuming to calculate accurately.
- EBITDA has the benefit of neutralizing the impact of ownership or financing decisions. Remember, buyers may choose to use a completely different financing structure post-transaction.
- Given its near universal usage, EBITDA permits us to directionally discuss opportunities in different sectors on an apples-for-apples basis. That said, some industries, such as equipment rental or financial institutions, have a wide disconnect between EBITDA and cash flow due to the

high amounts of capital expenditures or interest needed to run the businesses efficiently. We tend to see correspondingly lower multiples in those sectors to account for these distortions.

Buyers expect to earn a financial return on their acquisition, and an EBITDA multiple provides a rough estimate of an investor's annual investment returns. Multiples are mathematically the inverse to an investor's expected return on investment (equivalent to a *cap rate* in real estate). Put another way, the higher the multiple, the lower the expected returns, all other things equal. Analyzing nearly 5000 private equity (PE) investments over the past 20 years, GF Data reports an average EBITDA multiple of 6.8× (GF Data 2023, p. 2). That corresponds to an approximately 15% annualized return if the investment is entirely funded in cash. Accounting for average levels of inflation and using some debt to fund the purchase price, PE firms should be able to pay this multiple and still achieve their targeted investment returns of 25–30% annually. To pay multiples higher than this and continue achieving these desired returns, investors will need to improve growth, performance, or the multiple they achieve upon exit.

SMALL TRANSACTIONS

Small transactions are frequently valued based upon a multiple of the seller's discretionary earnings (SDE), which also adds back the owner's salary and benefits. Because these transactions are essentially buying a job, they also tend to be valued using much lower multiples (average 2–3× SDE).

THREE FACTORS DRIVING MULTIPLES

Regardless of these difficulties, multiples do provide us with directional guidance on what to expect. At the core, multiples are driven by three elements: Growth, risk, and supply and demand considerations. Let's take a closer look at each.

Growth

The more growth and/or potential for growth, the higher the multiple. This is because rapid growth allows the investment to grow into a higher multiple, allowing the investor to achieve the same targeted returns. A rule of thumb shared by Dennis Roberts in his book *Mergers & Acquisitions*: "... If a middle-market business's earnings are growing at a rate that will make the multiple paid today, whatever that multiple is, appear to have been a five times multiple when compared to the business's earnings approximately 18 months to two years from now, then that multiple is probably justifiable" (Roberts 2009, p. 275).

Just like stock market investors look ahead, middle-market acquirers buy the future. You need to convince them of the future growth potential of your company. I often justify higher purchase prices by selling based on the next full year's projected financials. For example, if we are in spring 2024, rather than sell on 2023 or March 2024 financials, I will try to sell on the 2024 projections. To successfully do that, I need to fully convince a buyer that those numbers are credible and will be achieved. A strong management team with a track record of consistently hitting or exceeding prior budgets provides a lot of comfort.

In order to get them feeling comfortable stretching on price, buyers need to be comfortable regarding the sustainability of growth. Market tailwinds or industry inflation that improve profits are easy sources of growth for some businesses. The market assigns more value to growing EBITDA through revenue increases versus improvements from cost-cutting measures. There's even the potential to get some credit for purely theoretical opportunities if you can credibly articulate specific quantifiable opportunities and the action plans to execute.

Risk

If a business could guarantee its profits going forward, you would see businesses trade for sky-high multiples consistent with US government bonds. Uncertainty results in lower values. Conversely, eliminating or reducing uncertainties provides prospective buyers with the confidence to offer higher multiples. Some sellers believe that buyers prefer businesses with room for improvement so they can add value. This is true as long as the buyer can purchase it cheaply. Investors care about returns and almost always prefer high-performing businesses because it means a higher likelihood of success and lower downside risk. A GF Data analysis reveals that high-quality businesses with above-average characteristics command a 15–30% premium on their EBITDA multiples – and that's on top of the higher EBITDA levels associated with better performance.

A variety of risks can spook buyers into considering an opportunity only at a low price. While many risks are external factors out of your control, others are qualitative and involve the buyer's judgment and discretion (a bad first impression does cost you real money). Here are some areas that can help de-risk the investment from the buyer's perspective:

- Business is professionalized with systematic processes that reduce dependency on any specific employees.
- Management team has a proven track record of execution.
- Stability of the culture and ability to retain critical employees.
- Strength of your relationships with your biggest customer(s).
- History of customer retention with high satisfaction levels.
- Products and services present a strong value proposition relative to competitors.
- Top customer relationships are managed by a wide range of team members versus just one superstar salesperson.
- Superior cost structure relative to your industry.
- Ability to control expenses and/or to pass along price increases to customers.
- Long-term contracts, patents, and other legal tools to shelter you from fierce competition.

SUPPLY–DEMAND FACTORS

Like everything else in a market economy, mergers and acquisitions (M&A) transactions are affected by the forces of supply and demand. From the supply side, value is all about scarcity. Just like a rarely available baseball card commands higher pricing, so will unique businesses. Conversely, values tend to go down if the market is inundated with similar businesses. On the demand side, valuation multiples are strongly correlated with size for a variety of reinforcing reasons (see Figure 2.1). First, valuations are directly related to the amount of financing lenders are willing to provide, and as size increases, they typically increase their lending as a percentage of the transaction value. Therefore, a bigger transaction is nearly always more competitive (both in terms of price and number of interested buyers) than smaller deals. Similarly, multibillion megafunds and large multinationals with the wherewithal to fund large transactions tend to have a lower cost of capital (i.e. lower investment return hurdles).

Larger companies can also command higher multiples because they tend to have greater sophistication and resources that can be leveraged to grow and scale. PE firms pursuing a buy-and-build strategy attempt to purchase a platform, which is a business with sufficient financial scale to support the systems, technology, and managerial talent necessary to successfully acquire and integrate lots of small acquisitions at scale. A platform can be acquired by virtually any PE firm, so it tends to receive tremendous buyer

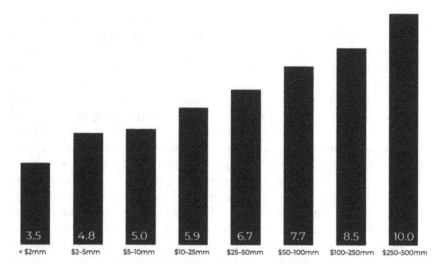

3.5	4.8	5.0	5.9	6.7	7.7	8.5	10.0
< $2mm	$2–5mm	$5–10mm	$10–25mm	$25–50mm	$50–100mm	$100–250mm	$250–500mm

FIGURE 2.1 EBITDA valuation multiples, by enterprise value range.
Source: GF Data M&A Report Feb 2024, p. 2; Pepperdine Private Capital Markets Report 2023, p. 90; Team Analysis.

interest. Consequently, there's a premium paid for the limited number of businesses that can serve this role.

Conversely, subscale businesses typically only attract interest from local competitors or strategic acquirers, who will consolidate your operations into their infrastructure. This is typically a fraction of the size of the broader PE universe so the valuations reflect this limited competition. In fact, investors often overpay for a platform, knowing they can acquire lots of smaller add-on acquisitions at lower valuations, resulting in a reasonable valuation multiple on a blended basis.

Similarly, businesses with revenues derived from vastly different business lines pursuing a conglomerate strategy are much less appealing. That's because there's a smaller universe of buyers that can capitalize upon its diverse strategy ("I like this part of the business, but we don't do that part"). Most buyers will value it as the sum of its smaller EBITDA parts, with their correspondingly lower valuation multiples.

Limited Buyer Universe Some businesses have great financials, but the universe of interested buyers is limited, even at a substantially greater size. Let's delve into a few of those reasons:

- Situations where few buyers can structurally participate. The highest valuations occur in industries where PE acquirers are actively doing deals. But, in some cases, the buyer universe is limited because of structural considerations that exclude PE from owning the company. In one example, construction firms must carry bonds that require personal guarantees that funds can't provide. In another example, franchisors and dealers often have total discretion over whether to approve or deny a buyer, and many dislike PE.

Conversely, this power of the franchisor also scares away a lot of otherwise interested buyers due to the potential chilling effect it could have when they choose to exit the business. A similar scenario is a business designated as minority- or woman-owned. Few buyers can purchase it without losing the designation and jeopardizing its revenues.

- Industries with reputational concerns. Institutional investors will typically not consider investments in industries considered to be unsavory (think e-cigarette businesses, etc.). The last thing that they want is to end up in the papers. Because most of their capital comes from large endowments and pension funds, there also tends to be significant sensitivity toward any investment that is not politically correct.
- Special situations. High-performing businesses receive interest from nearly the entire universe of PE firms, while a distressed business will only attract attention from the smaller subset of firms willing to do a turnaround.

TOP 3 TAKEAWAYS

- Deciding the value of a business is both an art and a science. It's often subjective, especially for middle-market businesses, due to the lack of comparable sales data.
- EBITDA multiples are the industry standard for valuation. They roughly correspond to an investor's expected return. However, various factors can influence multiples and they should primarily be used to provide directional guidance.
- Growth, risk, and supply–demand are the critical factors in valuation. High growth and low risk command the highest multiples. Supply and demand dynamics can also play a significant role.

CHAPTER **3**

What Are We Multiplying By?

I've seen it happen over and over. The founder/owner listens to me talk about reported EBITDA and adjusted EBITDA, and their face begins to go blank. "I know my company is profitable," they say. "I have the books to show it. Why can't a buyer just look at our track record and see that we are a very successful business and pay me what it's worth?"

BUYERS BUY THE FUTURE

Acquirers are buying the future, not the past. Specifically, they care about the business' ability to generate future cash flows, not what a business has done historically. However, buyers use historical financials as an imperfect guide to predict the future. For various reasons, historical numbers are adjusted to reflect the true economics that a buyer can expect to receive as an owner of the business post-transaction. These adjustments are referred to as *addbacks*.

By taking a company's reported EBITDA (earnings before interest, taxes, depreciation, and amortization) and including the various relevant addbacks, you arrive at *adjusted EBITDA* (Figure 3.1). Given that the adjusted amount will be amplified by a multiple, there's a natural temptation to throw in everything and the kitchen sink to enhance value. Sellers should rightfully push for all justifiable adjustments that are supported with corresponding documentation. However, author Jonathan Brabrand warns in his book *The $100 Million Exit* that "a desire to maximize the purchase price must be balanced against maintaining credibility and goodwill with the buyer, who at some point before closing will go through every EBITDA adjustment in excruciating detail." Brabrand also argues that overly aggressive

(USD)	FY21	FY22	FY23
NET INCOME	9,934.531	9,987.056	10,361.054
Addbacks:			
Interests Expense (Income), net	161.351	422.393	1,812.341
Taxes	-	-	-
D&A	1,189.284	1,618.086	1,570.436
REPORTED EBITDA	11,285.166	12,027.535	13,743.831
Adjustments:			
Board Fees	1,247.121	1,297.809	1,303.676
M&A Related Expenses	170.672	306.280	151.341
Severance Expenses	65.900	90.184	-
Life Insurance	22.053	22.420	22.567
Trust & Estate Planning	-	99.345	-
PPP Loan Forgiveness	(1,789.098)	-	-
Cash to Accrual Adjustment	-	-	(608.515)
Total Adjustments	(283.351)	1,816.038	869.070
ADJUSTED EBITDA	11,001.815	13,843.573	14,612.901

FIGURE 3.1   Illustrative adjusted EBITDA reconciliation.

addbacks "create unrealistic [seller] expectations that are later unmet, whereas [sellers] most likely would have been more accepting of the same outcome had their expectations been more realistic from the start" (Brabrand 2020, p. 109).

There are three general categories of accepted addbacks: personal expenses, nonrecurring or extraordinary expenses, and accounting adjustments. Let's look at each category.

NONBUSINESS OR PERSONAL EXPENSES

In the middle-market, it's common for owners to run personal expenses through the business in order to minimize their taxes. Legitimate addbacks that we frequently encounter include:

- Above-market compensation for owners. Or compensation to family members not actively involved in operations.
- Expenses associated with personal toys such as aircraft, boats, luxury or antique vehicles, second homes, jewelry, and artwork.
- Personal expenses and obligations, such as home remodeling, private school tuition, alimony, trust and estate planning, personal taxes, and personal litigation.

- Cost of activities unrelated to the business, such as season tickets for sporting events, concerts, vacations, etc.
- Donations to charities.
- Owner life insurance policies.
- Above-market rent or maintenance expenses that are typically covered by the landlord for related-party real estate.
- Excessive costs related to vendors owned by related parties or friends.
- Discounts or preferred terms to related parties or friends.
- Overstated expenses for the purpose of tax planning.

There is room for some subjectivity regarding the appropriate market compensation for an owner. Remember, whatever you assume needs to correspond with the go-forward expenses. For example, suppose you want to reflect a lower salary for your EBITDA calculation. In that case, you must live with that salary structure going forward. Regardless, buyers require that the compensation is within market ranges, as the budget must be sufficient to hire a third-party manager in case you leave.

NONRECURRING OR EXTRAORDINARY EXPENSES

Some items are one-time in nature and, therefore, the financials do not accurately reflect the likely picture for the next year and thereafter. To neutralize their impact on the financial statements, these items are treated as addbacks. Here are some examples:

- Costs associated with preparing the business for sale.
- Any expenses incurred in nonrecurring transactions like financings or mergers and acquisitions (M&A) transactions, including investment banking, legal fees, and associated success bonuses.
- Acquisition payments such as earnouts and ownership transition consulting agreements.
- Costs of starting up and stabilizing new locations or turning around unprofitable acquisitions.
- Litigation expenses or insurance claims without a historical pattern (note some industries experience frequent lawsuits, and litigation is just the cost of doing business).
- Losses associated with natural disasters, extraordinary insurance claims, and embezzlement.
- Any losses associated with sales and other disposition of equipment.

- One-time employment costs such as signing bonuses or severance.
- Professional or consulting fees associated with setting up new programs or restructuring.

While consulting and professional fees can often be included, there's a mistaken belief that they can always be added back. The key question is whether these expenses are expected to be ongoing. If you're consistently spending money on something every year, a buyer is likely to deem those expenses recurring and reject any associated addbacks.

ACCOUNTING ADJUSTMENTS

Generally accepted accounting principles (GAAP) require that business expenses incurred must be recorded to match associated revenues, often referred to as *accrual-basis* accounting. Nearly all transactions are valued based on accrual-basis financials. However, for simplicity's sake, many middle-market businesses operate on a cash or a quasi-accrual basis. Particularly for high-growth businesses, the difference between these methodologies can be meaningful. Even for those businesses that do capture their accounting on an accrual basis, many use cash accounting on a monthly basis and then make a one-time adjustment at the end of the year to convert to accrual. Here are some frequently encountered adjustments to address accounting factors:

- Validating revenue is booked correctly on a percentage-of-completion basis.
- Expensed equipment or IT projects that should have been capitalized over a longer time period.
- Prepayments for services that last more than a year (e.g. multiyear insurance policies, prepaid rent).
- Normalizing expenses that may have been unusually high for a particular year relative to their historical context.
- Recasting financials to adjust for any changes in accounting practices during prior periods.
- Reversing the impact of new lease standards (ASC 842).
- Bonus, retirement account, and vacation accruals.
- Reversing the impact of accounting clean-up, such as write-offs of inventory, obsolete equipment, uncollectable accounts receivable, or unusual prior-period adjustments proposed by accounting firms.

ART, NOT SCIENCE

Valuation is fundamentally an inexact art requiring subjective judgment about various factors. Many sellers get hung up on achieving a specific multiple, but you should be focusing on the actual purchase price (ideally after-tax proceeds). Many miscommunications have occurred when buyers and sellers discuss multiples but have entirely different conceptions regarding the EBITDA level that should be multiplied by. Buyers will often present a very high multiple in the letter of intent (LOI) but assume a lower normalized EBITDA figure – this problem is compounded by disagreements in addbacks, etc. At the end of the deal, it doesn't matter if you get to $30 million using a 5× multiple for an assumed $6 million of EBITDA or whether you receive a 6× multiple, assuming only $5 million of EBITDA. I view their relationship like a balloon – you squeeze on one side, and it often comes at the expense of the other.

When trying to provide sellers with realistic valuation guidance, I place disproportionate attention on transactions by financial investors. It's easier to have a high degree of confidence because investors are plentiful and generally arrive at similar valuation conclusions. On the other hand, the additional value strategic buyers can derive from a complementary acquisition is idiosyncratic. Unless they are private equity–backed, the number of strategics with the financial and operational capacity to successfully acquire is generally limited, and their interest levels can be fickle. Operators are already busy with their day jobs, so considering a deal is often driven by their bandwidth and other competing priorities. I treat a strategic buyer's valuation premium as a "cherry on top," as we can't rely upon their participation in any given sales process.

PRO FORMA ADJUSTMENTS

Pro forma adjustments attempt to *recast* the financials to reflect expected improvements and changes that have yet to fully materialize in the historical financials. Many businesses invest in growth initiatives that take time to mature and start paying back. These investments often present an immediate drag on earnings despite significantly improving the business's long-term prospects. Without a pro forma adjustment, the business would be penalized for doing the right thing. The magnitude of the adjustment is generally tied to budgets and other projections that were created when the effort was initially considered and approved. Some examples of pro forma adjustments include:

- Annualizing changes that occurred mid-year to reflect a full year's benefit.
- New locations yet to reach maturity.
- Acquisition of underperforming competitors.
- Launch of new product with a ramp-up period.
- New contracts with more favorable pricing or terms.
- Investment in technology systems expected to improve efficiency.
- Price increases above and beyond keeping up with inflation.

While you may not get full credit for these adjustments, if you highlight and quantify these potentially overlooked areas of value, you help buyers justify stretching on valuation.

SYNERGIES CAN BE IMPORTANT

Specific to strategic buyers who already have a related complementary business, sellers will often try to quantify expected synergies between them. Synergies involve a situation where the value of two businesses combined is greater than the sum of their parts. Here are some common sources of synergies:

- Elimination of duplicative overhead (i.e. IT, finance, etc.).
- Consolidation of redundant facilities.
- Reduced procurement costs due to greater economies of scale.
- Excess capacity that can be utilized by the buyer at a low incremental cost.
- Relative reduction in insurance expenses and professional fees.
- Access to new customers and sales channels.
- Complementary products that can increase sales to existing customers.

Does the buyer or seller receive the value of these synergies? Each adamantly believes that this value should belong to them. From a practical standpoint, it gets shared between them. If the seller has greater leverage, they can capture more and sometimes all. The absolute best scenario is a bidding war between two strategics, where neither wants the other to have it.

Alternatively, buyers generally will not pay for synergies when they have a strong hand. Michael Frankel, Founder and Managing Partner of private equity (PE) firm Trajectory Capital, explains he determines whether an acquisition is strategically a *must have* or *nice to have:* "If I'm doing a rollup and this is one of 20 companies I'm buying, it's a nice to have. I'm not going to give away most of my synergies, because I know I got 19 others I can go after" (Frankel 2023). Similarly, suppose only one legitimate strategic can benefit from the synergies. In that case, they have no pressure to pay you for those savings.

It's important to note that some major risks may be mitigated by the right strategic buyer. For example, a consolidator may not care that you have significant key-person risk as they already have a preexisting management team that they trust who can absorb your operations. The problem is the universe of potential buyers becomes very small (the bulk of the traditional aggressive buyers is eliminated), eliminating the chances for a highly competitive M&A process that will maximize your sales price.

ADDBACKS ARE A TWO-WAY STREET

Remember, addbacks go both ways.

Buyers and their due diligence advisors closely inspect both the adjustments and the underlying financials to determine sustainable revenues and profits. They will analyze ratios and trends, trying to identify attempts by sellers to artificially make the numbers look more favorable. Buyers will also be on the lookout for any negative addbacks that should be included to account for any extraordinary windfalls or other distortions that don't fully reflect the economic reality. Common areas that are scrutinized are sharp reductions in discretionary spending in areas such as maintenance and repair, capital expenditures, marketing, and research and development (R&D). Moreover, the buyer will ask detailed questions to ensure no revenues are being recognized prematurely.

While most accounting advisors will reach similar conclusions, the results are not black and white. For example, is the business suddenly performing more efficiently, or is it robbing from the future potential? This is one of the reasons why it's generally much easier to get buyers comfortable with a stabilized business that has been consistently running for a few years with improved efficiency relative to reflecting improvements that just occurred. To the extent they feel like the financials failed to reflect the full anticipated expenses going forward, they will often normalize the financials to account for these distortions.

Acquirers are more likely to stretch financially for companies they view as clean and straightforward to understand. Profits that you pay taxes on are nearly always taken at face value. However, addbacks are generally met with some level of skepticism, with the burden on the seller to substantiate their appropriateness and magnitude with *detailed* documentation. I recommend including a couple of obvious adjustments not in your favor. The buyer will discover these items anyway, and disclosure helps build trust. If a buyer views you as fair and reasonable, they're much more willing to give you the benefit of the doubt for other items on the margin.

Because of the challenge of fully proving that an expense is personal and would not be incurred under a different owner, I highly recommend to stop running personal expenses through your business for at least a few years before going to market. Sure, you'll temporarily pay higher taxes as a result, but you provide the buyer with greater confidence in your numbers and ensure you'll receive full credit in the valuation.

The total amount of adjustments relative to the adjusted EBITDA is also relevant. If adjustments represent a nominal amount of the total adjusted EBITDA levels, there will generally be less concern than if they represent a significant portion. As a rule of thumb, adjustments representing more than 25% of adjusted EBITDA will likely have a tough time receiving full credit. As a seller, you should understand that every addback raises questions about your credibility. Yes, addbacks are normal, and they can be perfectly justifiable. By all means, include substantive addbacks. But try to avoid trivial addbacks that will achieve little more than undermining your credibility with buyers.

IT ONLY TAKES ONE

Value is relative, and the same asset can have vastly different valuations by two separate buyers. For example, to me, a used aircraft part is a waste of space that I would pay to have removed. But for an airline who needs that part to get a plane back up in the air, it may be worth thousands of dollars. The reality is that value is derived not just by the seller's fundamentals but by various buyer assumptions, many of which are influenced by gut instinct and first impressions. These factors include:

- Sentiments and assumptions about the industry and its expected direction.
- View of the seller's upside and risks, based upon their assessment of the business, management quality, and various other business-specific factors.
- Views on the reasonableness of addbacks and interpretation of past performance.
- Perspective on the business' potential for improvement and growth under the buyer's leadership.
- Unique strategic motives and objectives of a given buyer.
- Perception of scarcity and competitiveness of the process.
- Buyer's range of alternative investments.
- Ability to generate unique synergies when combined with their preexisting assets.

In the end, you only need to find that one buyer who agrees with your worldview and is willing to pay you for it. It doesn't matter what the other bidders think your company is worth.

TOP 3 TAKEAWAYS

- While historical financials are used as a guide to predict future cash flows, they are imperfect. Historical numbers are adjusted to reflect the adjusted EBITDA that a buyer can expect to receive as an owner of the business post-transaction. Adjustments are generally met with skepticism, with the burden on the seller to substantiate their appropriateness.
- Addbacks generally fall into three categories: personal expenses, nonrecurring/extraordinary expenses, and accounting adjustments. Remember, buyers will be on the lookout for any relevant negative addbacks.
- Value is relative to each buyer and is shaped by their assumptions, including industry outlook, risk assessment, and unique strategic objectives. You only need one buyer who aligns with your viewpoint to determine the worth of your business: everyone else is irrelevant.

CHAPTER 4

Picking the Right Time to Sell

"Should I sell now or wait?" While I'm always tempted to ask my clients if they think I have a crystal ball in my desk drawer, I usually ask a few strategic questions about retirement plans, overall health, and future hopes. Unfortunately, I've seen people who have sold too soon, but many, if not more, who have waited too long. More than once, I've had to help a widow who knew nothing about the business try to make complex decisions because her husband had died unexpectedly. You don't want to add to your loved one's grief, so a forward-looking approach benefits everyone.

TIMING IS YOUR EDGE

While many things are outside your control, you can decide *when* to sell your business. It's to your advantage to proactively and intentionally choose when, how, and why to go to market rather than to be at the mercy of life's circumstances (more on that later).

Curiously, far too few sellers strategically take advantage of this opportunity. Most reactively sell based upon an inbound inquiry or a knee-jerk desire to exit after a disorienting life experience that has them reassess their priorities (e.g. health scare, death of a close friend).

As an owner, it can be hard to know if you're getting impatient and selling too soon or hanging on past your sell-by date. From my experience, most sellers err on the side of waiting too long. Many try to hold out just a little bit longer to capture every last penny of potential. They assume current conditions will go on indefinitely. Unfortunately, most of the time, the risk is asymmetric, meaning there's a greater chance of missing your expectations to the downside than an unexpected positive surprise. Other sellers simply procrastinate, focus on more urgent matters, and start thinking about selling when the dynamics become less favorable.

I advise business owners to take control of their own destiny as much as possible, but it's also important to understand that timing mergers and acquisitions (M&A) is challenging and subjective. To begin, there are hundreds of potentially relevant factors that should be collectively considered. All things equal, business, industry, and market conditions filled with uncertainty are not a good time for selling. However, having optimal conditions simultaneously is virtually impossible. There will always be a better time across some dimension, and real-time information is sparse. The goal is not to time things perfectly but to slightly tilt the odds in your favor.

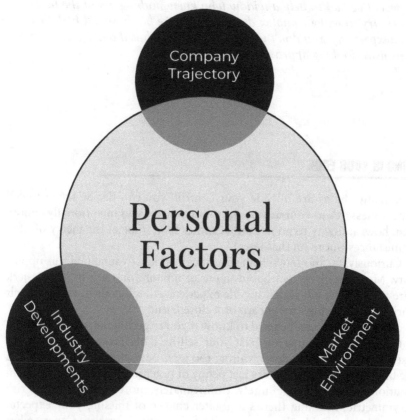

FIGURE 4.1   Optimal timing framework.

The uncertainty is also a function of the substantial time required to successfully market and close a middle-market transaction. Business performance and market conditions can be totally different when you're in the process of closing than they were when you went to market eight months earlier. Consequently, it's virtually impossible to outrun deteriorating business or market conditions.

Finally, the decision is frequently deeply personal. Two highly intelligent partners can have completely different opinions regarding the same business. Their outlook, weighting of each factor, and need for liquidity can all differ. Selling is ultimately a judgment call.

Ultimately, you should assess, weigh, and prioritize the different factors. To the extent you determine that now is not an optimal moment, view that as a gift of additional time. This presents an excellent opportunity to proactively improve and maximize your value.

Once they decide to consider a sale, my best-prepared clients systematically assess and discuss these relevant factors at their board meetings. These discussions also allow them to analyze how buyers might view various strategic operating decisions and how they may affect the purchase price.

The below framework summarizes the major factors to consider when deciding when to go to market (Figure 4.1). Let's deep dive into each factor and discuss what would constitute ideal textbook conditions.

COMPANY TRAJECTORY

The best time to sell is when both your revenues and profits have been consistently growing for a few years or more. Ideally, margins have remained constant or improved. It's important to assess the realistic likelihood of next year's performance objectively and whether it will be better than today. Of course, it's still possible to sell with financial volatility or stalled momentum but at materially less generous prices. After experiencing a down year, I typically recommend waiting another couple of years before returning to the market in order to be able to show a trend of positive growth.

Larger institutionalized businesses that have the capacity to serve as a platform will generally command much higher multiples than a subscale business with poor infrastructure (see Chapter 3 for additional details). This begs the question: Should going to market be delayed until all improvements have been implemented? The answer is specific to each potential improvement and largely depends upon a range of factors, such as:

- What is the potential upside?
- How long will it take to see the full benefit? Until breakeven?
- What is the required cost or investment?

- How will this impact EBITDA (earnings before interest, taxes, depreciation, and amortization) over time?
- What is the risk/likelihood of being successful?
- Are you personally willing and able to commit the time and energy to make those required changes?

From my experience, most owners have a timeline to sell based on personal considerations and then decide what improvements they can make with relative certainty within that time frame.

INDUSTRY ENVIRONMENT

An often-overlooked element of timing is analyzing how your industry's dynamics will impact your business strategically. Industries with attractive fundamentals enjoy widespread interest and premium valuations. Everyone would love to be a market-share leader in a sustainably growing industry, and have a well-positioned business strategy and product mix to capitalize upon that trend. But the reality is many sellers find themselves in the middle of a rapidly changing and increasingly difficult industry landscape, such as:

- Increasing consolidation among their customers and suppliers, often driven by private equity (PE), resulting in less pricing power.
- Industry risk of being disrupted by a new technology.
- Expanded universe of competition given the virtual world we live in.
- Shrinking labor pool insufficient to do the work.
- Industry perceived as *politically incorrect*.
- More intrusive regulations or government scrutiny of the sector.

During difficult industry environments, a lot of consolidation wrings excess capacity out of a market. Many owners decide if you can't beat them, join them before things start deteriorating. That said, buyers are aware of these trends and will likely adjust their valuations to reflect them. This is amplified at moments when the market is flooded with similar businesses.

Within any market, some sectors are more in favor than others. This is driven by the consensus regarding that industry's expected demand and prospects. Various trends and themes (e.g. artificial intelligence, climate change, etc.) also benefit some industries and harm others. If your industry has experienced large valuation increases relative to historical averages, there's a greater risk of reversion to the mean. Conversely, industries that did not have big increases in multiples are less likely to experience major corrections.

Similarly, industries tend to experience cycles where consolidators enter and drive up multiples. One of the primary factors I look for is the level of involvement of PE. Before institutional capital invests in an industry, the universe of buyers is small, the markets are inefficient, and valuations are low. Once one firm gets involved, you will generally start seeing many others follow. As PE becomes an increasingly prevalent and known buyer within the sector, you will typically see valuations spike. I have seen multiples double and triple from their initial levels. That said, the music eventually stops. A major failure within the sector can result in the entire industry going out of favor. Market cycles present windows of opportunity that come and go. Often, when you miss one, you will likely need to wait a long time for a similarly attractive environment to return. For example, in the late 1990s, public consolidators across multiple industries went bankrupt, and in some sectors interest from aggressive acquirers did not return for almost 20 years.

MARKET AND MACROECONOMIC ENVIRONMENT

The overall economic climate will also influence how much your company sells for. Macroeconomic factors, such as economic growth rates, inflation levels, labor shortages, and geopolitical risks (e.g. supply chain disruptions), impact companies differently. Some businesses are procyclical, meaning they follow the broader economy, and others perform the best during downturns. You should assess how your business will likely perform under these various environments and then compare against your best perspective regarding the likelihood of those conditions.

A number of macroeconomic factors also influences the market's receptivity to your business. Just as in real estate, some market environments are more favorable than others. A healthy M&A market is one characterized by high volumes of transactions. Your M&A advisor should be able to provide you with a clear pulse of market conditions.

These conditions and valuations are strongly correlated with the performance of the stock market and the lending environment. While they don't track perfectly, private transactions mimic the markets. Why would someone purchase a business for a high multiple if they can buy a correspondingly cheaper equivalent in the public markets? When lenders are willing to lend large amounts (high loan-to-value levels) at low interest rates with minimal restrictions (loose covenants), buyers are able to stretch and pay premium prices. Unfortunately, the credit markets are frequently binary. Most of the time, they are open and plentiful, and then the window abruptly slams shut (Marks et al. 2012, p. 137).

Ironically, the timing of your exit has much less impact than you'd think when viewed after a few years. This is because most people reinvest their proceeds into the public markets, and those markets are highly correlated with your private valuations. In *The Art of Selling Your Business*, John Warrillow equates it to "selling your house in a good real-estate market; unless you're downsizing, you usually buy into an equally frothy market. When you sell, you can't put your money under your mattress, which is why timing the sale of your business on external economic cycles is usually a waste of energy" (Warrillow 2021, p. 22).

PERSONAL FACTORS

Sellers should be emotionally prepared to sell. That's rarely easy. You've poured years of passion and work into your company, and now you have to decide if you're really ready to part ways. This involves mentally accepting walking away or having a boss to report to for a period of time.

Without coming to terms with this, many sellers start second-guessing and then holding out for unreasonable terms that will never materialize. This can do real, lasting damage to the value of their company, and when they do end up selling, it's often at less favorable terms and conditions. I advise sellers that if they're not emotionally ready, the timing isn't right for a sale. You also need to be ready to dedicate the required time and energy to successfully close. The process is grueling – you do not want to do it twice. If you decide to sell, you need to jump into the task with the same single-mindedness you've devoted to making your company successful.

What is your current level of job satisfaction? Life is too short to stay unhappy, and dread going to work. Fatigue drives many sellers to decide to exit for a more sustainable life. Before selling, I encourage sellers to design a compelling future life that they are excited to dedicate their time to post-transaction (whether it's another business venture, nonprofit work, or art). It's far better to sell to pursue something else than to purely sell to get away from something (for additional detail on the psychological preparation, please see Chapter 26).

The number one factor driving entrepreneurs to sell is a desire to retire and enjoy the next phase of life. Many owners have a specific age that they want to be fully retired by. To maximize your sale price and terms, you likely should go to market a minimum of four to six years ahead of this targeted date. This is because to maximize the chances of obtaining premium pricing, you need to assume a transitionary employment period of up to three years. On top of that, a sales process will generally take 6 to 12 months.

Finally, you ideally want to have the luxury of some buffer of time to be able to credibly postpone the sale if the offers don't make sense.

You should also consider your personal financial circumstances. Most business owners will have the majority of their net worth tied up in the business. Many choose to sell all or a portion of their business to secure their family's future, regardless of what may happen. Working with a financial planner, you should identify the minimum amount necessary to achieve financial independence given estimated taxes and your expected lifestyle.

Business

- Will next year be better or worse than today?
- Are margins increasing or decreasing over time? Have you been gaining or losing market share?
- Is your business of sufficient scale to be a platform acquisition?
- Do you have a viable internal successor?
- How much incremental work and investment is required to achieve a peak transaction? What's the risk/return calculus?

Industry

- How long has PE been investing in your subindustry?
- What is the industry's growth rate?
- What major trends are impacting your industry? How is your product mix, channel mix, etc. positioned for the future environment?
- Are there any regulatory risks?
- Is there consolidation of major competitors, suppliers, or customers? How is that affecting your business and its risk profile?

Macroeconomic

- When do you anticipate a downturn? Is your business pro or counter cyclical?
- How is your business impacted by interest rates?
- How will your business react in an inflationary environment?
- What is the exposure to geopolitical risks?
- What are M&A multiples relative to historic averages?
- Are there a lot of comparable businesses currently available on the market?

Personal

- Do you have something better to do? Personally, professionally?
- Do you continue to feel a passion for the business? Do you feel burnt out?
- At what age would you like to be fully exited from the business?
- Will a sale result in sufficient after-tax proceeds to achieve your financial goals?
- Are you psychologically/emotionally ready for your new life post-transaction?

FIGURE 4.2 Factors to consider when determining optimal exit timing.

Based on what they learn, some owners may delay a transaction until growth justifies a sufficient level of proceeds. On the other hand, if an owner has already become wealthy, the pressure to sell may be significantly less.

Other factors provide an owner with the optionality to not sell. For example, owners with interested and capable children may choose to keep it within the family. Alternatively, transitioning to a professional management team enables you to continue to enjoy the distributions while assuming a passive role. That said, it's important to be sensitive to your family and whether you will be leaving them a complex burden after you've gone. In general, the financial outcome will likely be better, with less stress for your heirs, if you handle the sale yourself.

Finally, anticipated changes in tax rates should also be a consideration. For example, in 2021, there were fears that capital gains treatment would be eliminated. Functionally, this would have doubled the tax rate and would essentially require that a seller grow significantly in order to achieve similar after-tax proceeds.

AVOID FORCED SALES AT ALL COSTS

The goal of every seller should be to sell on their terms from a position of strength. The exact opposite is becoming an involuntary seller who is forced to sell, regardless of price. This places you in a highly disadvantageous position, particularly during weak markets or periods of poor business performance. Without the ability to credibly choose not to sell, you are at the mercy of the market at that specific moment. Greedy buyers refer to the dreaded "four Ds" as a source of fire sales:

- Disagreements among partners. Major disputes devolve into impasses and costly legal battles. More frequently, co-owners simply have good-faith disagreements about the strategic future of the company. Sometimes, one partner can buy out the other. But if that's not on the cards, a sale to a third party is the remaining option. In this scenario, it's important for partners to put aside their differences and present a unified front. After all, the value of the company depends on cooperative sellers. The company's valuation will suffer if warring parties air their grievances during the marketing process.
- Death or disability. The unfortunate reality of aging business owners is that some suffer health issues that force them to step away from the company before they planned. If the owner is dealing with debilitating health issues, that complicates the sale process because no one is a more knowledgeable and forceful advocate than the owner.

- Debt or other financial pressures. Whether business or personal debt, overleveraged owners can sometimes be put in a position where they need to quickly sell to satisfy their obligations.
- Divorce. In some instances, a marital breakup triggers a sale. After all, privately held middle-market companies are illiquid, and the only acceptable way for the spouse to get the proceeds might be to sell the company to a third party.

Life can be messy and unpredictable so it's impossible to totally eliminate these risks. However, maintaining the business in a transaction-ready posture significantly reduces the downside risk should misfortune strike.

TOP 3 TAKEAWAYS

- You have the advantage of being able to choose when to take your business to market if you plan in advance. Too often, sellers act reactively due to sudden life changes or unsolicited offers. Being proactive about timing allows you to sell from a position of strength.
- Optimal timing is subjective and personal: Sellers should weigh a multitude of factors regarding company trajectory, industry environment, market conditions, and personal considerations when deciding to sell. While it's challenging to have all conditions align perfectly, the goal is to tilt the odds slightly in your favor.
- Avoid the four Ds: The absolute worst situation is being forced to sell quickly, regardless of price, because of debt, death, divorce, and disagreements among partners. Without the ability to credibly choose not to sell, you are at the mercy of the market at that specific moment.

CHAPTER 5

No Learning on the Job

I'm a successful investment banker who does this daily for a living, and even I chose to hire another M&A advisor to negotiate the sale of one of my business investments. Why? With potentially life-changing money at stake, I felt it was impossible to hide my eagerness, which would place me at a disadvantage. Poker players closely analyze slight changes in demeanor to obtain clues regarding the strength of someone's hand, referred to as a "tell." The same occurs in negotiations. Your words, body language, facial expressions, tone, and even responsiveness are all being assessed to determine whether you are bluffing or not. By using a neutral third party, I insulated my counterparty from any of my "tells." I felt confident they could easily achieve a better net outcome relative to their small percentage fee.

PENNY-WISE, POUND-FOOLISH, DO IT YOURSELF

Before we dig into some of the details of who might buy your business and how the sale will be negotiated, we need to talk about the importance of hiring a team to assist you. I understand that you might be skeptical of investment bankers and their substantial fees. As an entrepreneur myself, I get it. The urge to do it yourself is a strong one. But, study after study shows that hiring an investment banker yields a high financial payoff. For instance, a University of Alabama and Portland State University study (Agrawal et al. 2023) involving 4468 transactions over a 20-year period estimated that sellers who hired an investment banker received valuation premiums of an average 25%, depending on their methodology (consistent with another study that estimated a premium over 30%).

Perhaps more insightful, this study also found that more than 99% of the 1727 business sales by sophisticated institutional sellers (i.e. private equity [PE] and other "smart money") chose to use an investment banker. Considering that a majority of PE investors are former investment bankers themselves and typically have a large contact list of potentially interested buyers, that finding is pretty amazing. Clearly, these owners could easily sell a business themselves if they wanted to, but they know that hiring an external advisor brings them a huge return on investment.

Similarly, Northern Trust's Business Advisory Services group analyzed 4316 transactions and found that sellers represented by an investment banker obtained an average EBITDA (earnings before interest, taxes, depreciation, and amortization) multiple 1.5× higher, with more consistent outcomes (i.e. lower risk). This data reflects average performance, but these premiums are often much larger with top advisors based on anecdotal and personal experience. Bottom line: An experienced investment banker will make you far more than they charge in fees.

THE VALUE OF EXPERTISE

While an owner is the subject-matter expert of their business, investment bankers are experts in selling companies for top dollar. Most business owners have never sold a company before. As seasoned experts, mergers and acquisitions (M&A) advisors get the deal successfully across the finish line while minimizing the stress and anxiety associated with what is typically the largest, most fraught financial transaction of a seller's life.

Think about how much more effective you are now than on your first day in the industry – given the complexity, relevant experience is arguably even more important when selling a business, and the stakes are definitely much higher. And remember, this is likely not your buyer's first rodeo. In other words, if you go it alone against a more experienced counterparty, you could quickly find yourself overmatched.

Aside from the total purchase price, here are some other important advantages that savvy business owners can realize by engaging an investment banker:

- Greater cash paid up front with the best terms.
- Increased likelihood of a successful closing. You don't want to invest hundreds of hours of your time and significant money in legal and accounting fees only to see the sale fall apart and have to repeat the process. Because the market often interprets a business that fails to transact as "damaged goods," the business frequently gets taken off the market for a prolonged period before it's marketable again.

- Staying focused on your core business. Running the business at peak performance needs to be your highest priority. Given the significant time commitment involved, we often see a performance decline in companies where owners attempt to sell on their own while also juggling their day jobs. This creates an opportunity for the buyer to decrease their initial offer, putting you in the difficult situation of having to either sell the business at a discount or wait to restabilize the business.
- Reduced stress levels. The time and stress involved in selling a business are even more burdensome if you're trying to learn and master the subject on the fly.

In addition, hiring an investment banker adds credibility, giving the prospective buyer the impression that there are other informed buyers competing for the acquisition. I have a client who was told by a potential buyer that the valuation range would likely be 3–6× EBITDA. In my initial call with representatives from that same company, the buyers voluntarily mentioned that they understood that I knew that businesses in the industry were trading at 10–15×.

In other words, buyers know they are dealing with a sophisticated counterparty and that the seller will not entertain lowball offers. Investment bankers can attract buyers and add a sense of urgency without making you appear desperate and will keep the buyers anchored to a specific timeline, ensuring that there are multiple bidders at every stage of the process.

The bottom line: You can have peace of mind that you received the absolute best price and options possible by being represented by a professional M&A advisor.

NO TIME TO LEARN ON THE FLY

Selling your business is no time for learning on the job. You need an experienced expert. A 2016 study by Michael McDonald entitled *The Value of Middle Market Investment Bankers* surveyed business owners who sold their businesses for between $10 and $250 million, with its findings best summarized by quoting one recent seller:

> *Unless you have substantial expertise, a broad buyer network, and a lot of free time, partner with an investment bank. You may be able to get it done yourself, but you'll be leaving millions of dollars on the table as well as closing a higher-risk transaction (when it comes to representations, warranties, and indemnifications). (McDonald 2016)*

WHAT AN INVESTMENT BANKER DOES

Better outcomes from investment bankers don't come through magic. They result from a methodical process combined with insights developed from handling a wide range of deals. This should result in several compelling offers from buyers, allowing the seller to choose the right combination of price and overall fit. As you can imagine, this requires an extensive time commitment that averages 1000 to 2000 hours throughout the entire sales process. Let's delve into the specific tactics and formal and informal functions that any competent M&A advisor will handle for their clients.

Get the Company Ready for Sale

One of the keys to a successful sale is a proactive seller. When you're in control of the timing and circumstances of the sale, you're more likely to strike a deal that's favorable to you. An investment banker will alert you to issues that will serve as red flags to buyers. Examples might include outstanding litigation, unresolved regulatory issues, or past-due receivables. If your issues are easily addressed, this process of tidying up might take only a few weeks. More complicated problems might take months or even years to resolve. Whichever scenario you find yourself in, the investment banker's role is to position your business in the best possible light so that you go to market from a position of strength.

Manage the Transaction Process

An investment banker initially conducts their own due diligence to craft a confidential investment memorandum (CIM) that effectively communicates your company's value and to organize relevant documents in a data room (for greater detail, see Chapter 16). Another critical responsibility is to anticipate the tough questions that will emerge. They will then coach you to most effectively address the questions and will act as a helpful guide during meetings, making sure important points are covered and responses are reframed if necessary.

Other duties are tedious but valuable project management tasks, such as managing the workflow with other advisors and attorneys, ensuring that outreach and follow up occur quickly and consistently, customizing documents across various buyers, and keeping track of what was said and provided to whom.

Frame the Opportunity

The job of an investment banker is to *sell* the business by leveraging persuasion, market insights, and relationships to induce the best offers. Bidding wars occur when buyers engage emotionally – and the best way to engage someone emotionally is generally by telling compelling stories or narratives. A strong advisor can create an exciting and engaging story for the buyer while placing a positive spin on any negative elements of the business (even the best businesses have some blemishes).

Through prior deal-making experience and keeping abreast of market trends, investment bankers know what buyers are looking for – both the good and the bad – and will help reframe the business most favorably. For example, many bankers have been able to achieve outsized multiples in otherwise boring industries by characterizing them as "technology-enabled."

Craft and Execute a Tailored Process to Maximize Competitive Intensity

An investment banker assesses both your company and the potential buyers of your business and then creates a customized marketing strategy based on your company's unique circumstances.

Investment bankers know that maximum prices and other positive outcomes occur because of competition or the threat of it. Put yourself in the buyer's shoes: All other things equal, you want to pay the least amount possible for what you buy. If you know you're the only one competing, are you going to present your highest and best offer? Of course not, since there's no incentive to raise your offer.

Another key factor that is often overlooked is each of the interested buyers needs to be at roughly the same spot in the competitive process. Otherwise, you may be in a position to choose a suboptimal offer or decline and wait for something potentially better (see Chapter 21 for more details). A critical component of the art of investment banking is speeding up and slowing down various interested parties to keep them in sync.

Identify and Reach Out to Prospective Buyers

Sometimes, finding interested parties doesn't take much imagination. If an expansion-minded competitor is targeting your industry and geographic area, that company is probably interested in at least taking a look at your business. But potential buyers also can lurk in the shadows – perhaps they're PE funds that haven't yet taken the plunge into your industry or foreign buyers that haven't telegraphed their intentions. The investment banker's job is to look for less-than-obvious sources of interest in your company.

Another big advantage is that the banker preserves your confidentiality. If you were to contact potential buyers on your own, they'd quickly figure out your intentions. Often, your competitors are in the best position to offer the highest price, but engaging with them generally comes with significant risk. However, an investment banker is able to design a customized strategy to handle these communications to minimize the chances that your inside information will be used against you.

Serve As a Buffer Between You and Potential Buyers

Even if you have every intention of selling your company, you still need to run the business in the meantime. It's not easy if you're doing a hundred or more introductory get-to-know-you-calls with potentially interested parties. The banker will handle these initial calls on your behalf. Later, they will handle future data requests while also coordinating communications so that all interested parties have access to the same information. The banker can also smooth things over when the questions get tough. Savvy buyers will ask probing questions. They might criticize your strategy or express skepticism about your projections.

Similarly, when important unanticipated issues inevitably emerge further along, an emotionally detached advisor can interpret situations and provide an objective perspective on what's reasonable – unlike the owner, who has poured years of blood and sweat into the business. It's natural to get prickly in those situations; the investment banker is there to help manage your emotions.

Negotiate the Best Terms

The investment banker sets a formal timeline for buyers to submit their best offers and then works to persuade them to sweeten the terms. They will then take the lead in negotiating and documenting the agreed-upon terms in a letter of intent (LOI). These terms include not only the purchase price but also the terms and conditions, timing, and other major considerations of the transaction, such as the mix between cash, equity, seller notes, and earnouts (see Chapters 21 and 22 for additional details). Negotiations do not stop at the LOI. Dozens of smaller negotiations occur before closing regarding unexpected changes or ironing out unanticipated details that need to be satisfactorily resolved.

Investment bankers can structure each transaction to address the needs and desires of both sellers and buyers, thus providing creative solutions to find a middle ground to get to "yes." They also can serve as the "bad guy" who pushes hard without jeopardizing a strong working relationship with the buyer in the future.

Effective negotiation requires strategy and soft skills, such as the ability to establish rapport with the other side of a deal and discern when to stand firm and when to make concessions during the negotiation process. The best negotiators I know all have exceptional skills in reading their counterparty psychologically, particularly regarding their motivations. Their experience and insights allow them to *intentionally* select the most effective framing and phrasing, timing, and concession-making pattern.

Good negotiators also keep the emotional side of transactions at bay. Just as doctors don't treat their family members and lawyers don't represent themselves, investment bankers keep the negotiations going on a professional rather than a personal level.

Hold Your Hand

Successful entrepreneurs are often successful because of their bias toward action. Unfortunately, in negotiations, being impatient puts you at a disadvantage, making even the calmest owner antsy and anxious. Your advisor will frequently become your therapist during this emotional roller coaster.

Support Attorneys with Drafting the Sale Documents

Attorneys play an important role in drawing up the final documents, of course, but an investment banker can fill in the blanks regarding financial and other nonlegal details understood from the prior negotiations. They will also frequently assist in populating some of the disclosure schedules. Should the legal negotiations veer off course, the advisor can also provide a valuable third-party perspective.

FACTORS TO CONSIDER WHEN SELECTING YOUR BANKER

Unfortunately for sellers, no credential, license, or educational background is required for those who work in the Wild West of M&A advisory, so it's hard to identify who is competent. In recent years, an alphabet soup of credentials has been invented, often by for-profit companies looking to generate fees. This has been so problematic that the Securities and Exchange Commission (SEC) issued an Investor Bulletin warning that "some professional awards, rankings, and designations provide little to no basis on which to judge the skill or abilities of the financial professional

(U.S. Securities and Exchange Commission 2017). The Financial Industry Regulatory Authority lists 236 designations, many obtainable after just hours of coursework. The curriculum and rigor of some of these programs may be excellent, but I can't think of a single top banker who promotes having any of these designations. Consequently, there is no easy way to identify and select the best advisor.

Here's the strategy not to take: Do not select an advisor based on who provides the highest valuation guidance. Some investment bankers will pitch owners high numbers, fully knowing the company is unlikely to fetch such a lofty price, betting that they can blame an inconsequential item from diligence for missing their pricing guidance. Unfortunately, parting ways after figuring that out is almost impossible because, in standard investment banking contracts, the seller is contractually obligated to pay the investment banker for at least 12 months and sometimes up to three years. Getting out of the contract is tough; most will have to wait it out or pay a duplicative set of fees.

Like any professional you hire, advisors are not created equal. Quality, negotiating skills, and integrity differ dramatically among individuals, even within a single firm. And there is a huge difference in results between excellence and mediocrity. Given the dollars at stake, choosing the right advisor is crucial.

Remember, a typical selling process takes a minimum of six months and frequently in excess of 12 months, so you're going to spend a lot of time together. You might as well like and trust them.

So, what's the process to find the right advisor? If you're not already familiar with some, I suggest you start by asking other professional service providers and business owner peers for recommendations. Then, interview two or three advisors to select the best fit. You will learn a tremendous amount about the market and your business from this process.

Be prepared for a two-way interview in this initial introductory meeting. This is because the best and most coveted bankers – those you *want* to represent you – have more work than they can handle and, therefore, have the luxury of strategically selecting their engagements. Because the success fee drives the overwhelming majority of their compensation, they need to underwrite the deal themselves regarding potential payout and probability of success. Aside from the fee size, here are other factors that typically influence an investment banker's decision to represent a seller:

- Owner's true commitment to selling.
- Reasonableness of seller expectations.
- Marketability of the asset.
- Willingness of the client to listen to recommendations.

- Client reputation and integrity.
- Advisor's relevant experience and capabilities.
- Personality fit.

Once you begin interviewing advisors, try to get a general feel for their personality and approach. Also, delve into the details. Here are some specific areas to explore.

Take Time to Understand the Prospective Investment Bankers' Track Records

Ask to speak to former clients, and not only the ones they suggest. Ask these references about the attentiveness of service, the quality of guidance they received, and their overall satisfaction level.

Ask about the deals they worked on that didn't close. Failures can be more illustrative than successes. Statistically, many deals will not close, but it's generally insightful to dig into what may have gone wrong.

Only Consider Firms That Specialize in Your Company's Size Range

In my opinion, this is perhaps the most important consideration. Investment banks tend to focus on specific deal size ranges, each having a unique ecosystem of ideal buyers, lenders, and professionals. Continuously swimming in that water enables bankers to develop deep, relevant relationships and context.

If you own a lower middle-market company (selling for under $250 million), you are almost always better off going with a smaller boutique. This is because your deal size and its associated fees will be small and insignificant to larger banks. In fact, for relatively small assignments, they typically use these engagements as a "low-risk" opportunity to train their newer team members. You're unlikely to get the service, attention, and availability you deserve. There's nothing worse than having an advisor who makes you feel like they are doing you a favor by serving you.

Counterintuitively, many of the most sophisticated and effective senior advisors who focus on the lower middle-market work for smaller boutiques, from my experience. They typically strike out on their own to maximize their compensation and obtain greater autonomy than typical in large institutions.

Who Will Be Working on My Deal?

It's the specific people who staff your engagement that matter, not the firm. Investment banks employ a mix of junior and senior bankers. While it could make sense for a junior banker to handle tasks such as writing the (CIM), you want the senior professional to be front and center during negotiations. So, delve into the workflow and delegation. Many firms parade in their seasoned partners just to sell the engagement and then promptly hand your deal off to a junior resource before the ink dries. Make sure to ask who specifically will be leading your project, their relevant qualifications, and their expected time commitment.

How Many Deals Do You Typically Take On, and How Much Time Can You Devote to My Transaction?

You don't want to hire someone with so many transactions in process that you don't get the attention that your business deserves. So, ask the banker to describe how the advisory team juggles deals.

Ask Them to Walk You Through Their Proposed Marketing Strategy

Are they designing a bespoke process catered to your unique circumstances, or are they forcing you to fit within their standardized approach? Ask them *why* they made specific recommendations.

A word of caution: Contrary to popular belief, finding and accessing buyers is a commodity. Every successful M&A advisor uses the same databases, and if the deal is compelling, any legitimate buyer will answer their call (investors make money by deploying their capital). If an investment banker claims to have access to some secret pool of buyers willing to pay a premium, be suspicious.

Inquire about How Much Support Owners Get in Compiling and Organizing Materials for Prospective Buyers

Buyers expect documents – sometimes tens of thousands – to quickly be provided on a silver platter. Quality control is essential to ensure all shared data ties and reconciles. Will your investment banker help you slice and dice requested information in many different ways or is it fully on you to deliver? The latter could mean hundreds of hours of additional work during this critical period. A few also prepare quality of earnings (QofE) reports internally to minimize the chances that anything falls through the cracks. Remember, if you spend too much time on the sales process and business performance starts to decline, it will be very difficult to sell at a reasonable price.

Discuss the Similar Deals That They Have Completed over the Past Few Years

While it's valuable that your prospective banker has done recent deals involving similarly sized companies in your geography and industry, similarities involving relevant circumstances (e.g. selling a business with high concentration, etc.) are often just as important. This is important for obvious reasons: A banker who already knows the lay of the land begins with a head start.

Decide between Industry Specialists vs. Generalists

Aside from a handful of complex sectors – such as pharmaceuticals, insurance carriers, or oil and gas – it's generally a matter of preference whether you use an industry specialist (who focuses exclusively on your industry) or a generalist (who works across multiple industries) as they both have their pros and cons (Figure 5.1).

	PROS	CONS
Industry Specialist	• Understand industry-specific transactional nuances • Strong pulse on your industry, including who is looking for what • Deep, relevant buyer relationships important for less marketable deals where just trying to get something done	• Conflict of interest – more profitable for them to quickly coordinate a "fair deal" versus pushing the envelope • Risk of complacency calling on the same buyers • Tendency to use a cookie-cutter approach
Generalist	• Fully aligned to aggressively fight for the last dollar • More likely to execute creative, customized strategies • More likely to include buyers from other industries	• Takes time to fully get up to speed on the industry • Likely to utilize a broader process with a larger universe of buyer

FIGURE 5.1 Relative advantages/disadvantages of specialist vs. generalist bankers.

If you do choose to go with a specialist, make absolutely certain that their integrity is impeccable. Remember, as a founder/owner, you are a one-time transaction to an advisor versus your buyer counterparty, whom they make a living selling to and sometimes soliciting business from. It's a lot easier to quickly settle for an average deal than to ruffle feathers to obtain an exceptional outcome for you.

THE TRUST CHECKLIST

Of course, M&A advisors have rehearsed answering those questions and can be quite persuasive. To make the right choice, you need to listen to your gut. Fundamentally, this decision should come down to trust:

- Trust that they will always place your interests above their own agenda. This is the number one factor why someone ends up being dissatisfied with their advisor: The client perceived that the investment banker worked for the other side to ensure a deal got done and they got paid. During the pitch, do they reference options that would be contrary to their immediate financial interests (e.g. waiting to go to market, etc.)?
- Trust in their ability to be discreet and keep your information confidential. If they are disclosing confidential information about prior clients to you now, guess what's going to happen in their future meetings.
- Trust to fully understand the nuances and differentiators of your business to persuasively sell the business.
- Trust that they will aggressively go the extra mile (including ruffling feathers) to negotiate an exceptional deal versus settling for a *fair* deal. It's a lot easier to quickly arrange an average deal, particularly for specialists who spend their entire career in one niche negotiating with the same counterparties.
- Trust in their creativity to structure appropriate solutions and ability to negotiate superior outcomes.
- Trust in their willingness to proactively communicate their candid assessment of situations and the hard truths to you, when necessary.
- Trust that they will proactively get your permission and guidance before relevant strategic decisions are made.
- Trust that they will transparently disclose their uncertainties, limitations, and staffing arrangements.
- Trust that they will be accessible and willing to patiently educate you about the process and strategic rationales. Will they fully understand your unique needs and preferences, including nonfinancial considerations (e.g. cultural fit, accommodating family members, etc.), and take them into consideration when representing you?

M&A VS. BUSINESS BROKER

The business broker is another type of professional who often tries to play in this space. These deal-makers typically focus on smaller, mom-and-pop companies with lower revenues. Unlike M&A advisors, business brokers seek prospective buyers by posting a brief overview and an asking price on various websites and then negotiating with acquirers as they emerge. Relevant buyers tend to be local individuals looking to buy a job, so brokers typically spend a significant amount of time helping them to arrange financing, often from the Small Business Administration (SBA) in the United States. Business brokers can provide valuable advice to entrepreneurs, but they don't provide the level of technical support and marketing sophistication offered by M&A advisors. They typically collect a commission of 8–12% of the transaction but don't charge an up-front retainer. There's a role for business brokers because most M&A advisors and investment banks are not equipped to profitably serve deals less than $10 million in size (many top advisors have minimum thresholds that are much higher).

EXPECTED FEES

It's standard for investment bankers to charge a nonrefundable retainer up front, typically between $50,000–$150,000. This is often credited against the success fees due at closing. The idea is to make sure the seller is serious enough about selling to write a check, as a significant time and resource investment is made to take any business to market.

Success fees are generally quoted as a percentage of the total transaction size. After analyzing various surveys and reviewing available engagement letters, Figure 5.2 reflects my best estimate of fee ranges for M&A advisors. There are economies of scale running a transaction, so as deals grow larger, the percentage generally decreases until it hits a 1% floor – conversely, most advisors have a minimum dollar fee regardless of size.

While these percentages reveal the average blended rates, they are generally structured within the engagement letter in one of three ways:

- Flat percentage. In this straightforward compensation, the advisor takes a fixed percentage of the final sale price. If the fee is 4% and the company sells for $30 million, the investment banker gets $1,200,000.

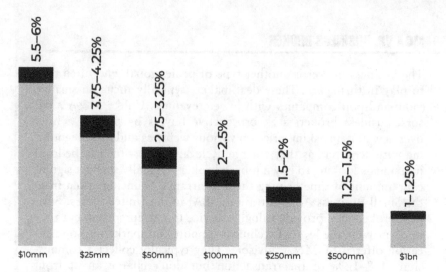

FIGURE 5.2 Typical investment banking success fee percentages, by total transaction size.

This approach is simple and easy to understand, and there's a lot to say for that.

- Escalating percentage. This involves a sliding scale that starts low and escalates as various targets are exceeded. Maybe the banker gets 1% of the first $10 million, 4% of the next $10 million, and 8% of any process above $20 million. This approach gives the banker a real reason to fight for a higher price on behalf of the seller.
- Declining percentage. This involves a sliding scale where the percentage declines as the deal size increases, often referenced as a Lehman scale or some derivative. This construct is often used because it allows an advisor to provide directional fee guidance without knowing the specifics of your company's value. This structure works well if you want to incent an advisor to help you in selecting the best fit, even at the expense of a lower purchase price.

When considering pricing, I recommend you focus on how much you will receive net of your advisor's fees. You will always find someone willing to undercut pricing. From my experience, when deciding between quality and rate, go with the former. Quality should give you an order of magnitude better result relative to saving a percentage point in fees.

ENGAGEMENT LETTER OVERVIEW AND NORMS

The engagement letter spells out a variety of the details of the relationship with the investment banker. In addition to language spelling out the retainer and the fee structure, here are the most important elements to focus on:

- Length of the engagement. A period of 6–12 months is standard, generally with automatic renewals. Most agreements enable either party to cancel at any point subject to the ongoing indemnification and tail provisions.
- Indemnification. This section on legal protection specifies that, if a disgruntled buyer later sues the seller, the investment banker is off the hook for any legal liabilities. These terms are generally standard across the industry, and most quality bankers find these sections non-negotiable.
- A "tail" period. This entitles the investment banker to their fee for a deal closed after the contract has ended with any party they were in contact with during the engagement period. A typical tail lasts between 12–36 months.
- Definition and payout of transaction value. Success fees are paid at closing based on the gross enterprise value, independent of any debt that needs to be repaid. Typically, any seller notes or equity received is valued at its face value. Where there is room for negotiation is regarding contingent payments (such as earnouts) that can take years to pay out. Relevant surveys indicate around 75% require full payment at closing, while the remainder of agreements delay payment of any success fees associated with contingent payments until the seller earns it.

TOP 3 TAKEAWAYS

- Studies show that an M&A advisor results in higher valuation premiums with greater cash up-front and an increased likelihood of a successful closing.
- Investment bankers prepare the company for sale by conducting their own due diligence to identify and mitigate red flags and craft a compelling narrative to engage buyers. They also handle initial calls with potential buyers, relieving owners of this time-consuming task.
- Choosing the right advisor is crucial. Like any professional you hire, advisors are not created equal – quality, negotiating skills, and integrity differ dramatically among individuals. Ask relevant, trusted contacts for recommendations and interview a few potential candidates. Fundamentally, choosing the right fit comes down to trust.

CHAPTER 6

M&A Is a Team Sport

One of my clients had played professional team sports. After we successfully concluded a sale, he said to me that he now understood the importance of having a team. "I was good," he said, "but I didn't win games on my own. I needed my teammates to make sure the game was won." I agreed and told him that each of us on his selling team had certain strengths . . . and weaknesses. It was only when we worked together could we be sure we were getting the best deal.

THE M&A ATTORNEY

An investment banker is one part of your selling team. The investment banker typically quarterbacks a deal through completion of confirmatory due diligence, with the lawyer providing input along the way. The baton then gets passed to the attorney who leads the transaction through the final closing. The lawyer expands upon the ten top business terms agreed upon in the three- to four-page letter of intent (LOI) and translates it into a set of contracts to effectuate the transaction with hundreds of pages of legal detail. The crucial role of the attorney should be straightforward. The deal attorney is there to structure the transaction, eliminate ambiguities, and minimize your risk exposure to various unforeseen situations while keeping the deal on track.

There's an inherently different personality and mindset between your mergers and acquisitions (M&A) advisor and attorney, yet both are essential to success. Just as you want your investment banker to aggressively market to maximize your outcome, a good lawyer is risk-averse, protecting your downside and minimizing the chances of getting sued post-transaction. The best outcome requires a strong working relationship between the lawyer and banker, where each respects and appreciates this healthy yin–yang balance.

Please, please, please hire an attorney dedicated exclusively to corporate transactions. Given what's at stake and the technical nature of the craft, this is not something you want to give to your generalist brother-in-law. Even with the right experience and pedigree, you will also encounter a wide degree of effectiveness. You want counsel that protects your interests while also trying to find a way to get deals done versus the deal breaker who says no to everything. Law school trains future attorneys to nitpick every possible legal quandary. In the real world, effective attorneys know which minor issues to stop pressing for. And when they do identify a potential issue, they also offer a potential solution.

Similarly, when selecting an attorney, it's ideal to select the right temperament. Rather than a litigator's win-at-all-costs mindset, the deal attorney seeks compromise and, ultimately, closing the deal. Not that your attorney should be a pushover – they must still protect your interests. But bringing adversarial tactics to the boardroom has killed many deals.

At the end of the day, you became successful by taking calculated risks as an entrepreneur. If you want an ironclad agreement with absolutely zero risk, you're unlikely to ever reach a deal. While your advisors will provide you with an invaluable perspective, it's *your* responsibility to fully understand the decision and its implications and to make the final call.

When searching for an M&A attorney, you'll have to choose between a big firm and a boutique law firm. Larger practices have more comprehensive resources, such as tax specialists. Just like selecting your investment bank, you need to make sure that your transaction is big enough to capture the firm's attention. Responsiveness from your deal lawyer is a high priority. Ask your M&A advisor and other business owners for referrals, and in particular, get a perspective on their attentiveness, their ability to educate you on the implications of various decisions, and how flexible they were in coming up with solutions.

OTHER DEAL TEAM ROLES

Tax Specialist

If your transaction is likely to trigger complex tax liabilities, consider bringing in a tax specialist who is generally a specialized attorney and/or accountant. This professional can walk you through the tax ramifications of the deal structure. For instance, how the purchase price that is assigned to different assets, including your noncompete agreement, can create tax issues outside the expertise of your day-to-day certified public accountant (CPA). Their input comes into play at separate stages during the deal:

- Before the company goes on the market, to find ways to minimize future taxes (often through estate planning).
- During early negotiations, to preemptively quantify and recommend structures that would be most advantageous to the seller.
- Immediately before closing, when final language and definitions within the sale documents are being drafted – with future ramifications for the seller's tax liability.
- After the transaction, as the seller files tax returns reflecting the taxable event triggered by the sale.

While sometimes handled by the same individual, another important role is that of estate planner. Through trusts and other tools, they can modify your ownership structure to minimize estate taxes. In general, the earlier they make these adjustments, the greater the savings potential.

The Accountant

Your CPA also plays an important role. While nearly every business owner uses an accountant to advise on taxes, not all use one to review and affirm that your financial statements follow generally accepted accounting principles (GAAP). In most accounting firms, different departments will handle these roles, given the distinct skill sets. Ideally, your financials are audited and if not, are reviewed annually by a reputable accounting firm. While many middle-market businesses successfully sell without them, I generally find the value of complying with their strict requirements and their seal of approval justify the incremental expense. If you and your team decide that a full audit is in order, this should be undertaken a few years before a sale.

In anticipation of a transaction, sellers should consider commissioning a seller quality of earnings (QofE), which is becoming increasingly popular. This report essentially performs the same rigorous financial scrutiny that a buyer is likely to perform during due diligence to identify and address any problematic accounting. Unlike an audit, which focuses on confirming historical statements comply with GAAP, a QofE aims to substantiate addbacks and pro forma adjustments that can better reflect the true, normalized earnings that a buyer can expect to receive post-transaction. This is ultimately detailed in a report providing a reconciliation between your financial source files, your tax returns, and the adjusted numbers.

EXPECTED FEES

Your counterparty will be staffed with experts who do this daily for a living. To stand a chance, you need to build your own dream team; unfortunately, it doesn't come cheap. Unlike the investment banker, the external team generally charges hourly fees, regardless of success or performance. Rates and required hours can vary widely, but I recommend mentally preparing yourself for these fees to cost an additional 1–3% of the purchase price. From my experience, legal fees can be as low as $100,000 for a small business and up to a few million dollars for a larger middle-market company, while accounting fees can be as low as $50,000 and up to a few hundred thousand dollars. Given the significance of these costs, you can see the importance and savings of getting a sale right on the first attempt.

BE TRANSPARENT WITH YOUR ADVISORS

It's essential that you're brutally honest with your advisors, erring on the side of proactively disclosing anything that might be relevant: common areas include your true bottom-line price, how fast you need money, and any negative developments that may arise within your business. Without the full picture, it's impossible for them to be effective in achieving your desired outcome. Many owners worry that disclosing this information to the advisor will result in them not pushing hard. Aside from professional integrity, every successful advisor is competitive and is driven to exceed expectations. If this is a legitimate concern, you hired the wrong advisor. Bottom line: Hire the right advisors and *trust* them to get the absolute best outcome for you that they can. Remember, you always maintain the option of not proceeding with a deal.

TOP 3 TAKEAWAYS

- You need a corporate specialist, not just a general lawyer. They should be good at solving problems and coming up with solutions, not just pointing out what could go wrong. Their attitude can make or break a deal.
- There's a yin–yang relationship between your attorney and M&A advisor. Just as you want your investment banker to aggressively market to

maximize your outcome, a good lawyer is risk-averse, eliminating ambiguities to protect your downside and minimize the chances of getting sued post-transaction. Typically, the former serves as the quarterback through confirmatory due diligence, and then the baton is handed to the attorney.

- Building this dream team isn't cheap. You'll pay them by the hour, and it could end up being a small percentage of your selling price. But, considering what's at stake, this is an investment worth making. Think of it as buying peace of mind and the assurance that you're getting the best deal possible.

CHAPTER 7

Who's Going to Buy My Business?

I had one client who came in with a laundry list of qualities they wanted in a buyer. They were adamant that they wanted to sell to someone who wouldn't change the business. They explained that they had worked hard to make the company a place where people wanted to work, and they didn't want any significant change, especially no firing of employees. They were even opposed to remodeling the office, saying that it was "historic." I had to have a hard conversation explaining there are ways to accommodate these interests contractually but the problem is in doing so that he would exclude a lot of his best buyers. I pointed out that most buyers don't want to commit to restrictions that may impede their ability to effectively run the business down the line.

Nothing is perfect, a reality that applies not just to life in general but also to buyers of middle-market businesses. There's just an array of imperfect options, each with its unique trade-offs.

There are always exceptions to any stereotype, but I want to share the typical experience and reputation of each buyer category.

STRATEGIC BUYERS

A strategic buyer is a corporate acquirer within your sector. This buyer is typically a direct competitor or an indirect rival, but it can also be a supplier or even a customer. To them, an acquisition is a strategic business move, with the primary motivation of building up their competitive position. Consequently, they often attribute value beyond the seller's current financial performance.

Brabrand explains that "strategic buyers always have a *make versus buy* decision. Would it be quicker and/or more cost-effective to acquire a given business or to invest in creating the same capabilities from scratch in-house?" (Brabrand 2020, p. 136).

Strategics can typically pay the highest prices due to synergies and the ability to improve their acquisitions operationally. However, you can never assume that a buyer in a similar business will automatically offer a reasonable price. Some veteran industry buyers only consider deals opportunistically if the pricing is low enough. Author Dennis Roberts mentions that "unless an industry buyer has mounted a conscious (formal) plan to acquire other competitors, [they] will not likely be a good buyer" (Roberts 2009, p. 25). Particularly for strategics who have never purchased a business before, a steeply discounted asking price is generally required to induce them to engage and participate in a process. Determining the appropriate valuation, structure, and terms for a deal, quickly finding the capital, and developing an integration plan are all monumental challenges well outside of their skill and comfort zone.

Playbook

As larger organizations, they tend to have a slow, bureaucratic decision-making process with lots of stakeholders who need to provide input (multiple departments, boards of directors, etc.). Identifying the true decision-maker can also often prove challenging. Those responsible individuals tend to be operations executives who already had a full plate before the transaction presented itself, so acquisitions can be a low priority relative to daily operations. Many times, the interest and commitment level to a transaction are independent of the deal's fundamentals but rather their available bandwidth. Similarly, a strategic's appetite can quickly change due to shifts in their strategy, lack of capital, missed earnings, and other factors that are hard to predict. As a result, strategic buyers often move at a glacial pace, which is often inconsistent with the timeline of a competitive sales process.

It's important to understand that your business will likely be unrecognizable post-transaction. Given their preexisting management team and resources, strategics frequently eliminate duplicative headcount (typically within finance and accounting, IT, and HR) and may shut down facilities. Similarly, your independent identity will likely be erased as your business gets absorbed into the buyer's brand. To gain full discretion in integrating the seller and making improvements, strategics typically purchase 100% of the seller. While owners may remain as head of a relevant division for a few years, they often provide the flexibility to retire after a short transition period.

Key questions to ask:

- What is the process and timeline for deciding whether to invest? Who is the decision-maker? Does anyone have veto rights?
- Where do you see the areas of value between our businesses?
- What is your intention for me and my team post-closing?
- What is the culture of your organization?
- How many of your last five letters of intent (LOIs) closed? What was the reason for those that failed to close?

In contrast, buyers who make acquisitions as a way of generating financial returns on their investments are called *financial buyers*.

PRIVATE EQUITY FUNDS

Private equity (PE) funds invest in or acquire private businesses with the objective of generating investment returns through distributions and/or capital appreciation (i.e. exiting at a higher price). PE funds raise pools of capital that get depleted after three to four years, so they are continually in fundraising mode. The fund managers share in the upside, generally receiving 20% of the profits generated. They also receive an annual management fee (typically 2% of the entire fund's assets) to find and manage investments, so their investors expect the money to be quickly invested to justify these fees.

While PE funds with committed capital frequently advertise their assets under management, they seldom have it as cash on hand. Rather this number refers to the amount of cumulative commitments the investors have obligated themselves to. When the fund decides to make an investment, it issues a *capital call* requiring those investors to send in their proportionate allocation of the purchase price a couple of weeks prior to closing. Once the money has been committed, the PE fund's partners have total discretion over the investment decisions, subject to their internal investment committee approval.

Generally speaking, PE aims to minimize the amount of capital they put into a deal, preferring instead to borrow from banks, other lenders, and even the seller to fund the bulk of the purchase price. This is because the cost of capital associated with debt financing – functionally, the expected interest rate – is lower than that of equity (particularly since interest is tax deductible). Minimizing the cash outlay also provides investors with the option to walk away from the business more easily if the performance deteriorates, minimizing losses.

PE funds are frequently measured and compared based on the investment return they generate, often referred to as an internal rate of return (IRR), which is equivalent to the return you receive on your investment portfolio. What is important to know is this return is highly influenced by how quickly the money is returned. Because of that, the funds often have a tendency to flip their acquisitions as quickly as possible. While the average fluctuates over time, the median hold period for a PE investment is around five years.

Playbook

Investing money is their full-time job; if they fail to deploy their capital, they will likely be unable to raise any future funds. Moreover, it's easy for fund managers to be aggressive with their investments because they're investing other people's money (OPM). Consequently, if they really like an opportunity, funds are nearly always responsive and generally can make decisions and fund quickly and decisively. While the norm is around 75 days, some funds can close as fast as 30 days after signing an LOI.

Structurally, funds prefer sellers to retain a meaningful minority stake in the company post-transaction, with an average of around 20%. The proceeds to the seller from this second transaction can be meaningful and can sometimes result in a greater payout than the initial sale.

Most PE funds frequently pursue a consolidation or rollup strategy (also called a *buy and build* strategy), which typically involves a platform company aggregating and integrating smaller add-on acquisitions to achieve rapid growth and scale. Upon exit, the investment benefits from the spread between the higher EBITDA (earnings before interest, taxes, depreciation, and amortization) multiples that larger enterprises command and the lower multiples paid for smaller acquisitions.

This results in a natural investor food chain as companies consolidate. Small lower-middle-market funds eventually sell the bigger company to a larger middle-market fund, which will then pursue a similar strategy, aggregating and (sometimes) integrating similar assets that are packaged with the intent of selling to an even larger fund. This process continues as the asset gets progressively larger and eventually ends with an acquisition by a large (often public) company or an initial public offering (IPO) (less common nowadays).

In many ways, these platform buyers present the best of both worlds between the previously discussed strategics and a PE firm. They have PE's aggressiveness and drive to do deals while also benefiting from the synergies of a strategic buyer.

Key questions to ask a PE buyer:

- What is the process for deciding whether to invest? Who is the decision-maker? Does anyone have veto rights?
- How much debt will you be using? What is the lender's level of commitment?
- How many of your last ten LOIs closed? What was the reason for those that failed to close?
- Post-closing, what level of involvement can I expect from your fund? How are decisions made, and what kinds are made by the board versus delegated to management? Who will be my point of contact?
- What is your plan to add value to my business?
- Do you charge ongoing management fees? How will that impact my rollover equity?

INDEPENDENT SPONSORS

Independent or fundless sponsors are essentially PE funds but without the guaranteed pool of capital. They tend to focus on the lower end of middle-market companies, with the majority acquiring businesses with less than $5 million of EBITDA. They are typically a rite of passage for entrepreneurial PE professionals who want to create an investment track record before eventually raising a fully committed fund of their own.

They pursue investments and then fund them individually on a deal-by-deal basis. Their investment capital tends to come from family offices and a growing number of institutional funds and mezzanine lenders. Given the additional decision-makers who have discretion on whether to participate, their speed tends to be slower, and there's the risk that the necessary money will not be successfully raised.

Anyone can pursue deals as an independent sponsor, so there is a wide range in quality, capabilities, and likelihood of success. Personally, I have made various investments as an independent sponsor and can confidently say that the first deal is by far the hardest. Independent sponsors can close deals, but they require heightened scrutiny from sellers, particularly if this is their first solo transaction or if some of their prior investments are performing poorly.

Typically, they are agile and able to pursue more flexible structures and strategies. For example, independent sponsors are frequently early adopters, considering investments in sectors before traditional PE funds will participate. They can also be a great solution for smaller businesses below the size criteria of funds.

Key questions to ask:

- What is your prior experience with similar PE investments?
- How many investments have you previously completed in your current firm? Walk me through your current portfolio investments and their performance to date.
- Who are your funding sources? What is their process for deciding whether to invest? At what point in the process will they be fully obligated to provide the capital?
- Are the investors committed to injecting additional capital for growth opportunities or unexpected issues?
- How many deals are currently under LOI?
- How many of your last five LOIs closed? What was the reason for those that failed to close?
- Post-closing, who will comprise the board? How are decisions made, and what kinds are made by the board versus delegated to management?
- What is the governance if you and your investors disagree?
- How many companies does your firm operate at the moment? How do you split your time and resources between them?
- Do you charge management fees? How will that impact my rollover equity?

SEARCH FUNDS

Often referred to as Entrepreneurship through Acquisition (ETA), search funds are the "younger sibling" of independent sponsors. They are run by one or two searchers (frequently recent MBA graduates) on a quest to buy a single business and operate it themselves. They focus on the smallest businesses within the lower middle-market, with EBITDA typically between $1–$3 million.

Their investment capital tends to come from a group of five to ten high-net-worth individuals or family offices. Additionally, there are a handful of institutional funds dedicated to investing in various search fund efforts.

Because there tends to be a common universe of investors for search funds, their investment criteria have a narrow, consistent strike zone. They typically focus on simple businesses that are more forgiving for an operator with limited experience. These buyers typically only pursue complete buyouts.

Key questions to ask:

- How long have you been searching?
- How many prior businesses have you had under LOI? If any LOIs failed to close, why was that? Do you currently have other deals under LOI?

- Who are your funding sources? What is their process for deciding whether to invest?
- Does my company fall within your investment criteria? If not, why will your funding sources make an exception?
- What role do you intend to assume post-closing? What is your relevant experience?

FAMILY OFFICES (ULTRA-HIGH-NET-WORTH INDIVIDUALS)

Family offices are the investment arms of ultra-high-net-worth individuals. Some invest their capital directly into private businesses. Because they are discreet and hard to access, there's often a mystique around them, and they are often viewed as Goldilocks buyers. However, like any family, no two are alike, and there are pros and cons relative to other buyer categories.

While some family offices represent inheritors of wealth, the legitimate buyers are nearly always affiliated with a successful entrepreneur who doesn't want to retire and wants to beat the markets in investments they can control and positively influence. Because they can choose not to make any investments and there are frequently other business and personal opportunities competing for their time and attention, they have a reputation for flakiness and being slow. From my experience, a large percentage enjoy reviewing and discussing private investment opportunities but rarely pull the trigger. Unfortunately, it often takes various meetings to separate the wheat from the chaff. Focus your efforts on those with a sophisticated team with a history of successfully making PE investments.

Playbook

Family offices tend to be a more patient and creative capital source because they have total discretion over their money. For example, they may offer a phased purchase over time or provide sellers with the ability to eventually regain control. Most of these individuals have an aversion to borrowing too much as it's their own money. Without the benefit of high amounts of debt, from my experience, they tend to offer prices 15–25% lower than their institutional counterparts.

Family offices have a range of involvement, from being totally passive to being highly involved in decision-making. There's a consensus that family offices represent a friendlier capital provider. From my experience, this is a simplistic viewpoint. Former successful entrepreneurs come in all stripes, and it's important to acknowledge that a handful earned their money because of their unsavory tactics. The most successful family office investments generally occur in industries and situations that can capitalize upon its founder's relationships and expertise.

Key questions to ask:

- What other private investments have you made?
- How many of your last five LOIs closed? What was the reason for those that failed to close?
- What is your level of involvement in your investments – highly involved or passive?
- How do you feel about debt? Risk?
- What resources and support do you provide your portfolio companies?
- How long do you expect to hold your investments?

MANAGEMENT BUYOUT

This type of transaction involves selling either to a current minority owner or a long-time management team member. Often, this structure is motivated by the seller's altruism: the owner wants to reward the loyalty and service of a key manager. Most of the time, these individuals don't have sufficient personal capital to make the acquisition. This often results in the seller deferring substantial amounts of their proceeds by self-financing the transaction. In some instances, one of the other mentioned financial buyers will back a manager to fund the transaction and the characteristics will be similar to a PE buyer.

Selling to management should be considered cautiously during a traditional sales process because the management team is critical in selling your business for maximum value. There's a conflict of interest if they are also competing with the buyers they need to *sell* on the opportunity. Moreover, if other interested parties are aware they are competing with management, many will choose not to participate. For that reason, some sellers expressly forbid considering managers as buyers. If you choose to consider this option, they should be presented with an up-front appraised price and given 60 days to accept and fund it. If they fail to do so, they should be expected to wholeheartedly support the sales process.

ESOP

An Employee Stock Ownership Plan (ESOP) offers the opportunity to sell to your employees while leveraging some tax advantages, which help sellers on an after-tax basis. ESOPs are regulated by specific laws of the US

BUYER TYPE	ADVANTAGES	DISADVANTAGES
Strategic Buyer	• Potential for the highest price • Ability to retire fastest • Often purchases 100% • Easier due diligence – understands your business	• Slow decision-making due to bureaucratic processes • Significant change likely (e.g. employees fired, plants shut, brands absorbed, etc.) • Heightened confidentiality risks
Private Equity Fund	• Aggressive, needs to invest money • Speed • High certainty of closing • Opportunity for a second bite of the apple	• High debt load can risk the business' survival • Frequently maximizes the short term at the expense of long-term value • Legacy and culture at risk
Independent Sponsor	• Greater attention and focus of managers • Good solution for smaller businesses and those in industries where PE is not involved • Greater flexibility	• Certainty of closing risk • Generally slower process due to their need to arrange capital • Complexity of ambiguous roles and responsibilities
Search Fund	• Good solution for smaller businesses below other groups thresholds • Ability to retire fast • Buyers are all in on this single investment	• Certainty of closing risk • Limited experience of searchers • Only applicable to businesses with specific characteristics • Governance complexity
Family Office	• Patient, creative capital • Generally the least disruptive to the organization's culture and values • Good solution for debt-averse sellers who want to remain involved	• Purchase prices are generally 15–25% lower than PE • Reputation for being slow and flaky • Generally unavailable for larger businesses
Management Buyout	• Solution for industries and situations where third-party buyers are not available • Minimal due diligence required	• Generally requires seller to lend buyer most of the capital • Low purchase price • Conflicts of interest – can chill interest from other buyers
ESOP	• Tax benefits • Solution for industries and situations where third-party buyers are not available • Shares wealth widely across broader employee base	• Significantly lower purchase price • Amount received at closing is limited to the amount lender will lend • Burdensome Department of Labor rules and requirements

FIGURE 7.1 Advantages and disadvantages by buyer type.

Department of Labor that are quite complicated – whole books have been written on the subject. ESOPs are so complex that it's almost impossible for this type of buyer to be viable in a competitive bidding process. It just takes too long for an ESOP to work through the legalities and get to the finish line.

The price is subject to a formal valuation with rules that typically result in a materially lower price, so this type of deal can make you a hero in the eyes of your workers, but it won't maximize your returns. ESOP deals are typically funded by debt, with the remainder of the purchase price funded by the business' own profit. In reality, this means you are lucky to receive 50% of your cash at closing. Ownership must be distributed widely. Given the complexity and lower valuations associated with ESOPs, they're rarely used. The entire United States currently has fewer than 7000 ESOPs.

Note that individual buyers are missing from this list. Unlike in very small transactions, individuals are generally not an attractive buyer for middle-market businesses since there's less certainty about their ability to close (both financial wherewithal and their willingness to psychologically pull the trigger).

TOP 3 TAKEAWAYS

- The perfect buyer doesn't exist. You will ultimately need to select from various imperfect options, each with their own advantages and disadvantages.
- Strategic buyers are corporate acquirers within your sector who make acquisitions as a strategic business move, with the primary motivation of building up their competitive position. Financial buyers make acquisitions as a way of generating financial returns on their investments and include groups such as PE funds, independent sponsors, search funds, and family offices.
- Recognizing the core motivation for a prospective buyer – whether it's strategic positioning, investment returns, or gaining market share – can help you better frame the opportunity and negotiate. Prepare questions beforehand to gain insight into relevant considerations, ranging from their decision-making process to their long-term plans for your business.

CHAPTER **8**

The Siren Call
of the Unsolicited Offer

I got a call from Michael (not his real name), who had been consid-ering selling for a couple of years. "I got an offer today," he said excitedly. "I think I want to accept it." Such an unsolicited call can be flattering, but it should be dropped into the same category as the mass mailer indicating they want to buy your house. Frequently owners think they received an offer that they can accept when it's super early in the process and is just something to build momentum.

In the Greek myth *The Odyssey*, the sirens were dangerous temptresses who used their voices to lure sailors into treacherous waters. As the hero's boat approached the sirens, he ordered his crew to clog their ears so they couldn't hear the sirens' calls and had the crew lash him to the mast so that he could listen but not act. As a business owner, your defensive tactics need not be so dramatic, but it is wise to understand the role of modern-day sirens with the allure of "saving" fees and the threat they pose to your business and your net worth.

INTERESTED PROSPECTS AREN'T NECESSARILY SERIOUS

If you own a thriving business, you've undoubtedly received a call from a buyer who expressed a desire to acquire your business. The attention is flattering. Perhaps the interested party is a competitor you know or an industry acquaintance who has for years expressed interest in acquiring your business.

Or maybe the caller is someone unfamiliar. Many of these calls come from brokers posing as buyers who are scouting for an opportunity that they can intermediate for a fee. In general, legitimate buyers fall into one of two categories: first, a strategic investor with a related preexisting business looking to consolidate (generally publicly traded or private equity [PE] owned), and second, a PE fund casting a wide net (often referred to as a "spray and pray" strategy) to find their next platform investment.

One of the dirty little secrets of the mergers and acquisitions (M&A) world is that PE funds routinely retain finder firms who eagerly cold call potential acquisition targets. There's a high probability that you're just one of hundreds or even thousands of business owners being contacted by these lead generators. The enthusiasm of these finders is often more a reflection of their incentives and aggressiveness than any specific interest of their client. They typically get paid a fee when a deal closes. I am frequently contacted by excited prospective clients who engage me to respond to one of these inquiries. Despite the initial caller's eagerness, the tone is much more subdued when I speak to the investor they represent. In fact, I estimate one out of two of these calls don't even progress to a subsequent meeting, let alone an offer.

To understand the motivation behind these calls, let's take a step back and consider how PE funds work. When marketing their funds to prospective investors, one of the key highlights is their ability to originate deals directly with a seller, bypassing a formal process, often referred to as off-market or proprietary opportunities. With no competing bids and with no professional representation on behalf of the seller, the sale price and terms tend to be much more favorable to the buyer and less favorable to you. After all, without competition, all the leverage belongs to the buyer.

PE firms find this approach so valuable that they spend significant money on resources and finder fees to uncover these opportunities. With a friendly demeanor, they will often flatter you to lower your defenses. Their tactic exploits the optimism, resourcefulness, and frugality inherent in an entrepreneur's DNA. Once in a while, these cold callers catch an owner who chooses to do it themselves in order to save fees.

RISK OF TESTING THE WATERS

Any decision to sell your life's work should be made on your terms, and you should proactively manage the process. Responding to a cold call is the opposite of being proactive. You're reacting to someone else's expression of interest in your company and relinquishing control of the process and timing.

Many sellers reckon that there's no harm in entertaining a discussion and "testing the waters." Perhaps your suitor will blow you away with an offer that combines unusually generous terms with modest requirements for due diligence. That's possible, but the too-good-to-be-true bid is a rare occurrence. The more common scenario is they will induce you to invest a lot of time and energy responding to detailed requests to make it more likely you'll accept an offer that's mediocre to fair.

When you choose to sell, you should be 100% committed. Otherwise, I highly discourage entering into substantive sale discussions because they unleash forces that are hard to reverse. After all, you can't unscramble an egg.

Not being fully prepared and reactively addressing their information requests is not optimal for creating the best first impression. Moreover, entering into talks when you're not ready to let go of your company can be a recipe for bad blood in the future: The buyer will feel they've wasted their time. If the bidder was serious, they're unlikely to make an offer in the future when you are ready to sell.

There are other risks, too. Given the volume and time sensitivity of data requests, there's a high likelihood of management distraction and associated declines in performance, making it more difficult to sell at a good price in the near future. It can also be demoralizing for your employees to work on a deal that falls through as they begin to wonder whether the company is damaged goods. This is particularly true if they had a success fee at stake. The bottom line: Don't take this decision lightly.

Many sellers quickly receive a letter of intent (LOI) and mistakenly believe that the battle is nearly won at that point. Studies show that a signed LOI results in a successful closing less than 50% of the time, with that number dropping significantly for these kinds of off-market deals. This occurs because misunderstandings and surprises are more likely with less prepared sellers. Counterintuitively, the transactions that do close generally take much longer.

It's important to understand that an offer is only as valuable as the rigor of the underwriting and analysis that went into it because it's nonbinding. Many buyers treat signing an LOI as a free option – heads I win, tails you lose.

I'm aware of some less scrupulous PE investors, whom I will not publicly name, that close fewer than 10% of deals they sign. They will issue offers they have no intention of honoring to get a term sheet signed while fully expecting to make substantial downward adjustments during the due diligence phase. This approach, known as *retrading* the deal, happens when the seller is exhausted, and their negotiating leverage is at a low point (see Chapter 23 for additional details). This vulnerability is compounded because the buyer knows you have no alternate buyers. Even worse, the LOI requires exclusivity, preventing you from soliciting interest from any potential competitors (with serious legal risk to you if you violate the terms of the LOI).

Remember, while the deal may be the most important thing in your life, it's likely one of dozens of prospective opportunities the buyer is considering. Because of the lower close rate for these proprietary deals, attorney and other professional fees are often counterintuitively higher because the process gets repeated multiple times.

HOW TO HANDLE THE CALLS

My recommended approach for business owners is to thank callers respectfully and politely for their unsolicited interest and indicate that you're not entertaining offers but will contact them when you do decide to sell. Then, file away their contact information and share it with your advisor when you do choose to go to market in an organized and methodical fashion.

Many sellers worry that introducing an advisor into the mix will jeopardize the interest of the suitor. This is often fueled by some callers who mention their preference for negotiating directly with owners because advisors tend to get in the way (of them getting a steal). From my experience, only a bottom-feeder trying to take advantage of you would be deterred by professional representation. Any legitimate buyer understands and expects you to seek expert advice regarding your most valuable asset. These same professional buyers use investment bankers themselves in 99% of their sale transactions, according to a University of Alabama and Portland State University study (Agrawal et al., 2023) (see Chapter 5 for further details). Many serious buyers actually prefer you to have an M&A advisor because it improves the likelihood of closing, reducing the chances of wasting their time.

To the extent you choose to entertain a conversation or meeting, be careful not to reveal something you might regret. Even with a nondisclosure agreement in place, you never know their intentions. Under the guise of a potential acquisition, competitors can be fishing for valuable information or opportunities to poach your top managers. In fact, I recommend taking control of the conversation and letting them do most of the talking, gaining as much relevant intelligence from the interaction as possible.

TOP 3 TAKEAWAYS

■ Buyers spend a lot of money and resources cold calling because avoiding professional representation and a competitive process results in a lower sale price.

- While it might seem safe to find out what a prospective buyer thinks your business is worth, there are irreversible risks involved in entertaining these discussions. Selling should occur with the same single-mindedness and intentionality that made your business successful in the first place.
- An unsolicited offer can often come under the guise of a "friendly" approach, suggesting that advisors might complicate matters. However, professional representation is almost always in your best interest. It signals to the buyer that you're serious and well advised, which can actually make them more confident in the deal.

CHAPTER 9

What Does a Buyer Want?

I have worked with many buyers (as well as sellers), and the one indisputable fact is that buyers want the lowest possible price, and sellers want the exact opposite. When Marcos (not his real name) came to me wanting to sell his business, I asked him to put himself in the place of a prospective buyer. "What are the downsides of buying your business?" I asked. He drew a deep breath and said that maybe he was looking at things through the eyes of all his hard work, not necessarily what his business was like to an outsider.

Your company is only worth what someone is willing to pay for it. Therefore, it's an invaluable exercise to view your business through the vantage point of an acquirer and to understand what attracts their attention. Just as a military general studies his battlefield enemy's tactics and weapons to devise the most effective strategy, you can leverage your knowledge of potential acquirers and their preferences to make informed strategic decisions prior to selling and to better tailor your messaging to address potential reservations. Put yourself in a buyer's shoes and think hard about what characteristics would make you most comfortable with any given opportunity, not to mention excited enough to pay a premium.

The majority of middle-market transactions involve private equity (PE) buyers. They look for certain fact patterns, and their criteria tend to be consistent with what any other prudent buyer or lender would prioritize. Strategic buyers (please see Chapter 7 for an explanation of the different kinds of buyers) may prioritize some other factors, but it's harder to generalize since they tend to be specific to their individual strategies.

FEASTING ON BIDS OR STARVING FOR ATTENTION

From my experience, the mergers and acquisitions (M&A) market tends to be feast or famine. From a quick conversation with a prospective seller about their business, I can generally determine if the number of interested parties will be plentiful or not. Fit within the PE strike zone and you're likely to be overwhelmed with interest and receive dozens of healthy offers. Collectively, PE has trillions of dollars of "dry powder" waiting to acquire businesses so there's no shortage of demand. Conversely, many good, profitable companies struggle to obtain a single offer because the interested buyer universe is so limited. If you can fit your company into the characteristics buyers are scouting for, you can greatly improve your chances of a highly competitive process and a strong outcome.

WHAT CREATES VALUE FOR BUYERS

PE investors are expected to generate annual returns between 25–30%. This is not easy, given the realities of market valuations. Assuming they are not buying something for a steal, this is generally accomplished through three critical levers: utilizing debt to supercharge their investment, growth/performance improvements, and maximizing the exit. Given the frequent need to maximize the amount of debt placed on the business, there is a strong emphasis on stable cash flow, which provides lenders comfort. The grease that keeps M&A deal activity going strong is the plentiful availability of credit; without it, everything grinds to a near standstill.

Growth or performance improvements allow buyers to justify paying higher prices. Before buying, they generally develop a perspective on the extent of improvements they can realistically make as well as a game plan for how they will achieve them, often referred to as their *investment thesis*. In Pepperdine University's annual survey of lower middle-market PE firms, the average fund expects earnings to grow between 12–18% annually, far greater than their associated industry growth rates (Everett 2023).

Given the importance of a strong exit, buyers are also concerned about the ultimate sellability of the asset. An investor perceives a business as more valuable, the greater the number of exit alternatives. Remember, PE funds are expected to return their capital in a predefined period of time (generally with a maximum of ten years), so to realize profits, the investment needs to be resold. They are unlikely to buy companies where there's a limited buyer universe or worse. This functionally means thinking about a business's outlook and sellability beyond a buyer's ownership period. In *Private Equity*

Toolkit, author Tamara Sakovska explains investors' focus on industries that "have good prospects and stand on solid footing for the next 10–15 years. Why? Apart from supporting [their] investment thesis, there should be plenty of room for another investor, who will be buying the company from [them] at exit to construct [their own] viable investment thesis 5–7 years down the line" (Sakovska 2022, p. 72).

Whenever a business transitions to a new owner, there's always a level of risk of it not going smoothly. Consequently, there's a much greater preference for more forgiving businesses with downside protection. Many of a buyer's desired characteristics are associated with greater resilience and, therefore, reduced risk levels.

So, what qualifies as a textbook acquisition? A perfect business is functionally a cash machine with little to no competition that automatically and consistently produces a predictable amount of money on autopilot. Short of that, I reviewed the investment criteria of over 2000 PE firms that my firm follows, and I found there are certain characteristics that nearly all funds target (they often use very similar language to describe their checklists):

- Recurring revenues with a stable, diversified customer base (ideally, the largest customer represents less than 10% of sales, and the top five customers represent less than 25%).
- History of resilient financial performance through various business cycles (i.e. Great Recession, COVID-19 pandemic).
- Preference for high margins (which insinuates a higher value-add business with less risk of commoditization), with most expecting an EBITDA (earnings before interest, taxes, depreciation, and amortization) margin greater than 10%. Note, however, that margins *dramatically* higher than your industry average are viewed as a red flag. Buyers either worry the company is temporarily capitalizing upon an opportunity that will eventually experience competition and reductions in margin, or there's underlying compliance or fraud risk (particularly in heavily regulated industries).
- Leader in a fragmented niche or market, ideally with further consolidation opportunities.
- Defensible market position (sustainable competitive advantage) based upon differentiation, brand reputation, etc.
- Favorable growth prospects (either organic or through acquisition) and industry trends.
- Strong management team in place, particularly if they intend to use the business as a platform.

Although often not explicitly mentioned, one important factor for nearly any buyer is the concept of revenue quality. Not all revenue is created equally. Regardless of the customer type, the most coveted businesses – those that generate the most competition among bidders – tend to have predictable recurring revenues. Revenue quality can be viewed along a spectrum. At the bottom is the least coveted – discretionary, project-based revenue, such as home renovation contractors. Customers can defer spending on projects when times are bad so that those companies can have wild swings between significant profits and losses. The gold standard at the top of the spectrum is long-term contracted revenue, such as software subscriptions. There are various permutations in between. Greater certainty in the stability and predictability of revenues provides acquirers and their lenders the comfort to stretch.

WHY YOUR CAR WASH SELLS SUBSCRIPTION PLANS

One way to create value is to modify a business model to create higher-quality revenues. For example, you might have noticed that your car wash has overhauled its pricing plan. Instead of pitching a $10 single wash, now your car wash wants to persuade you to buy a monthly subscription. That's because car washes traditionally experienced low-quality transactional revenue. In boom times, a customer might come in once a week for a $10 or $15 car wash. But in a recession, or even in a rainy month, that same customer washed the car at home or just let it get dirty. But in recent years, creative PE investors have moved into the business. They began marketing subscriptions, a shift that provided sufficient predictability to enable banks to provide significant financing. *Voila!* A low-multiple business is now selling for valuation multiples in the mid- to upper teens. Sharp-eyed readers will notice that car wash subscriptions qualify as noncontractual revenue rather than the contractual revenue that's at the top of the revenue hierarchy. Depending on your industry, there are logical limits to how high up the revenue spectrum you can move. The idea is that with some creativity, you can push your company's revenue stream higher up the desirability ladder.

You often see investors pursuing similar industries with more favorable trends and economics, with the most common being:

- business services, particularly ones enabled by technology
- healthcare services
- technology/software as a service (SaaS) businesses
- niche manufacturing
- consumer products
- value-add (specialty) distribution

Some sectors and business models inherently have less attractive fundamentals, such as low barriers to entry, commoditization, and risk of obsolescence (can I interest you in a buggy whip or film camera manufacturer?). While PE likes to fund the growth of a disruptor playing offense, they are wary of industries experiencing significant disruption that jeopardizes the business model.

Lastly, size matters for PE firms. All other things equal, bigger is nearly always better for them. Even if the deal is larger than their fund can accommodate, they prefer to find a way to fundraise additional capital than to invest in a deal below their thresholds. This is because their cost structure makes small deals inefficient and, therefore, less profitable. Those businesses that don't check most buyer boxes are unlikely to get offers, let alone command a premium multiple.

MEASURING UP

Nearly every owner I've met believes their business's organization, team, and processes are above average. Some of the most important factors in assessing these factors are qualitative and involve discretion. To help you calibrate, here's what a world-class acquisition target looks like:

- Management team has worked together for a long time.
- Management represents the business in a way that showcases their competence and strength.
- Designated successors for all key roles within the organization.
- Low employee turnover across the organization.
- Track record of achieving or beating their annual budgets.

(*Continued*)

(*Continued*)

- High customer retention and customer satisfaction levels.
- Detailed reporting showing performance relative to plan for strategic initiatives.
- Accounting books are consistently closed by the 7th or 15th of each month.
- Culture of making decisions by data versus opinion.
- Key performance indicators (KPIs) are tracked and reported on a frequent basis (monthly or weekly).
- Significant availability of data across all functions. Some examples of what middle-market businesses should be able to quickly provide:
  - Financial reports showing profitability by customer, segment, category, etc.
  - Operational reports showing target vs. actual for various metrics.
  - HR reports showing historical employee turnover by department.

TYPICAL BUYER TEAM

Your initial interaction with most buyers will likely be with a member of the Corporate Development or M&A team who is responsible for proactively "scouting" for new opportunities. Eventually, the relationship is handed off to a hierarchical investment team that analyzes, negotiates, and executes deals, if warranted. While the titles can slightly differ across buyers, the team is typically comprised of a young analyst or associate (generally in their early 20s and responsible for doing detailed financial analyses and handling the details through closing), a vice president/director (generally in their late 20s to early 30s, who leads the execution and will likely be your daily point of contact during any confirmatory due diligence), and a partner (anywhere from mid-30s to 70+ years old, who is responsible for negotiating the major decisions). While the partner has a great deal of influence, they may not be the final decision-maker, particularly in funds that require decisions by a formal investment committee. Investment committees generally meet weekly to approve or deny potential investments. Many of those members will have no knowledge of the opportunity outside of what is presented in the deal memo prepared by the team members pursuing a deal. Strategic buyers are even more complicated as they tend to be bureaucratic and have a wide variety of stakeholders with influence on a transaction. Always ask prospective buyers early on who makes decisions and how they are made, as everyone does things differently.

BUYER REVIEW PROCESS

PE buyers, on average, review approximately 100 deals for each transaction they consummate, so it is valuable to understand how deals typically progress from their vantage point. In general, an analyst or business development team member will eliminate any opportunities that exhibit deal breakers or are clearly inconsistent with their investment criteria. From there, most buyers have a standardized review process that analyzes prospective opportunities in depth and qualitatively compares the attractiveness of the deal against other investment or acquisition alternatives.

As a seller, it's important to remember that you are competing against a buyer's opportunity cost. There's functionally an endless supply of alternative prospective deals. Professional acquirers are not only looking at how your company stacks up but also comparing your business's risk and return potential against other acquisition targets.

Junior team members will typically begin by digging into the financials and other technical matters, with the more senior team members typically focusing on more qualitative and strategic topics, such as your competitive landscape, strategic vision, bench strength, etc. A Harvard Business School survey of PE firms representing approximately $750 billion of capital found that the quality of the seller's business model was their number one consideration (Gompers et al. 2014). Warren Buffett often describes his ideal business as one protected by an economic moat (sustainable competitive advantage). Some relevant questions that are frequently discussed include:

- What differentiates the seller's products and services from others?
- Why do customers choose to buy from the seller relative to its competitors? Would customers miss the company if it went out of business?
- Does the company have market power? Are they a price setter or price taker?
- Does the seller control its sales channels? Who owns the customer relationships?
- What is the seller's cost structure relative to the rest of its market?
- Are prospects good for the next 10–15 years, providing opportunities for the next buyer?
- Do we trust management and the organization's capacity to successfully execute and capture the expected opportunities?

Aside from these company and industry characteristics, investors are particularly focused on understanding the seller's motivations to get comfortable with why they are selling *now*. A nightmare scenario for buyers occurs when owners jump ship right before it sinks. A management team bullish on the future and willing to invest their own capital into the business can provide significant confidence. PE typically prefers situations where ownership is older and looking to retire, or the business is at an inflection point where it is performing well and poised for future growth. PE acquirers understand that middle-market companies often face a hurdle to unlocking this growth potential. That challenge could be insufficient talent, a need for new machinery, or various other issues. Their most preferred obstacle is insufficient growth capital, as they're in the business of putting money to work.

COMMON BUYER DEAL TACTICS

Most buyers are tough negotiators who try to use every opportunity to strike the best deal. Their methods are predominantly fair and ethical, but some bidders will cross the line. In the interest of knowing your enemy, here are some tactics throughout the sales process that you should be on the lookout for (along with the best defense):

- Leveraging friendliness. Yes, you want to build rapport with buyers. But you also need to keep bidders at arm's length, particularly early in the process. Some smooth operators push to meet early and will try to charm you with the goal of convincing you they share your values and that they are uniquely suited to take over the business and carry on your legacy. But the hidden motive can often play on your emotions to pave the way for a less competitive situation. Solution: Leverage your investment banker to serve as a buffer.
- Hiding their true character. Sure, every buyer will be on their best behavior during the bidding process. But some of the sneakier players engage in outright deception. They feign respect, fake empathy, and generally overpromise until the deal is done. Solution: Conduct deep character references before signing a letter of intent (LOI) with any buyer.
- Circumventing the auction. Every bidder would prefer to negotiate behind closed doors rather than in the open light of an auction. They will indicate a desire to move quickly and ask for exclusivity. Circumventing the process not only reduces the level of competitiveness but it also reduces your effectiveness in future negotiations as it places them in the driver's seat. Solution: Immediately and directly address any

attempts to bypass the process by redirecting them back to your M&A advisor.

- Dividing and conquering. Similarly, some buyers will try to circumvent the advisor and contact the seller directly to gain an advantage. Often, this devolves into an *if Mommy says no, go ask Daddy* situation. This also undermines the power and influence of your advisors, which will hurt their ability to effectively negotiate on your behalf later on. Solution: While you should feel free to engage with the buyer regarding diligence questions or the mechanics of future integration efforts, hold firm that all deal terms must go through your advisors.

- Testing the waters to lowball their offer. If given the opportunity to negotiate directly with an owner, many buyers will informally float various ideas to gauge your body language. They are probing to understand the bare minimum deal you'd be willing to accept, particularly if competition is lacking. Their objective is to make an offer where you are slightly disappointed, however close enough that you want to counter and negotiate instead of walking away. They often attempt to lessen the sting by referencing some specific element that they incorporated into their offer to try and address a previously mentioned preference. Solution: Once again, make sure to redirect any price or term discussions to occur through your advisors.

- Bidding far more than they plan to pay. Conversely, unscrupulous bidders can gain commitment by offering a big number. Taking advantage of the nonbinding nature of an LOI, they entice you to sign. Sure, all bets are off for any legitimate material misrepresentations or omissions that are made. However, many times, buyers will intentionally express alarm at some minor issue to negotiate the price down when your leverage is low. This dirty trick is most effective when brought up right before closing. Solution: Push for a highly detailed LOI and incorporate language that allows for exclusivity to terminate if the buyer exhibits bad-faith behavior. Make it crystal clear up front that you will walk away from any retrading.

- Dragging out the process. Some bidders may attempt to gain an advantage by intentionally slow-playing the confirmatory due diligence. The objective is to force you to invest time, dollars, and energy, making it harder for you to walk away. It also eliminates your plan B by reducing your ability to revisit the market. Solution: Ensure your financial performance remains strong during this period. Prepare for likely data requests beforehand and ensure that requested information is quickly provided so they can't blame delays on you. Last, the window of exclusivity should also be minimized to provide you with the leverage of potentially walking away.

- Co-opting their future employees. While your frontline workers might not know a deal looms, some of your management team will. A scheming bidder knows that these execs are eager to impress their new owners, so the bidder might try to sweet-talk your managers into divulging details about the number of bidders or pricing expectations, or even worse behavior, such as promising them lucrative compensation in exchange for biasing the deal toward them. Solution: Other than chaperoned environments, all communications and follow-up data requests should occur through a limited number of individuals, generally your M&A advisor and/or CFO. I would reconsider proceeding with any buyer attempting unscrupulous behavior.

TOP 3 TAKEAWAYS

- PE firms and strategic buyers are looking for specific business characteristics that often include recurring cash flows, a diversified customer base, and strong growth prospects. Highly marketable businesses generally receive numerous bids, resulting in the best negotiating position.
- PE buyers, on average, review approximately 100 deals for each transaction they consummate. It's important to remember that there's functionally an endless supply of alternative prospective deals. Professional acquirers are comparing the risk and return potential of your business against other acquisition targets.
- Buyers may employ various tactics to gain an edge in negotiations. While hopefully you don't encounter them, preparing yourself for these potential tactics ahead of time will ensure you maintain your negotiation leverage. Better safe than sorry.

CHAPTER 10

Choosing the Right
Transaction Type

"I don't want to sell because there are some opportunities coming that that I'd like to capture. So, I think I'll just hold off and keep running the business myself." I've heard this innumerable times because many owners mistakenly believe there's a binary choice: continue operating as is or sell. Early in my career, I was shocked by the number of owners who would swing wildly between seemingly opposite tracks: selling or wanting to double down on their business. I've come to realize this disconnect often occurred because the sellers wanted to pull some money out to diversify their wealth and secure their future. At the same time, they wanted to continue running the business and felt that there was significant upside potential that they wanted to participate in. Thankfully, there are options to do both.

Fundamentally, an investor's capital can be used for one of two purposes: cashing out the owners or funding growth. To differentiate between them, the operative question is whether the money is going to the shareholders to buy their stake (no net increase in cash in the business) or whether the cash is going into the business with nothing paid out to the shareholders. Luckily, it's not an *either–or* decision because most investors have the flexibility to accommodate both objectives.

A highly marketable business will always have a variety of options available to it. In fact, without being guided regarding seller preferences, you'd be surprised by the dramatic range of approaches that buyers will propose in a single transaction. There's no one-size-fits-all answer – the best option depends upon the seller's specific conditions, timing, strategic objectives, outlook, and preferences. And remember, many businesses have multiple owners, each with their own perspective. An optimal solution may need to creatively accommodate the exit of some shareholders while supporting the continued growth of those that remain. One of the advantages of a strong advisor is their ability to ask the right questions and translate them into an optimal deal structure that best addresses the ownership group's unique needs. Some of the relevant factors to consider when determining the most appropriate approach include:

- How much cash do you need now?
- What is your confidence in the future prospects of the business?
- Is now the right time to sell the entire business for maximum value, or do you believe waiting would be strategically advantageous?
- What is your risk tolerance?
- How much value-added support (e.g. relevant customer relationships, M&A know-how, etc.) do you need from a partner?
- Are you comfortable having external partners?
- Do you want to continue operating, or would you like to exit?
- What is your time frame for having a full exit?

While there is a near-infinite array of permutations, I'd like to cut through the noise and showcase the four primary solutions available to owners, when each is most appropriate, and what you can expect.

TOTAL EXIT

This is the classic structure that most sellers think of. It is most frequently associated with a strategic buyer purchasing and integrating the business. While seller financing and contingent payments may represent a small portion of the deal, this approach allows the seller to maximize their up-front cash payment (although at the expense of receiving a greater total amount over time) and allows them to walk away after a minimal transitional period.

CONTROL BUYOUT

A control buyout involves a private equity (PE) investor purchasing a majority stake in the business. These transactions involve the sellers retaining some equity in the company post-closing (often referred to as "rollover equity"). This structure aligns interests by providing both a carrot and a stick:

■ Meaningful upside if things go well. Incentivizes owners to ensure a smooth transition and to assist in maximizing the investment's value.
■ Share in the pain if things go poorly. Skin in the game incentivizes sellers to manage the downside as well.

The amount of equity retained by sellers tends to average around 20%. For businesses where the sellers have unique skill sets and will continue to run the business, investors will often mandate that owners retain far more – up to 49%. Sellers will ultimately get fully paid out for this remaining equity when the business eventually gets sold again.

The financial investor will actively manage the business as an investment and will almost always want to improve and grow it for a future exit in four to seven years. These new owners will generally use significant debt and will pursue aggressive strategic moves. For many owners, this presents an ideal outcome, as they can de-risk and swing for the fences (although many times this structure will allow a seller to transition out as well) – attempting that ambitious growth plan that they always wanted to do but were too risk-averse to try with their own money.

Governance

Just as the new owners will be responsible for daily operations, they will also control a majority of the board and are in the driver's seat. They can unilaterally make most important decisions. They will also put in place a number of processes and formalities that you, as an entrepreneur, may not be used to.

Most crucially, they select when to ultimately sell the business. It is important to understand that there is generally no practical way to monetize your stake before the ultimate sale. Sellers will receive standard minority shareholder protections.

MINORITY GROWTH PARTNER

Other owners are looking for an aligned, professional partner as an intermediary step to help accelerate growth and institutionalize the business in anticipation of a much more meaningful sale down the road. Sellers will continue running the business and use the provided funding to capitalize upon an opportunity, whether through organic growth (e.g. purchasing new equipment or opening branches in new regions) or making acquisitions. Additionally, most of the time the seller will be able to cash out a portion of their stock and immediately take some money home (or use it to buy out other minority partners).

There's a minimum amount of money that a PE investor needs to deploy for this strategy to be worthwhile, so there's an inverse relationship between company size and the minimum percentage they are willing to accept – at a bare minimum of 10% and generally more than 20% of the company. They also want to own a large enough percentage to capture a meaningful share of the upside that they help create. Institutional growth capital will only be available for larger businesses. For smaller lower-middle-market companies, the best option tends to be raising capital from a former entrepreneur with a successful exit in their industry.

Particularly because an investor will only receive a minority of the proceeds (corresponding to the equity percentage), valuations are of low importance if they can help dramatically grow the business. Consequently, disproportionate emphasis should be placed on finding the right partner who can expand the pie. Conversely, this can be a miserable option if you have the wrong partner – one who doesn't share the same vision or business philosophy.

Governance

To best protect the investor's position, the deal is generally structured using preferred or structured equity. While there are technical differences, the investor generally gets their money back plus a preferred return first.

The new investor will generally be actively involved and will typically assume a board seat. Since they don't have control, investors will generally require their consent for any major decisions that can materially impact their business interests, such as incurring debt, issuing more equity, or selling the business or its assets. To ensure a return on their investment, the investor generally has the right to force a sale after a certain number of years – typically seven or more.

DEBT RECAPITALIZATION

Sometimes, an owner needs some cash but is bullish about the company and would like to maintain ownership without any outsiders. In a debt recapitalization (or recap), a lender provides the company debt to fund a special dividend to the shareholders. Funding with a loan allows the owners to maintain full control of the business without experiencing dilution. No new owners are introduced, so the business remains fully within the seller's control. However, debt also increases the risk of insolvency, and many owners prefer not to incur high debt levels to sleep well at night. Furthermore, this option might not be practical in many situations, for example, if the business already has high debt levels.

Depending on size and industry, it's not uncommon to distribute 3–4× EBITDA (earnings before interest, taxes, depreciation, and amortization) as a dividend (assuming the business has no other preexisting debt). A recap typically occurs with rates and fees that are significantly higher than bank loans. This is because of the higher leverage available and the fact that these loans are nonrecourse, meaning there are no personal guarantees. In the absolute worst-case scenario, you can walk away free and clear. Consequently, many owners choose to do this to secure their future and view the further upside as playing with house money. Moreover, these loans provide significantly greater flexibility, such as delaying the repayment of the principal for a period of time or allowing some of the interest to be accrued and paid only at the end.

Lenders may also participate in some of the equity upside by receiving a small amount of warrants (i.e. stock options). To ensure the investors can exit, they will typically be able to force the owners to cash out these warrants at some point (generally 7+ years), using a predetermined formula.

All in all, these lenders frequently earn an annual return north of 15%. However, this remains significantly cheaper than selling equity. Equity does not have an interest rate that must be paid annually, but the associated dilution typically generates a 25–30% annualized return for middle-market investors.

Lenders generally play a hands-off role with investments and will assume a board observer role at most. They typically just want periodic (generally quarterly) financial and operational reporting to ensure that their investment is secure. Correspondingly, there is very little support or value-add that is provided.

As you weigh these options (Figure 10.1), you should keep in mind that there's no single right answer. Smart and successful owners can disagree on the optimal approach as this decision is just as much personal and psychological as it is financial and logical.

TOP 3 TAKEAWAYS

- Owners often think the only option is a total sale of the business. However, a highly marketable business will always have a variety of options available to it. The choice of transaction type should be influenced by a range of factors, including your need for immediate cash, your views on the future prospects of the business, and your comfort level with external partners.

	IDEAL SELLER CIRCUMSTANCES
Total Exit	• Wants as much up-front proceeds as possible • Desire to retire and walk away as quickly as possible • Potential concerns about future business prospects
Control Buyout	• Desire for the majority of proceeds today with the ability to participate in future upside • Often higher valuation received relative to total exit • Owner can retire or continue running the business
Minority Growth Partner	• Wants a value-added partner to help prepare them for a substantially greater exit in a few years. • Desire to buy out departing minority owners without primary owner exiting themself • Company already has debt and is ineligible for a debt recap • High confidence in business prospects • Owner intends to continue running the business
Debt Recapitalization	• Company is currently undervalued (due to market conditions or pending improvements) but owner would like to access some money now • Wants to have the option to never sell • Value-add support is not needed • Prefers operating without an external partner • High confidence in business prospects • Owner intends to continue running the business

FIGURE 10.1   Best exit options by *seller* characteristics.

- When reviewing a proposal, focus on whether the money is going to you to buy your stake (no net increase in cash in the business) or whether the cash is going into the business (generally to fund growth) with nothing paid out to you. Luckily, it's not an either–or decision because most investors have the flexibility to accommodate both objectives.
- Regardless of the transaction type, governance plays a critical role regarding how you interact with your partners and your level of control post-transaction. Whether it's a majority sale or a minority growth partnership, take the time to fully understand how the partnership will operate going forward and your expected rights and responsibilities.

CHAPTER 11

Bad News

"What do you mean 'my business can't sell?' It's making money and has been for years!" My client's face began to get redder and redder. Telling a client that their business is unsellable, at least as it is currently structured, is hard to say and even harder for a client to accept. But sometimes it's just the cold, hard fact. This has nothing to do with the profitability and desirability of the industry or business. In order for a business to sell, a buyer needs to want it and to choose to buy it over the available alternative investment options.

As mergers and acquisitions (M&A) professionals, we love to talk about successful transactions, but we implicitly fail to talk about the businesses that can't sell. The reality is that it's statistically more likely that a business cannot sell than that it is marketable. Studies indicate that just two out of ten businesses with revenues above $5 million successfully sell. While I would expect this number to be higher for larger businesses, and some may be transferred internally, my best guess is that approximately 50% of middle-market businesses fail to sell because they are considered unsellable.

Many business owners have illusions that their business is much more marketable than it really is. This thinking is typically fueled by a boasting competitor or friend at the local diner. In this fantasy, many buyers are waiting to quickly buy their business for record-breaking valuations.

As an entrepreneur and business owner myself, I know how it feels to consider the business you built through hard work and sacrifice to be your baby. In the eyes of a parent, their children are the prettiest, the smartest, and the best. One hundred percent of owners I have encountered believe their business to be above average and worthy of premium valuations. However, the real-world reality is your business is only truly worth what someone else is willing to pay for it.

Of course, you can monetize your business's value, by liquidating the company's assets, but you're likely to receive a fraction of your potential value. Accountants use the phrase "going concern" to describe a company that can continue indefinitely independent of its owners (with the difference between going-concern value and the value of the underlying assets referred to as *goodwill*). Selling as a going concern results in a much higher sales price – in some asset-light industries, like technology or pharmaceuticals, it can be hundreds of times greater than if the assets were just sold off (how many physical assets does Facebook or Google have?).

GOOD NEWS

The good news is that nearly any business can be modified over time to become coveted by buyers. By addressing key value detractors now, you can not only sell a previously unsellable business, but you will also dramatically expand the universe of prospective buyers, their demand levels, and, ultimately, your valuation. This pre-sale process can require a lot of time and effort. The not-so-good news is you're going to have to put time and energy into changing, which no one, including your team, is going to be excited about.

EXISTENTIAL RISKS

The best way to explain what makes a business unsellable is to briefly put yourself in your buyer's shoes. The number one reason a business cannot find buyers is because of what I call existential risk, meaning a threat with such severe repercussions that if it were to occur, it would be financially catastrophic. For a buyer, it would be career suicide to pay millions of dollars for a business that could lose a substantial portion of value shortly after closing because of some foreseeable risk. Consequently, even if the danger is unlikely and there is significant upside potential, most buyers will pass on opportunities when there exists a single point of failure.

Yes, investors get paid to take risks, and every business has its risks. But the risks they get paid to take are less catastrophic, such as changes from competition, operational declines, or a recession. These are easier to effectively mitigate or navigate because they take time to dramatically disrupt the business. Existential risks, on the other hand, devastate a business overnight.

Every buyer is paranoid that they are missing some hidden risk or skeleton in the closet. Three individuals won the Nobel Prize in Economics in 2001 for their work revealing that the side that loses when there's an imbalance of information is counterintuitively the party with greater information. Buyers understand it's impossible for them to get a full picture from their limited, often curated interactions. Sellers inherently know a lot more about the risks of the business they own, and buyers ultimately overcompensate by assuming the worst-case scenario.

Here are the most common types of existential risk:

- Key-person risk. This hazard generally concerns the owner. Can you take an uninterrupted four-week holiday and come back to a business that's in the same state you left it? If you can't, you don't have a going concern business but a job. But key-person risk can occur farther down the hierarchy, for instance:
    - Sales: When a large amount of the sales are dependent upon the relationships with a single personality. This is the most typical risk. When that superstar salesperson leaves, customers may shop elsewhere.
    - Operations: Daily operations depend upon a single person. If they were to leave, the company would be put in a tailspin.
    - Know-how: Does one engineer or manager possess unique, specialized knowledge that few others have?
    - Nepotism: Having a management team formed of related family members is also perceived to be a risk because if one member becomes disgruntled or is terminated, it risks multiple disruptive departures.
- Customer concentration. Your largest customer leaving you could halve your revenue overnight. This can often be mitigated by signing long-term contracts and raising the switching costs to make it much harder to replace you with a competitor.
- Regulatory risk. A pending or expected change in the law can drive whole industries into extinction. While most companies are marginally impacted by laws and regulations, some business models can be rendered obsolete overnight.
- Compliance risk. Any investigations involving regulators, whether criminal liability is a possibility or not, are highly likely to scare off potential buyers. Not only can these present huge direct or indirect costs, but also most buyers do not want to be associated with the reputational risk.
- Legal risk. Pending litigation involving a large, disputed amount could result in the business becoming insolvent, and buyers generally do not have the expertise to independently form an educated opinion regarding the likelihood and costs. While carving out these liabilities through an asset sale may reduce this risk, most buyers are concerned about successor

liability. In other words, if you are not around to pay the judgment, the plaintiff will come looking for the deep pockets.

- Accounting risk. Financials and record keeping may be so unreliable that they prevent a buyer from having any confidence in the company's true condition.
- Supplier risk. As supply chain problems during the COVID-19 pandemic revealed, the inability to get product from a critical supplier, particularly if few alternatives exist, can be incredibly disruptive. You can't sell if you don't have the product.
- Location risk. If a business is perceived to be dependent upon its specific location, and a long-term lease cannot be guaranteed, all of the value could evaporate if the lease does not renew or if rates go up substantially.

OTHER COMMON VALUE DETRACTORS

Existential risks are just an extreme category of risk. Savvy buyers are on the lookout for a number of other scenarios that would cause them to either not consider your business as an acquisition candidate or to discount its value dramatically. Often, there is a willing buyer for the business, but at a price point you likely will not find compelling.

Here are some factors that have scared away buyers from otherwise great businesses:

- Management. The leadership team is a critical component of a buyer's transaction rationale. A revolving door in the executive ranks can be a red flag for buyers. A potential owner is looking for stability, and high turnover can be a warning sign. While a buyer can incur the hassle and risk of building their own team post-closing, top dollar is reserved for businesses with a strong functioning leadership team that provides the comfort of a seamless transition.
- Customers. Just as high turnover in the C-suite is a sign of trouble, instability in the customer base can be a reason for a buyer to walk away. The buyer will conclude that the turnover is a result of poor customer service or intense competition. In either case, it's up to you to create a detailed explanation to address potential buyers' concerns. For example, if you've experienced a spike in warranty claims, the buyer will likely have quality concerns. You should explain what went wrong and what you've done to fix it.
- Tax issues. If you've been fast and loose with business expenses and other tax issues, it's time to tighten up. In some transactions, the buyer

retains liability for the acquired company's tax issues. Off-the-books transactions – including cash deals and other unrecorded arrangements – are likely to receive partial credit, at best. If this applies to you, get together with your certified public accountant (CPA) or tax attorney about these problem areas before starting the sales process.

- Legal liabilities. Buyers are rightly skittish about getting involved with even minor legal issues. They aren't all that interested in hearing your side of a dispute – they just see the potential for a costly headache. And liens are yet another problem area – either for unpaid taxes or from unpaid vendors and suppliers.
- Employee classification. Another common legal issue surrounds employee classification and the distinction between contractors and full-time employees. If there's a gray area surrounding how you've classified your employees, consult with an employment attorney to determine how to proceed. Worker's comp and overtime are other areas that can scare off would-be buyers.

TOP 3 TAKEAWAYS

- An estimated one out of two middle-market businesses are unsellable. In order for a business to sell, a buyer needs to want it and to choose to buy it over the available alternative investment options. The alternative is to liquidate the company's assets for a fraction of its going-concern value.
- The number one reason a business cannot find buyers is because of some catastrophic risk (even if the probability is low) with such severe repercussions that if it were to occur, it would devastate the business overnight. Most existential risks involve a single point of failure, such as customer concentration, key-person risk, regulatory exposure, etc. Buyers can typically address other more manageable risks with a lower valuation or less favorable structure.
- The good news is that nearly any business can be modified over time to become coveted by buyers. By addressing key value detractors now, you can not only sell a previously unsellable business, but you will also dramatically expand the universe of prospective buyers, their demand levels, and, ultimately, your valuation.

CHAPTER 12

Reverse Engineering
Your Business

I walked with my client into his office. When I asked about financial statements, inventory accounting, and employee records, he yelled to his secretary. "Where are all of our records?" His secretary came in and handed him a bundle of papers. "Here they are," she said. My client looked a little sheepish. "I've been meaning to get them in order, but I've just been so busy . . . ."

Before selling a house, you invest time and money to improve its curb appeal – and yet many owners fail to prepare their business to sell for an optimal price. First impressions are even more important to investors who are presented with thousands of investment opportunities in order to make a handful of acquisitions a year. Once a value has been ascribed to your business by a potential buyer, they mentally anchor off of that number, and it becomes challenging to get them to reprice it later.

Sellers are hopeful that buyers will give them credit for the long list of potential improvements that can be made to their business. The reality is buyers are skeptical about these unproven opportunities and are generally reluctant to pay for them. If they were so simple, why haven't you made the changes already? Full value comes from showing buyers actual results rather than telling them about the upside.

Taking steps to build a more valuable business boosts your company's marketability and improves your ultimate exit value. It's key to selling from a position of strength on *your* terms. Even if you choose not to sell, these same steps will enhance your cash flow, reduce your downside risk, and improve your lifestyle as an owner as you minimize your day-to-day decision-making. After all, the ultimate objective of a "sale-ready" business is one that can successfully run independently of its owner.

USING PRIVATE EQUITY AS A ROLE MODEL

A deliberate, disciplined examination of your company is a must. After all, building a business to appeal to buyers is too important to be left to chance. Luckily for you, a playbook already exists. Private equity (PE) firms are experts at buying, improving, and growing businesses with the intent of reselling them for a profit. Given their expertise in maximizing an exit, it's informative to observe – and to borrow – many of their techniques.

Reverse engineering is the core of how PE makes money. At a high level, they work backwards, designing the specific intermediate milestones needed to create their desired end-state business. PE firms are ruthlessly disciplined on this front – even when initially analyzing a business, they're thinking about the ultimate sale. During their due diligence, they underwrite the transaction and their proposed valuation based on detailed financial projections. As selling is mandatory and how they achieve their payout, they will even develop a perspective on who the most likely buyers are and what those buyers are willing to pay the most for All future budgets and strategic plans are typically directly tied to achieving and beating these projections. Before the PE firm even closes the transaction, it creates an initial value creation plan (often referred to as a "100-Day Plan") that kicks these efforts off with a sense of urgency.

Similarly, I recommend determining what potential buyers value the most and then using that as your North Star to guide your efforts. It's a straightforward – if difficult – exercise: View your business through the lens of a consultant advising a well-capitalized PE buyer with access to professional managers. To the extent possible, try and implement these strategies yourself. I know, I know – this is just one more task to add to your already full schedule and likely requires a change in mindset.

You must proactively confront difficult issues and instill a level of discipline that most private businesses don't possess. Consider bringing in external consultants to help, particularly because these can be added back to your EBITDA (earnings before interest, taxes, depreciation, and amortization) as a one-time expense. I promise it's worth the effort and money since you will be paid a multiple of these improvements.

SALE READINESS: SHORT-TERM TIME HORIZON

If you're taking your company to market in less than a year, you don't have time to dramatically reshape your fundamentals and strategy. But you can make some meaningful improvements that will make your company less objectionable to buyers, more valuable, and more likely to successfully get over the goal line and close. Here are some of the areas that I have found move the needle the most:

- Clean up the financial statements. Insist on accurate and timely *accrual-based* financials and associated reporting. You need to finally address all of those accounting adjustments you have been procrastinating about. Some common problematic areas:
  - Ensure revenue recognition is appropriate.
  - Check year-end payroll and benefit accruals.
  - Write off bad debt, receivables, and obsolete inventory.
- Eliminate as many personal expenses within the business as possible. While these can usually be added back, buyers always mentally discount addbacks, often providing only "partial credit" versus real profits that you have paid taxes upon. Regardless, make sure to keep and organize all supporting documentation for addbacks.
- Proactively address situations where a third party could have influence over the deal. They hold all of the cards if you need to approach them and get their consent right before closing.
  - Lock in the management team by putting employment contracts in place (with nonsolicitation and noncompete agreements essential) with financial incentives to motivate key managers to drive a transaction forward enthusiastically. Also, consider putting in place deferred compensation plans with vesting that will help retain critical leaders post-transaction. Most buyers will not proceed with a sale unless your key people are fully on board.
  - Clean up any outstanding litigation. Settle, if possible. Some important matters, particularly those that are large or unquantifiable, will essentially preclude you from successfully selling the business. Do not initiate lawsuits, as they will likely invite countersuits and other escalations that can come back and bite you.
  - Modify important supplier, customer, or landlord contracts to permit them to be assigned or transferred to the buyer.
- Organize all legal contracts, leases, insurance policies, and HR records in a centralized place so they are accessible and ready to show. Create a spreadsheet to summarize the key terms, such as termination rights and change of control provisions. When a buyer quickly receives nearly everything requested in an orderly fashion, you signal that you are a well-run, sophisticated organization, and they will need a strong offer to buy.
- Consolidate all relevant legal entities under a single holding company with a clean ownership structure to the extent applicable and practical.

- Ensure you are fully compliant with all major laws and regulations. Nothing will kill a deal faster than some government investigations in the mix. The laundry list includes state and federal Departments of Labor (proper classification of 1099 vs. W2s, including overtime hours), state and federal Occupational Safety and Health Administrations (safety requirements), and dozens of other industry-specific agencies.
- Improve your working capital efficiency. Collect your receivables more aggressively and stop holding any unnecessary excess inventory. This will ultimately directly impact your cash at closing as it helps your working capital adjustments at closing (see Chapter 23 for more detail).
- Spruce up your facilities. Many business owners are frugal, sometimes to a fault. And if you come into a building every day, you might fail to notice the fading paint in the entryway or that machine on the shop floor that's been broken for years. But you can bet a buyer will notice all of those things. So, take some time to declutter and make some cosmetic upgrades. A full renovation isn't necessary, but a freshening up goes a long way toward subtly improving buyer confidence.
- Redesign your website and marketing materials so you present yourself as a successful, modern enterprise.
- Check review sites (Yelp, Google, etc.) to ensure you have flattering reviews. If not, look into reputation management services, whose job is to improve these ratings and bury negative reviews as far down as possible in search results.
- Try to get as much positive press about your company as possible. If possible, apply and win relevant industry awards, such as Best Places to Work.
- Start expanding the scope of responsibility for your direct reports, delegating as many duties as possible. You must be able to address the question: If you stopped showing up to work, who could keep the business moving forward?
- Have a strategic plan and budget in place and measure your progress against it. A history of consistently executing and delivering on your budget makes your future expectations more credible and gives buyers the confidence to buy based on next year's financials.
- Hold yourself accountable for achieving your goals through a board of advisors, a business coach/consultant, or a CEO peer group (such as the Young Presidents' Organization [YPO] or Vistage).

These are all smart business moves anyway, and not doing them leaves real money on the table. It is important to analyze the various improvements that can be made through the lens of return on investment (ROI), both in terms of money and time. Will you get a premium, or even your money back, for installing new blue kitchen cabinets in a home? Apply that same sort of thinking to your business. Similarly, you may be punished for a partially implemented growth strategy that hasn't yet reached stabilization. They will take advantage of your increased costs and the uncertainty of whether the expected profitability will materialize. Counterintuitively, you may receive more credit for presenting that same business case as a future opportunity that the buyer can capture.

As you approach going to market, refrain from making any drastic strategic changes or new long-term commitments while continuing to run the business under the assumption that a deal will not get done. This helps maintain a strong plan B – continue running your business profitably.

LUXURY OF TIME: MID- TO LONG-TERM TIME HORIZON

What if you don't plan to sell for three or more years? If that's the case, you have the luxury of taking the long view and making structural changes that can significantly improve both your bottom line and the expected multiple. Generally, the highest ROI comes from systematically addressing the various existential risks and value detractors that plague some middle-market businesses. Fundamentally, you want to improve the amount of cash and the certainty of that cash. With the luxury of time, you can be ambitious. Some areas to address:

- Tilt future growth toward product, channel, and customer mixes with the most attractive profiles. Work backwards from what buyers most value and then execute a strategic plan to start emphasizing that category, geography, etc. Ideally, focus on building what a broad base of buyers wants so you can maintain competitiveness (versus building to suit a specific buyer's ideal acquisition candidate).
- Work on improving the quality of your revenues (shift to subscriptions or longer-term agreements). An alternative approach would be to modify your business to make it painful to leave. For example, I don't love my bank but won't switch because it's too much of a pain to reschedule all those automatic payments I've set up.
- Design yourself out of a job by hiring a full-time CEO or President and shifting to a passive Chairperson role. If you can successfully do this, the buyer will likely exempt you from having to stay and transition the business.

- Upgrade your management team so a strong stand-alone team remains with the business post-transaction. Sure, buyers can hire to replace departing team members, but they perceive this to be riskier than sticking with tried-and-true managers who already know the business well.
- Modernize your software. If you use antiquated software, it's time to consider the merits of upgrading. You don't need to make costly, disruptive investments in your technology, but you should spend enough so buyers perceive you as a technologically savvy operator. If you want to be more aggressive, boldly adopt a suite of technologies to assist you in marketing as a technology-enabled business. For instance, WeWork received insane valuations, being perceived as a tech rather than a traditional real-estate business.
- If you have customer or supplier concentration, focus on slowly growing with others to diversify your business.
- Develop new or more robust online sales channels to drive additional growth and increase diversification.
- Implement digital transformation programs. Automating various back-office functions will drive long-term value.
- Consider creative staffing arrangements. Many clients have been strategically offshoring more sophisticated professional roles and achieving improved performance and employee retention at a significantly lower cost.
- Pursue various efficiency/cost reduction efforts:
  - Procurement.
  - Supply chain optimization.
  - Lean Six Sigma efforts to improve efficiency.
  - Renegotiating key contracts.
  - Overhead reduction.
  - Improved sales force effectiveness.

One useful construct is to try and convert *but's* to *and's*. Often, we say this is a wonderful business, *but* it has this one flaw. We want to systematically address the deficiencies so we can credibly say this is a wonderful business *and* it also has all these other great highlights.

The possibilities for growth and improvement are likely endless. However, you and your team have limited bandwidth. Consequently, I find it most practical to systematically assess and prioritize the various efforts across various dimensions (Figure 12.1).

No matter how many years in the future you intend to sell, the decisions you make today can result in a better business and the best positioning for success. It's often said you should build a business today as if you will own it forever but could sell it tomorrow.

Opportunity Prioritization

Items and Key Elements	Estimated Valuation Impact	Required Investment	Timeline (months)	Implementation Difficulty/Risk
Maximize economics of e-commerce customers (i.e. increase active users by 11% and increase frequency of orders from 4.3 to 5 annually) - CRM e-mail campaign - Loyalty program introduction	$3.9–6.9mm	$250K	6–12	▬▬▬─────
Renegotiate national account pricing to improve EBITDA margins by 2%+ - Retain corporate attorney - Prioritize southeast market	$2.0–2.8mm	$150K	3–6	▬▬▬▬▬───
Eliminate unprofitable service line	$0.5–0.7mm	$100K	1–2	▬▬───────
Launch acquisition campaign to acquire new web customers - Significant shift in capabilities - Advertising and marketing spend	$10+mm	$1,500K+	6–18	▬▬▬▬▬───
Pursue strategic alliances with major retailers	$20+mm	$500K	12+	▬▬▬▬▬▬▬
Financial statements reviewed by accounting firm	N/A	$50K	2–3	───────

FIGURE 12.1   Illustrative opportunity prioritization of potential projects.

TOP 3 TAKEAWAYS

- Prepare your business ahead of time. First impressions matter to buyers, who often have many options to choose from. Focus on quick wins that clean up your business and make it more appealing. It's also much more valuable to show buyers actual results rather than telling them about upside potential.
- Taking steps to build a more valuable business boosts your company's marketability and improves your ultimate exit value. Even if you choose not to sell, these same steps will enhance your financeability, increase your cash flow, reduce your downside risk, and improve your lifestyle.
- PE investors are pros at buying businesses, making them better, and then selling them for a profit. They start by figuring out the end goal, then reverse engineer to ensure accountability in making it happen. For your business, identify, analyze, and prioritize the largest value drivers through an ROI lens, both in terms of money and time.

CHAPTER 13

The Art of Selling

One of the deals I remember the most involved listening to a client talk about how he founded the business. He was a master story-teller, and by the time he finished his narrative, I swear that he could have been selling a company that made rotary phones, and the buyers would have wanted to continue negotiating. That's when I realized that in M&A transactions, success requires a significant amount of art.

Buyers stretch and participate in bidding wars when they are buying emotionally and concluding that they *must have* something. These emotions are best stirred through storytelling. Every story presents an opportunity to connect more authentically and build rapport. This is the seller's opportunity to control the narrative to focus on areas where it shines and has a distinctive comparative advantage.

Whenever possible, the pitch should be customized for each buyer and what they will find most exciting and persuasive. For example, vividly describing what a merger with a specific strategic acquirer would look like and quantifying the associated benefits and upside is far more effective than referencing vague benefits. Remember, a buyer's decision-makers tend to be singularly focused on advancing their own strategy and products. So, place disproportionate emphasis on how a combination will assist *them* in accomplishing their corporate objectives and priorities rather than how a deal has the potential to boost your company's potential or profitability.

Buyers are buying the future, so it's important to paint a high-resolution picture of all the growth opportunities available if the business had the capital and resources to capture them. The ideal fact pattern for most buyers is a proven business model that just needs rocket fuel poured on it to rapidly scale.

At the same time, stories can help explain and put in proper context deficiencies or choppy performance. Never be defensive about your weaknesses – try to nonchalantly mention them as a strength whenever possible. At some point in the process, you will inevitably be asked about your founding history. Everyone loves a good American Dream story, so try to weave in relevant highlights and wins as you describe how you built your business against the odds.

PACING IS IMPORTANT

Nothing better exemplifies the art of selling than pacing. The adage "time kills deals" is true, yet there are many situations where patience and allowing the other side to unilaterally respond is the best course. In an effective sales process, every decision – timing, disclosure of information, structure – is made intentionally. As a seller, you have the unfair advantage of selecting every detail to tilt the odds just a little bit in your favor. Stakes are high; the payoff can be enormous. The difference between top dollar and the deal blowing apart can drastically change your life.

The alternative – reactively addressing a buyer's requests – puts you in a defensive position of trying to counter their various tactics, which were designed to advantage them. Just like your sales efforts for your business's product or service, persuasive delivery can have a significant impact on a buyer's interest level and willingness to pay. John Warrillow points out, "you make a few hundred or a few thousand dollars when you sell your product, but if you turned those same skills to selling your company, you can make exponentially more. You have the right skills, but you're selling the wrong product" (Warrillow 2021, p. 40). The fundamentals of effective selling are equally applicable and important in the sale of a business.

FRAMING MATTERS

Through your research and in the course of discussions with a prospective buyer, you and your advisors will be able to uncover the buyer's objectives and motivations. Don't be afraid to ask direct questions regarding their strategy and priorities. These can then be utilized to frame the opportunity more effectively, in a way that is most relevant and persuasive to them. For example, during the course of the discussions, you may be able to determine that increasing their market share determines their performance bonus. You can then use that information to emphasize how this acquisition would further this goal over other potential areas of focus.

How buyers perceive your industry and business model is also highly influenced by how it's positioned. Since certain subindustries or themes, such as artificial intelligence (AI), can quickly get hot, there may be the opportunity to successfully reframe the company. For example, just because they utilize some software to run their operations, I've seen car washes, manufacturers, and even janitorial service businesses successfully market themselves as tech-enabled businesses. Similarly, referencing an opportunity in the context of a sexy trend that everyone knows and is excited about can be helpful. For example, this is an opportunity to invest in the "reshoring of American manufacturing."

HANDLE OBVIOUS OBJECTIONS EARLY

There's a tendency to want to avoid the elephant in the room. These issues could range from a regulatory investigation to declining performance. The reality is any buyer or their advisors will be sophisticated enough to eventually identify these problems.

I advise sellers to voluntarily put these issues on the table early for a couple of reasons: First, the transparency helps build trust and allows you to spin the messaging and show them the issue is not insurmountable. Additionally, delaying the inevitable can be counterproductive. It raises the risk that the prospective buyer will quietly assume you were trying to avoid disclosure and question your trustworthiness. This risks them backing out. Trying to revive the deal and induce them to reenter the process is far more difficult and can make you appear desperate and lacking alternatives.

STAGING IS CRUCIAL

First impressions matter because judgments are quickly made. Just like a home seller strives to maximize curb appeal, it's vital to physically clean and organize your facility so it appears safe and functional. This indicates a level of efficiency (implying Lean Six Sigma has been

(Continued)

(Continued)

implemented) and attention to detail that provides buyers with greater conviction in proceeding with a strong offer. Present an environment that a buyer can connect with emotionally and can see themselves owning.

A buyer's first exposure to a seller is generally through an Internet search and its financial statements. With that in mind, search your business and its key employees and objectively review your public image relative to the 800-pound gorilla in your industry. Proactively identify and try to address areas where you're lacking, such as improving or updating your website or addressing negative reviews. Similarly, do your housekeeping on your financial statements beforehand to minimize the chances of awkward discussions about that "Ask my accountant" entry.

FORWARD PROGRESS

At its core, all sales processes are designed to maximize competition or the implicit threat of it. Synchronizing all of the interested parties is a fundamental yet challenging aspect of this. As a seller, you want to be able to assess all of your available options at the same time so you can make a fully informed decision. Otherwise, you may be put in a position of having to choose between accepting a standing offer or declining it in the hope of encountering something better later along.

Deviations from the initial timeline and exceptions may need to occur, but they should be made strategically and intentionally. While some eager buyers may need to be stalled, others will need to be prodded to speed up. Your banker is expected to be aggressive, so he has the advantage of pushing along the process without you being perceived as overeager or desperate.

A sense of urgency throughout the process is important and signals to prospective buyers that you are selling on your terms. All conversations and interactions should have next steps and be geared toward moving things forward. While uncelebrated, consistent follow-up is also critical to keeping things on track and ensuring that good bidders don't fall through the cracks. Good investment bankers will make various follow-up calls (in addition to e-mail outreach) to keep the ball moving. For example, they should call immediately after the confidential information memorandum (CIM) is sent to confirm receipt, around ten days after receipt of CIM, asking about their reaction to it and asking for any questions they may have about it, and approximately a week before offers are due to provide a friendly reminder.

BACK TO DATING

To return to the dating analogy, desire cannot be imposed on a buyer. Trying to force interest is like pushing on a string. Not only is it pointless, but it also signals weakness and a lack of compelling alternatives. The best a seller can do is to lay down breadcrumbs to entice the buyer to pursue it.

Buyers tend to be herd animals and often get spooked when they sense you don't have other alternatives. They start to wonder whether they missed something others noticed and you're damaged goods. How do you feel when you visit a new restaurant which turns out to be empty?

There needs to be some challenge and tension. Even in the worst of circumstances, I find it's best for the seller to confidently feign a hard-to-get mentality of one who has options. This is generally not mentioned in direct discussions about the competition but rather signaled in indirect hints (or even "accidental" leaks) referencing other interested parties.

Relationships take time to blossom, and it may take time for a buyer to fully buy in, particularly for jaded private equity (PE) investors who review hundreds of opportunities annually. The goal is to lure in a buyer emotionally to ensure that they have sufficient commitment to follow through. Without the buyer taking the initiative to chase a target, there's likely insufficient momentum to go through the closing gauntlet.

TAKING A BUYER'S PERSPECTIVE

Whether you realize it or not, you are constantly communicating information to the world by what you do and even by what you don't do. Buyers are constantly trying to read between the lines, attempting to infer your motivations and positions based on your reactions (or lack thereof), your tone, and the consistency of explanations.

Sellers tend to have a blind spot regarding how their actions are being interpreted by prospective buyers. Specifically, many sellers inadvertently undermine their intended outcome through inconsistent actions. While there are a million different examples, here's one I frequently encounter: Sellers will frequently try to convey indifference about doing a deal, yet they act impatiently. Lean on your advisors to convey how your behavior may be coming across to others.

Deals will throw plenty of curveballs, so in situations where it's unclear what is the best approach to take, I default to asking: How would a seller with many compelling alternatives act under those circumstances? In theater, "method acting" involves the performer becoming the character and fully taking on their life. The same applies here. Be that confident seller with attractive options, and find that you will be treated as one. Perception becomes reality.

TOP 3 TAKEAWAYS

- In order to get maximum value, you need to create a narrative that addresses the goals and objectives of the buyer. That means you will need to customize your pitch to each buyer, always being aware that along with the bottom line, there is an emotional component to a sale. The buyer has to have the desire to buy your business and buy it now.
- Every business has weaknesses. As a seller, it is your goal to be proactive about weaknesses and obvious objections. Transparency builds trust, and trust enables sales.
- Analyze your actions from a buyer's perspective. It's always best to act a bit hard to get. Being overeager or seeming desperate to sell will be used against you.

CHAPTER 14

Negotiating Strategy

"Wow," Monica (not her real name) said. "You were really tough in there. Don't get me wrong. I appreciate what you did, but I'd hate to be on the opposite side of the table from you." While I was flattered, having studied negotiation at Harvard Law School, I've found most academics tend to focus on collaborative negotiating styles designed to expand the pie for mutual benefit. However, my experience in the real world hints at a different reality: Most negotiations are overwhelmingly geared toward the pie's allocation and trying to gain an advantage over your counterparty. My responsibility is not to achieve a mutually fair outcome but to obtain the best possible deal for my client.

The final days before signing a letter of intent (LOI) generally involve a significant amount of negotiation. Most sellers think that the negotiating is complete at this point. The reality is this is just the beginning of dozens of smaller negotiations that will occur through the final day of closing. This occurs for two reasons: First, changes and new information emerge that now must be accounted for. Second, the standard 100 pages of legal documentation involves lots of detail that was not anticipated or resolved in the LOI.

While some issues can be quickly resolved, plenty of others can become major stumbling blocks to consummating the transaction. You need to acceptably resolve 100% of outstanding issues in order to successfully close a transaction. Unfortunately, a single sticking point has the potential to become a deal killer.

While it's generally not to your advantage to get directly involved in negotiations yourself, it is helpful, if not essential, to understand some of the common tactics your advisors and counterparties will use and their rationale.

The right approach tends to be highly contextual. My objective in this chapter is to highlight some important fundamentals and areas to be on the lookout for in your transaction.

THEORY, MEET REAL WORLD

Both parties willingly transact because they believe it is in their best interests to do so. While, of course, sellers want to negotiate the best possible outcome, most agreements require compromise and finding a middle ground where the buyer feels satisfied enough to willingly proceed.

Interestingly, it's the negotiating process itself that assists both parties in perceiving a sense of fairness with the outcome. In his book *Smart Negotiating: How to Make Good Deals in the Real World*, author and Wall Street lawyer James Freund points out that people "need to see the other side move from its opening position – to feel the satisfaction of having engaged in a strenuous undertaking – in order to arrive at the finish line reassured that [they] got the best deal possible and didn't leave too much on the table" (Freund 1992, p. 25). This is similar to a bargain hunter who enjoys finding a discounted item and haggling about it. The actual item purchased is an afterthought. A negotiation needs to unfold and run its course. Counterintuitively, we psychologically prefer the thrill of the pursuit relative to proposing and quickly agreeing to the exact same outcome.

EVERY INTERACTION IS A NEGOTIATION

From the initial instant that the buyer and seller meet, negotiations have begun, with each side trying to gain the upper hand. From that moment on, each continuously tries to posture, with the intent of best positioning themselves going forward. Be aware that small things can inadvertently undermine your posture. For example, being overly accommodative, such as a willingness to meet anywhere, anytime, can often make you appear overeager.

Good investment bankers take nothing at face value and continuously observe and listen to what is really being portrayed. They also keep track of relative leverage as events unfold in real time. Throughout the sales process, I am constantly assessing where we stand and how new developments impact our position across various dimensions (not just price but also various structural things I'm advocating, such as not needing an escrow). While individually each piece of information is inconsequential, the goal is to understand how it directionally impacts your leverage: Is it helpful, hurtful, or irrelevant?

Information is the lifeblood of any negotiation. Without it, you're just stabbing in the dark. Consequently, a lot of efforts are geared toward trying to uncover and evaluate information about the buyer and their willingness to budge from their stated position. They are directly and inadvertently conveying information all the time, both truthful and bluffs. It's valuable to listen closely to what the buyer says and compare the consistency with their prior positions, nonverbal cues, and reactions (or lack thereof). Collectively, these provide the raw materials to make educated inferences about the buyer's true motivations and positions. Rest assured, the buyer will be doing the same with you during your limited interactions. So, take care to filter your words and actions through a buyer's ears and eyes, and try to understand how they might be interpreted or misinterpreted.

DON'T FORGET THE HUMAN ELEMENT

Negotiations occur between two or more human beings who do not always act rationally. We have the capacity for a wide range of nuanced emotions, which impact our judgment, decisions, and behaviors. Consequently, it's important to be attuned to these elements and leverage them to your advantage. What separates good investment bankers from excellent ones? Their ability to psychologically size up their negotiating counterparties and to use it to their advantage.

One of the most destructive emotions in a negotiation is vindictiveness. When someone feels disrespected, there's a risk they respond by hardening their positions and trying to retaliate, even at their own expense. You may encounter some situations where you hold all of the cards and can dictate the terms. Particularly in these situations, it's critical that logical reasons for your positions are presented and there's a perceived openness to being influenced by your counterpart's arguments. It's important not to be perceived as overbearing or arbitrary, as it can potentially bruise the buyer's pride and backfire. It often causes your counterparty to lose trust, rapport, and their motivation to close. Like anything else in life, showing courtesy and respect goes a long way.

In nearly all middle-market merger and acquisition (M&A) transactions, the buyer and seller continue to interact and be financially intertwined for the next few years. Consequently, it's vital that your buyer counterparty leaves the negotiation feeling like you are a reasonable person who keeps their word and acts in good faith.

Understand that a deal's roller coaster of emotions is likely to affect the quality of your decision-making as well. Many sellers panic if they perceive the deal at risk of dying with each issue that emerges. Lean on your advisors, and don't be afraid to take the time to pause and reflect.

MANAGING RELATIONS WITH THE COUNTERPARTY

While I reference the buyer as a single entity, remember there are actually two different counterparties being engaged: the individual negotiator seated opposite you and the buyer that employs them. Their objectives and interests frequently diverge. In some environments, your buyer counterparty may be a salaried operator with no upside for taking a risk. Conversely, the individual may have strong financial incentives to do deals without responsibility for their outcomes. These factors should be understood and leveraged to your advantage.

Significant research and preparation should go into understanding as much about both as possible. I frequently reach out to prior sellers and their service providers to get a sense of the buyer's negotiation style and character.

Whenever possible, your advisor should actively be looking for opportunities to allow your counterparty to save face. One of the easiest approaches is to concede something of minor importance or accept changes where their request is undeniably reasonable. Your buyer counterparty needs the psychological satisfaction of having scored some points, too. Always try to allow them to celebrate a win with their constituencies, even if the victory is inconsequential.

PREPARATION IS HALF THE BATTLE

It's critical to develop a game plan beforehand. Most negotiations are won *before* any formal haggling begins. You wouldn't compete in a championship fight without training and analyzing video of your opponent. This deal is your equivalent of a prize fight – and the bout of a lifetime is not the time to *wing it*. In *Smart Negotiating*, Freund introduces a four-question framework for effective preparation beforehand (Freund 2006, p. 92):

- What do I want?
- Where do I start?
- When do I make concessions?
- How do I close?

Work with your investment banker to quantify your walk-away price and terms before the negotiation. Similarly, assess and categorize the true deal breakers, those concessions that are preferred but not sacrosanct, and those that can easily be used as bargaining chips. Trying to make these decisions in real time under the influence of emotions makes it too easy to rationalize and accept suboptimal outcomes.

While an argumentative mindset is not constructive, good negotiating is like a debate. The chances of resolving a point are significantly increased if the most logical rationales to support it are presented in a prioritized fashion. The argument grows even more persuasive if it can be framed as to why it's in the buyer's best interest as well.

Consequently, having a strong grasp of all of the relevant facts is advantageous. Without it, it's virtually impossible to understand the implications of various proposals and solutions in real time. For example, before advocating for a certain approach to handling working capital, I calculate the various versions of the metric beforehand. Depending on what's most advantageous to us, I will then attempt to nonchalantly advocate the merits of using that approach.

LEVERAGE

It's definitely a lot easier and more fun to negotiate when you come from a strong position. A highly marketable business practically sells itself. The mark of a high-quality negotiator is their ability to achieve a successful outcome in environments where they are poorly positioned.

What impacts negotiating leverage? Here are the characteristics of a weak seller position, with the opposite representing high leverage:

- Fundamentals
  - Lukewarm buyer interest or feeling that they believe they are already overpaying.
  - Single buyer that is dramatically higher than all other interested parties.
  - Lack of a senior champion within the buyer's organization.
  - Buyer has invested relatively little time and/or money into third-party due diligence.
  - Deteriorating seller financial performance.
- Timing/urgency
  - Seller needs to move quickly.
  - Seller is fatigued and ready to capitulate to get things over with.

- Scarcity
  - Deal is a commodity with lots of suitable substitutes currently on the market.
- Detachment
  - Buyer is indifferent and can easily live without the acquisition.

In the real world, these factors are likely to be a mixed bag, with some advantageous and others harmful to your cause. Where you draw the line and the aggressiveness of your negotiating strategy may be vastly different depending on these factors and the specific context.

To the extent you have a weak position, it's best not to advertise it, as buyers can and *will* use it against you. I always pay particular attention to how the timing, manner, and substance of my responses can be perceived and what they may inadvertently convey about the strength of our hand.

BATNA

BATNA, or Best Alternative to a Negotiated Agreement, is essentially your Plan B if a negotiated solution cannot be agreed upon. Strong alternatives give you the confidence to walk away from an unfavorable deal. Conversely, if your options are substantially less attractive, then you should assume a more flexible stance.

It's critical to continuously analyze and attempt to improve your BATNA. Since things change, and options can fall through, there's never a downside to proactively soliciting other options (i.e. Plans B and C). In a sale transaction, you essentially have two alternatives: pursue another competitive offer or choose not to sell. One of the most powerful things you can do is to optimize your business's sustainable value (see Chapter 12 for specific tactics). If you're running a profitable, fine-tuned business, there's no financial pressure on you. Without pressure forcing you to sell at the current market value, the buyer will need to make it worth your while to transact.

At the same time, it's also wise to try to understand your buyer counterparty's BATNA as well, to extrapolate how flexible (or inflexible) they're likely to be on contested deal terms. A classic guide to negotiating, authored by Herb Cohen, is *Negotiate This! By Caring, But Not T-H-A-T Much*. I like to say that the party who wants it the least is in an advantageous position. If I am eager to get a deal done and you're indifferent, I am going to have to make a lot of concessions to induce you to participate. Conversely, if the acquisition is a must-have, buyers are much more willing to stretch on price and terms than if it's just a nice-to-have.

THE DANGERS OF BLUFFING

While bluffs come in all shapes and sizes, the most common version of this gambit is "the best and final offer." (Sure, it is.) Appearances of leverage are critical, yet appearances can often be manipulated through brinkmanship and bluffing. Consequently, buyers will naturally question your side's position, probing to gauge the true firmness of your stance by suggesting minor modifications. They are also highly attuned to any inconsistencies with your behaviors and actions relative to a seller with strong alternatives.

Like the boy who cried wolf, a seller caught bluffing or making an empty threat will struggle to be taken seriously going forward. Perhaps worse, with their credibility in question, the buyer may think the seller to be bluffing on real non-negotiable positions.

Bluffing is appropriate in certain circumstances. But it comes with risks and should be saved for extremely important matters, ideally toward the end of the sales process. This is because there are three potential scenarios when you bluff, and only one is favorable:

- It's believed and accepted – your desired outcome.
- It's called out, and you lose credibility.
- It's believed, and it causes the buyer to walk away from a deal you would have agreed to.

To the extent you do authorize your advisors to bluff, here are some typical approaches to minimize the risk:

- Present a plausible reason for why your position doesn't have any leeway.
- Tie your bluff to prior positions you have been asserting consistently.
- Show flexibility on some other issues to emphasize the firmness of your bluff. You're unlikely to maintain credibility if you are claiming a hard line on everything.
- Frame your bluff with some wiggle room in case the buyer refuses to budge. Freund also advocates preparing a *changed circumstances* story beforehand to help you save face if you need to backtrack from your position (Freund 2006, p. 75).

I consider threats a more serious and riskier version of a bluff. If you're not willing to live with the consequences, do not make a threat. Moreover, I find they tend to be counterproductive since buyers often want to escalate and respond in kind.

STRIKING A BALANCE

Freund offers smart advice on this topic: "The secret of effective negotiating is to achieve a functional balance between what you do to gain an advantage at your counterparty's expense and what you do to move the two of you closer to an eventual compromise" (Freund 2006, p. 79). In other words, you don't need to go for the kill on every point. Restraint is a virtue, particularly because conditions can quickly move against you. It's frequently valuable to strategically concede something of relatively low importance to prime the pump and induce movement from your counterparty.

YOU MAKE THE CALL

You will need to make decisions with imperfect information, often a result of the buyer trying to bluff or misrepresent their true position. Based upon the counterparty's behavior, reactions, and tone, a skilled negotiator has an intuition regarding the negotiation's position within the broader life cycle. In his book *Mergers & Acquisitions*, Dennis Roberts points out that buyers "gradually will squeal louder and louder for negotiations to be concluded and the deal to be done. Such buyer 'noises' should be scrutinized carefully: is the buyer just testing the seller in hopes the seller will fold (a strong possibility in the early goings), or is the buyer communicating genuine frustration that should be taken very seriously?" (Roberts 2009, p. 206).

Let me make a comparison to fishing. When you've got a fish on the line, there's a fine balance between tiring the fish out and creating so much tension that the line breaks, and your catch gets away. While most sellers generally perceive an overexaggerated risk, there's always that chance that using aggressive tactics (such as strategically choosing to walk away) will end up hurting or even killing the deal. Your investment banker's instincts and objective perspective will prove valuable.

Make sure your advisors fully educate you on their proposed negotiating strategy, their rationale, and potential risks. Then, it's your responsibility to make the final call. The buyer will ultimately hold you responsible for your side's tactics, particularly if they are perceived to be unreasonable. As the seller, you have the ultimate responsibility and authority to decide how aggressive or conservative you'd like to be. Your advisor will then use that guidance to inform the thousands of microdecisions that are made during actual discussions.

FLEXIBILITY PLUS CREDIBILITY

As a seller, it's vital to communicate in ways that allow you the flexibility to backpedal without losing credibility. For example, John owns a large, profitable payday lender business, an industry with some regulatory and reputational risks that will make garnering widespread buyer interest difficult. Interest will likely be lukewarm and require significant effort to induce any buyer to invest the time to engage.

If he tries to approach a couple of potentially interested buyers and fake an auction, there's a good chance of it backfiring. That's because the pacing of a competitive process has specific milestones and moves along at a fast pace. Consequently, it is virtually impossible to hide the inconsistencies between negotiating with a single buyer and an auction. As time passes by, the truth will come out. The mere fact that the seller continues to engage after a couple of months conveys that the seller has a weak hand and they are possibly the only buyer.

Once you lose credibility with a buyer, it results in significantly less trust and leverage going forward. In this circumstance, I would subtly insinuate that there are other interested buyers and that fit is an important objective to my client. This provides the flexibility to continue to engage over a long, drawn-out period without getting caught lying.

NO-REGRET MOVES

While there are few universals in negotiating, here are a handful of recommendations I nearly always provide to my clients:

- Don't bid against yourself. Some buyers will ask for concessions without making any movement themselves. Unless your position was wildly unreasonable, don't negotiate against yourself and revise your offer without receiving a counteroffer.
- Don't jump at the first offer. No buyer will expect you to make an important decision regarding the sale of your company without taking the time to discuss it with your advisors and to reflect on the answer.

Even if the buyer presents a perfect offer as is, I highly recommend taking an appropriate amount of time to respond and creating the impression that you're, at a minimum, slightly displeased. Additionally, I recommend countering, even if the change is cosmetic. The alternative risks the buyer feeling like he offered too much unnecessarily. Later in the negotiations, there will be plenty of details for the buyer to water down the offer's attractiveness and even the score. When it comes to negotiating, slow responses are nearly always better than quick ones.

■ Demand to deal with ultimate decision-makers. Insist that your negotiating counterparty has the full authority to negotiate the transaction without additional approvals. If additional parties are needed to provide consent, demand that they also participate in the discussions.

■ Let your advisors do the negotiating. During negotiations, one of the benefits of working with an advisor is the ability to negotiate with limited authority. As an agent, an advisor cannot agree to concessions and commitments, so there's always the chance to "take stuff back." When negotiating as the actual decision-maker, you don't have this luxury. Car dealerships often use this tactic. There's a reason why the store manager never just comes out and negotiates directly with you.

■ Have only *one* lead negotiator. There can be only *one* lead negotiator who serves as the quarterback at any given time, with all of the other advisors playing a supportive role – typically the investment banker until the confirmatory diligence is completed and then the attorney through closing. Having multiple negotiators on your team risks things falling through the cracks and adds friction to the process. It creates confusion and headaches for the buyer, who needs to spend more time and money on arriving at a solution. Perhaps worse, it leaves you vulnerable to the buyer trying to capitalize upon your team's inconsistencies to cherry-pick the most favorable elements.

■ Leave room to negotiate. No matter how impatient you are to get the deal over with, it's important that your starting position provides some leeway to negotiate. We have been indoctrinated that initial offers always have room for improvement. Freund advises "making a first offer that is sufficiently reasonable to be viewed constructively by the other side and thus to evoke a positive response. On the other hand, it should give you enough room to move deliberately to your expectations without being forced to stretch" (Freund 2006, p. 119). To the extent you do need to present numbers, he recommends starting a buffer of 15–25% above your realistic expected outcome. The optimal magnitude and timing of concessions will be highly dependent upon how the buyer responds.

■ Do not accept bad behavior. Permitting boorish moves only emboldens your counterparty. For example, if they backtrack on a concession previously agreed upon, conveniently misremember, or intentionally distort your statements, a dramatic response from your side may be warranted to convey that those tactics will not be tolerated. Similarly, if the buyer overtly threatens you, it's important to call it out and show that you will not be intimidated.

TOP 3 TAKEAWAYS

■ Recognize the human element of negotiations, especially the individual negotiator. Businesses don't negotiate; people do. Allowing all parties to save face by making certain unimportant concessions can make the final negotiations much easier.

■ Leverage dictates your options and strategies. You have a lot more leeway with a strong hand versus a weak hand. Trust your advisors. That's what they are there for.

■ It's vital to communicate in ways that allow you the flexibility to backpedal without losing credibility. Once you lose credibility with a buyer, it results in significantly less trust and leverage going forward.

CHAPTER 15

Overcoming Inertia

"When is this going to be done?" Even if a client doesn't say it out loud, I know they think this at least once, so don't be surprised when it happens to you. What I tell my clients is to stay the course. Selling your business is going to take more time than you think it should . . . and more time than you want it to.

Before we continue with the sales process, I'd like to take some time to talk about the role of inertia in every sale. Just as a rocket needs sufficient velocity to escape the Earth's atmosphere, a deal doesn't happen unless both parties channel their energy to close. Under the best of circumstances, pursuing an acquisition consumes a significant amount of time, energy, and money. Each challenge, misunderstanding, and setback in the negotiations adds a small grain of sand to the gearwork, reducing the likelihood of success. The greater the initial momentum and trust, the higher the likelihood of success. Conversely, if the buyer starts out lukewarm about the deal, a small issue can derail the transaction (or significant price concessions will be needed to induce them to continue). Applying the laws of physics to mergers and acquisitions (M&A), you always want to deposit as much currency into the momentum bank as possible – you never know when you might need to draw upon it.

BUILDING MOMENTUM

When a letter of intent (LOI) is initially signed, both sides are typically in a honeymoon phase. Buyer and seller feel an excitement that energizes them and provides momentum to continue to push the deal through the inevitable hard times in the future.

Every deal has a cadence, and the pace should be continuously monitored with the goal of maintaining it. Impasses sap momentum, while success begets success. Your advisor will keep an eye toward making progress and resolving outstanding items and issues, no matter how small. Every day should bring you closer to closing.

Just as you're busy, so is a prospective buyer. Numerous other responsibilities and opportunities vie for their attention. Particularly for strategic buyers, an M&A opportunity is just another burdensome task for an operator on top of their already full day. The easier it is for potential buyers to go through the process, the higher the likelihood of closing.

At the same time, momentum can also go in the other direction. The opposite of momentum is *deal fatigue*, when the participants reach a level of exhaustion and exasperation profound enough that they begin to question why they are even devoting time and energy to the deal. The risk is compounded when trust levels are low. Eventually, one side loses the will to transact and concludes enough of this.

The adage that *time kills deals* is true. Delays rarely provide upside but rather create more friction and costs that make it easier for one of the sides to walk away. The longer that journey takes, the more room for unanticipated surprises, which can disrupt the deal, such as:

- Declines in your company's performance – a possibility that grows increasingly likely as time passes and your team is distracted with the sales process.
- Changes in market availability of capital or financing.
- Angst over growing legal bills and resource commitments.
- Shinier alternatives present themselves.
- More opportunities for misunderstandings and feeling that the other side is "playing games."

First-time sellers who don't have the context of previous transactions are at the greatest risk of falling victim to it. They are either oversensitive and blow up the deal or start making unnecessary concessions to get the transaction over with. Buyers will often use this to their advantage: Once you reach the point of giving in, it's nearly impossible to hold your ground later on. Your advisors will serve as a buffer, helping to minimize the chances of this happening.

MINIMIZING FRICTION

Deals tend to stall and die because of the cumulative result of lots of small friction points. Minimizing friction is the unsexy part of closing deals, but its importance cannot be overstated. In an environment where buyers literally have hundreds of alternative investments, making it easy for them to pursue a deal is a critical but underappreciated differentiator. Someone recently pointed out this instructive truism: Put a bowl of fruit on the table, and the bananas are the first to go, with the oranges languishing until last. Why? Bananas are easiest to peel.

Reducing friction starts with avoiding unforced errors, such as a lack of responsiveness. In *The Art of Selling Your Business*, author John Warrillow observes, "When an excited acquirer asks for a piece of information, and you can't immediately give it to them, a little bit of their enthusiasm for the deal is lost. Fumble too many information requests, and the acquirer may lose patience and walk" (Warrillow 2021, p. 23).

As a seller, you are being judged not only on the content of your responses but also their timeliness. Slow answers insinuate poor systems, as companies with world-class systems can quickly provide the requested information with little manual intervention. Timely, professionally prepared due diligence responses signal you are a sophisticated counterparty.

On this front, preparation beforehand is invaluable. It comes as a surprise to most sellers, but the requisite documents that will be produced in a middle-market due diligence can be massive, in some cases involving 100,000+ pages of requests.

PROCRASTINATION IS A TERRIBLE STRATEGY

As a fellow entrepreneur and business owner, I fully understand that you have a million other priorities to take care of. The reality is a lot of work is required, and there's never a good time to start.

I've heard just about every excuse a seller can come up with for why they should delay preparing anticipated information requests ahead of time. Many sellers attempt to rationalize to themselves that buyers may not request or need it. The majority of sellers want to procrastinate in preparing these materials until a real buyer has materialized. This is a mistake because it shifts the burden to an intense, time-sensitive period when you will have your normal day job operating your business, *plus*:

- Searching for documents that you signed years ago that are not easily found (and, frequently, you're the only person in a position to find them).

(Continued)

(Continued)

- Trying to recreate and address any deficiencies in the required documentation.
- Pulling large amounts of data in ways you've never previously done may require significant manual intervention.
- Interpreting and negotiating long and dense legal agreements.
- Approaching key suppliers, customers, and employees to modify their agreements to comply with the buyer's requirements.

Given your desire to keep confidentiality, many of these responsibilities cannot easily be delegated to others. If you're trying to juggle all of these distractions, it's highly likely that your and your team's attention will drift, reducing the likelihood of meeting or beating your performance goals.

It's informative to analyze how professional portfolio companies owned by private equity (PE) firms handle this: From Day 1, the CFO will be responsible for keeping a full repository of relevant information that is continuously updated, providing them the ability to go to market at a moment's notice. The reality is having these key documents in a central, organized fashion is a *no-regret* move anyway.

SPEEDING UP BY SLOWING DOWN

Out of impatience and a lack of understanding regarding the intensity of the sales process, many sellers frequently push to prematurely go to market. They tend to push their advisors to start approaching buyers before the relevant homework has been completed in an attempt to speed up the transaction. However, from my experience, the more work you do up front, the smoother and faster future efforts with the buyer will be, ultimately increasing your likelihood of successfully closing at full value. Counterintuitively, slowing down and being deliberate during the preparation process nearly always results in a faster closing timeline.

With the luxury of time, sellers minimize the chances of errors associated with rushing (which are common) and gain the ability to intentionally shape how to most effectively and impactfully deliver the information. The alternative of reactively addressing buyer requests risks catching you surprised by your own information. Author Jonathan Brabrand, in his book *The $100 Million Exit,* describes the awkward position where a buyer is "waiting for a report you had only run in response to their request that shows a negative trend you weren't previously aware of. Now you're under the gun to figure out a response" (Brabrand 2020, p. 108).

MAKE IT EASY FOR THEM TO SAY *YES*

Your investment banker will help identify what a buyer naturally wants to know to assess and approve the opportunity, with the goal of preparing all of those items beforehand, along with the corresponding backup details. Ultimately, if you can do as much of the work as possible for the buyer, you significantly reduce the effort needed – and you make it far easier and more likely they say yes.

This logic is also why investment bankers will sometimes prearrange a financing package from a lender, called *staple financing*. The buyer may or may not choose to use this loan, but it lets them immediately know the financeability and general range of terms, with no effort on their part. This is particularly valuable in circumstances where market uncertainty or the unique elements of the business make obtaining a loan challenging.

Whether because of too much on their plate or just plain laziness, many of your buyer counterparts are strongly biased toward whatever is convenient and easy. Remember, while a buyer will ultimately be a corporate entity, your counterpart will be an individual who likely is unable to single-handedly make final decisions. These buyer team members have their own internal constituencies that they will need to sell. They may personally enthusiastically believe in and support an acquisition, but they first need to convince their investment committee or board to formally proceed. This normally occurs through an investment memo and an associated presentation. Provide them with the ammunition needed to persuade their stakeholders why they should stretch to make the acquisition. The more you put on a silver platter, the faster and easier they can produce a high-quality investment memo that will be approved.

Having been a buyer myself, here are some of the things that save time for buyers and make their life easier:

- High-quality financial and operational data, with little reason to question its accuracy.
- *Real-time* information so they can monitor current performance and trends.
- Quickly responding to and addressing data requests (to the extent something is not easily available, suggesting and providing a relevant proxy that addresses the core need).

- Minimizing discrepancies between different data sources and reconciling, if necessary.
- Logically organized documentation with a summary sheet condensing the critical aspects.
- Digesting complex issues with easy-to-understand explanations.
- Providing background industry information so they can confidently get up to speed and understand relevant nuances.
- Neatly formatted information in Excel files.
- Providing backup information, verification, and relevant independent sources for claims made.

MINIMIZE MISCOMMUNICATIONS

At the end of the day, a buyer is purchasing a business because of its people. It's a lot easier to negotiate with a counterparty you like and respect. If it becomes too adversarial (especially early in the process before significant time and energy have been invested), there's a greater chance the other side will say it's just not worth it.

Be mindful that it's easy to misinterpret the tone of e-mail and other written communications. In the stressful environment of a big-dollar deal, a message that you intended to be innocuous and straightforward can metastasize in ways you never envisioned. In his book *Mergers & Acquisitions*, author Dennis Roberts reminds us to "never forget the communications corollary to Murphy's Law: If a written communication of any sort, and in particular the rapid electronic variety, can be misinterpreted, it will be. And each and every miscommunication forces the seller and his/her investment banker to backpedal frantically to save a deal and/or keep a prospective buyer on board" (Roberts 2009, p. 192).

Humans are superstitious and often look for signs *not* to proceed with a deal. Psychologists have identified a cognitive bias called *ambiguity aversion*. Closely related to the "only thing to fear is fear itself," we frequently prefer to impatiently get a known negative result over with (killing the deal) than continue along with uncertainty, even if it has the potential for a much better outcome. Small things can easily be used as an excuse not to go through with an opportunity.

Without the full context, misunderstandings can often be interpreted by the other party as a lack of trustworthiness or good faith, which is particularly corrosive. I pay particular attention to minimizing opportunities for these misinterpretations, as it significantly increases the probability of success. At the same time, I find it most constructive to err on the side of over-communicating and giving the other side the benefit of the doubt.

TOP 3 TAKEAWAYS

■ Every deal reaches a point where it feels like inertia is taking over. While some things simply take time, you can do your part by doing everything possible to help create momentum, which is critical to successfully closing.

■ Keeping friction and conflict to a minimum is the unsexy part of closing deals, but its importance cannot be overstated. In an environment where buyers literally have hundreds of alternative investments, making it easy for them to pursue a deal is a critical but underappreciated differentiator. Do your homework, making sure you have all of the necessary information ready ahead of time.

■ A disproportionate effort should be placed on anticipating and minimizing miscommunications. Misunderstandings can be seen as a lack of trustworthiness or good faith. Strive for straightforward, transparent communication at every step.

CHAPTER **16**

Documents and Deal Process

The amount of documents involved in the deal process can be over-whelming. Unfortunately, even with the advent of electronic copies, lots of documents are only available in hard-copy format. One of my clients, upon seeing a stack on my desk, asked if I was cleaning out some old file cabinets. I smiled and told him that these were all his documents . . . and that there would be even more to come.

Let's dive into the critical documents the seller produces that comprise the foundation of the sales process. Your advisor will create each of these documents on your behalf. You will play a vital role in refining these documents as their content will ultimately be attributed to you, and you will be held accountable for it.

TEASER

The teaser is your written elevator pitch. This one-page document presents the highlights of your business and the investment opportunity without revealing your identity. Assume that the reader will only skim it and will decide in the first 15 seconds whether to read further. Remember that most private equity (PE) firms review three to five teasers per day. If you want to keep yours out of the trash can, it needs to be succinct and compelling.

The goal is to concisely convey the basics about the business, its competitive advantages, its financials, and your goals/desired transaction. A good teaser assists in attracting ideal prospective buyers while enabling the unsuitable ones to self-select out, saving you time and allowing you to focus your efforts where they have the greatest impact. This saves valuable time and minimizes the number of unnecessary recipients who receive your confidential information.

Given this document's nonconfidential nature, you need to assume it will be blasted widely to an audience that includes your competitors and everyone else in your industry. Your goal is to provide enough information to pique someone's interest without outing you as the seller. To ensure that no one can make an educated guess about your identity, it's important to review the document through the lens of an industry insider. Try to keep the description vague enough that it describes 20 or more potential companies.

This game of cloak and dagger can get tricky. If your universe of competitors is small, you could broaden the geographic scope (instead of describing your company as headquartered in Florida, you might say it's based in the eastern United States) or refer to the industry more generally (instead of saying orthopedic services, you might say healthcare services). Similarly, you may leave out telling aspects of the business model that are unique to you or to just a few players. Providing specific figures can make it easier to identify you, so it's common to share directional ranges for number of locations, number of employees, and founding date.

A word of warning: It is critical that this information is entirely consistent with everything that will be presented in the confidential information memorandum (CIM). As a seller, you never want the buyer to be in a position to wonder which numbers to trust. Any inconsistencies will start you off on the wrong foot by making you look disorganized or incompetent. Because of this, I highly recommend not sending teasers until the numbers and CIM are fully finalized.

NONDISCLOSURE AGREEMENT (NDA)

This is a legal agreement that protects the information you share with a buyer. The nondisclosure agreement (NDA) is typically one to three pages long and will be signed by your advisor on your behalf. Only upon its signature will your name be revealed. While the definition of confidential information tends to be pretty standard and accepted, here are the critical areas that frequently get negotiated:

- Term. This ranges between one and three years, but most of the time, this ends up being 24 months.
- Nonsolicitation. This prevents buyers from using the process to poach your employees and customers. A lot of negotiation is to be expected regarding the scope of employees covered and the length of restrictions.

■ Dual hat exceptions. Given that the individuals seeing these documents often serve as board members in their other business investments, PE buyers will frequently stipulate that the NDA does not apply to these other businesses unless the information was actually shared with them.

The NDA is a legal necessity but can also give you insight into bidders. After all, this document is the first "negotiation" that occurs with a prospective buyer. I find it to be an informative preview of how reasonable your counterparty will be in future negotiations.

CONFIDENTIAL INFORMATION MEMORANDUM (CIM)

The CIM is where the real action happens. This is the primary document that presents the business in detail, covering all of the facets a buyer would want to know about. You might also hear the CIM referred to as the pitch-book, the offering memorandum, or simply "the book." The CIM is a foundational document as various future documents and activities will expand upon it, clarify it, or reference it.

In the past, CIMs were prose-like books that ran dozens of pages. But it turns out that – surprise! – no one really read them. In an age of shortened attention spans, the norm now is 20–30 bulleted PowerPoint slides customized to showcase all of the business' highlights in an optimal way. This is often accompanied by an appendix that can easily be two to three times its length. A corresponding set of more streamlined slides is also prepared for management to present during future meetings.

Above all, the CIM acts as a marketing document. The goal is to create a compelling narrative that describes your business as a story of growth and opportunity. The CIM also helps you set the agenda and control the messaging. Buyers inevitably find out about any problematic issues. You should attempt to objectively reframe potential weaknesses in a positive light. To the extent something is undeniably negative, I generally bury it in the appendix.

Here are some sections that are nearly universal across CIMs:

■ Executive summary.
■ Business overview, including composition of business lines.
■ Highlights of the business' unique competitive advantages.
■ Growth opportunities.
■ Generic overview of customers (specific names are generally withheld until after the letter of intent [LOI] is signed).

- Management team bios and organizational chart.
- Historical financials, ideally with breakdown by business line.
- Reconciliation tying adjusted EBITDA (earnings before interest, taxes, depreciation, and amortization) to audited or internal numbers.
- Financial model with projections for the next two to five years (a corresponding Excel file can accompany the CIM).

A professional look and feel of the CIM is essential as it influences buyers and their interest. While all have some common elements, a good one is not formulaic. It should anticipate and proactively address likely buyer questions and concerns, given your unique business. Extreme care should be taken to ensure all information is consistent and all statements can be corroborated. The buyer almost always independently validates the details later in the process. You don't want to erode trust and lose credibility. As Filippell observes: "Without fail, the facts on which [a CIM] stretches the truth are the very ones about which sophisticated buyers will be most inquisitive" (Filippell 2011, p. 91).

The CIM also serves as a preliminary due diligence document. The goal is that it alone provides sufficient information so that a buyer could realistically provide a general sense of valuation. This document should be able to stand on its own. The CIM often fills in as your surrogate to pitch and persuade deeper into the buyer's organization (e.g. board and investment committee), whom you may never meet. In some sale processes, sellers request indications of interest (IOIs) without providing any additional information. To the extent that a buyer proceeds, they will then receive access to a trove of more detailed information. The CIM is also frequently customized for specific strategic investors to highlight the unique synergies between the two businesses.

VIRTUAL DATA ROOM (VDR)

The virtual data room (VDR) is a repository where detailed backup information about the business is stored and shared in a digital format. The buyer and its advisors need this data to complete their due diligence. In the old days, the data room was a physical space in the lawyers' offices. Buyers had to take turns physically sifting through numerous banker's boxes of materials. Now, the materials are stored in the cloud. Many of these documents will end up being referenced within the schedules of the final purchase agreement.

A virtual data room is certainly more convenient than the earlier incarnation, but with an obvious downside: providing widespread access to sensitive information can be scary with or without an NDA. Theoretically, a traditional file-sharing program, such as Dropbox or Google Drive, could be used. However, sophisticated advisors insist on the advanced security features and controlled access provided by dedicated virtual data room providers. They are expensive, costing thousands to tens of thousands of dollars, but I find the cost to be worthwhile for a variety of reasons:

- Buyers perceive sellers to be more sophisticated and serious sellers.
- The program allows the sellers to track buyer usage and activity, providing valuable insight regarding their likely probability of closing.
- A dedicated virtual data room provider has features that greatly reduce the chance of leaks.

VDRs provide a number of security and convenience features, such as:

- File organization based on folders and tags.
- File-level access/permission management.
- View-only access, preventing printing or copying.
- Customized watermarking per user.
- Page-level user activity monitoring.
- Automatic notifications for new and updated files.
- Automated redaction.
- Drag-and-drop and bulk file uploads.

HOW THE PROCESS UNFOLDS

The timeline of the merger and acquisition (M&A) process comes as a surprise to most sellers, who dramatically underestimate the amount of time required to successfully sell a middle-market business. After you've chosen an advisor and agreed to move forward, the sales process spans seven to ten months, on average (Figure 16.1). Most of the variability depends upon the preparedness of the seller and the marketability of the business.

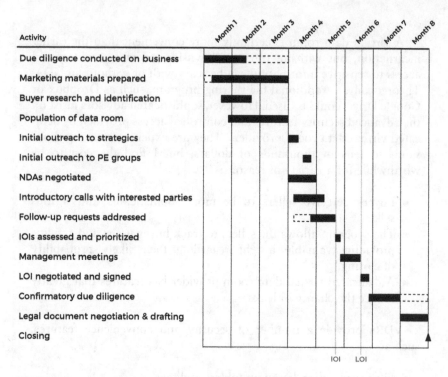

FIGURE 16.1 Timetable for a typical sales transaction.

While you can accelerate the closing date somewhat by being well organized, there's also a point at which speed comes at the expense of losing the participation of some bidders who cannot engage quickly enough, resulting in less competition and lower pricing. From your perspective as a seller in the midst of a life-altering deal, any delay in the transaction can feel excruciating. But prepare yourself now. The deal will drag on longer than you want it to, but in the end, a timeline that encourages competition among bidders and gives them sufficient time to do their homework will benefit you.

PREPARATION

The M&A advisor kicks off the engagement by conducting a full due diligence as if they were the buyer. This examination is crucial for a few reasons.

First, a dry run allows the advisor to fully get to know the seller and their business so they can craft a compelling CIM and serve as an effective advocate. Through analyzing the information in detail, positive attributes of the business are often uncovered, which can be highlighted. Conversely, the advisor aims to identify any challenging areas in order to prepare an appropriate response. A difficult topic or an operational shortcoming can often be reframed into an opportunity. For example, imagine that your company has grown despite operating with a rudimentary finance department. So, the pitch becomes something like, "Yes, this company's finance department is subpar. But imagine how much more the seller could accomplish with a world-class reporting function."

Another goal of this due diligence is to compile the information needed to populate the VDR. A work plan is then created to address any missing items or deficiencies. In parallel, you will decide how widely you want to shop the business around, and your advisor will prepare a targeted buyer list to approach (see Chapter 17 for more detail).

ENGAGING BUYERS

Going to market involves executing an appropriate process to maximize value and terms. There are variations, but the norm is a two-stage bidding process, which is reflected in Figure 16.1. The initial outreach involves reaching out to dozens, if not hundreds of potentially interested buyers.

Teasers along with an NDA are sent out. Upon signing the NDA, the name of the business will be disclosed, and buyers will receive a copy of the CIM. After reviewing the CIM, buyers will typically conduct an initial call with the bankers to discuss the opportunity. If they are interested, they will generally have follow-up requests and additional calls to clarify areas of importance to them. Remember, one of the primary benefits of an advisor is the ability to assume many of these time-intensive responsibilities to minimize the burden on you and your management team.

To not waste anyone's time, before the buyer is introduced to the seller, the buyer is requested to provide a rough preliminary offer, often called an indication of interest (IOI) or term sheet. If everyone is in the same ballpark, then the top few – four to six – interested parties will be invited to meet with the seller for half-day sessions. After these management meetings, it's typical for buyers to pose detailed follow-up questions. Ultimately, interested parties must submit their LOIs before the stipulated deadline. Generally, the top few offers are heavily negotiated until the seller feels comfortable signing one.

EXECUTION AND CLOSING

During this period, two tasks are performed: The buyer conducts its confirmatory due diligence to validate everything the seller previously conveyed to the buyer, and both parties negotiate the final legal documentation to effectuate the transaction. From the signing of an LOI to closing, you can expect approximately 60 days to pass. Signing the LOI generally kicks off the period when the seller commences spending money on third-party professionals (e.g. legal and accounting fees, etc.). Until that point, the team typically tries to do everything themselves in-house. Real commitment is shown by the buyers when they start spending money on professional fees; after all, advisors are not cheap.

Most buyers like to sequence these two tasks by starting the legal drafting once the financials and any other key areas have been affirmed in due diligence. Their aim is to minimize expenses should the deal fail to close. To the extent a buyer wants to close quickly, they will likely need to conduct both of these in parallel.

TOP 3 TAKEAWAYS

- The selling process involves many documents from start to finish. All the various documents are complementary and should reinforce your desired narrative. Remember that you will play a vital role in refining these documents.
- The typical timeline for a middle-market sale is seven to ten months. Acceleration often comes at the expense of competitiveness and ultimately obtaining the best outcome. Once again, trust your advisors to help provide perspective on the process.
- A two-stage bidding process is generally the most effective approach to maximize competition and minimize the risk of needlessly wasting time.

CHAPTER 17

Tailoring the Process

"So, when does the auction happen?" My client was used to bidding wars in his industry, and I could tell he was itching for that to happen with his business. "What do you mean by 'auction'?" I asked. "You know, lots of people bidding up the price until we finally yell, 'SOLD!'" I hesitated before telling him that wasn't going to happen. His face fell, and his shoulders sagged. "Why not?" he asked.

Over the years, I've become aware of a clear disconnect between the ivory tower view of deal-making and the reality in the trenches. Academics and economic theorists overemphasize the different kinds of auctions and the various brands of negotiating styles. The reality is that true formal auctions occur only in Wall Street transactions involving large public companies. Middle-market transactions nearly always happen through an informal, blurred approach that is customized to each specific situation. Selecting the right process is both an art and a science. The best advisors tailor each sale to provide the seller with maximum leeway and discretion.

HOW WIDE SHOULD YOU GO?

As a seller, you need to select how wide a process to utilize. At the far end of the spectrum, you can mass distribute the opportunity to hundreds of prospective buyers. At the opposite end, you strategically invite a single high-conviction buyer to negotiate. So, which is the right approach for you and your company? There are pros and cons to both.

No simple formula exists. This is a complex, multidimensional decision requiring careful judgment. The best approach depends on your specific circumstances, motivations, and preferences. Every deal proves different.

At a high level, it's common knowledge that maximum pricing comes from competition or even from the bidder's perception of competition. Theoretically, inviting the largest universe should create the optimal conditions for a bidding war, enabling you to sleep well at night knowing you received the best possible offer.

However, this logic does not always play out in reality. Many buyers will rationally choose not to participate in a wide process because the time and incurred expenses of assessing and pursuing a transaction aren't justified relative to the low probability of success. Put yourself in a bidder's shoes and do the arithmetic: If there are 100 parties, the mathematical odds of any single bidder prevailing are just 1%. In general, professional investors tend to be particularly disciplined regarding the allocation of their limited time and resources, especially when other compelling opportunities vie for their time and attention (i.e. high opportunity cost).

As much as academics love to study auctions, good luck finding a buyer who relishes this type of process. To them, the word *auction* is a dirty word. All buyers worry about the value they receive in one. The best-case scenario is they pay a fair market rate, and the worst-case scenario is they overpay. Effective mergers and acquisitions (M&A) advisors balance subtle references of competition while also making the potential buyer feel special as if the seller handpicked them from a curated list. As you can imagine, communicating this requires finesse; veteran buyers have heard it all before. Your actions ultimately speak louder than words. Buyers are unlikely to enthusiastically engage if they think they aren't receiving high-quality attention from a seller. This manifests itself in a seller's responsiveness, their level of customization in addressing questions, and several other small factors.

Similarly, to the extent a buyer feels a process to be unfair, they are less likely to participate. That means it's crucial to lay out a clear framework with a level playing field. While deviations from the initial process often occur, great care should be taken to ensure it's not perceived as favoritism.

QUALITY OR QUANTITY?

Like anything in life, there's a trade-off between quantity and quality. Given the volume of participants, large processes also tend to focus on what's most easily measured – price. Often, this means that other important factors, such as certainty of closing, are overlooked. Sellers tend to incorrectly assume that the probabilities of closing are similar across each prospective buyer. In truth, the close rate tends to be higher with a small number of bidders because the substantial high-quality exposure to buyers prior to a letter of intent (LOI) allows you to better assess their commitment level, intentions, and fit.

WEIGHING THE VARIABLES

As you determine the optimal scope, here are some common factors to consider, and, spoiler alert, many of these factors carry implications that conflict with one another:

- Unique, coveted assets. Unique assets that are highly coveted are frequently good candidates for wide processes such as auctions. After all, the seller holds a strong hand. Conversely, if your deal is viewed as a commodity (your company is similar to alternative businesses currently on the market), a targeted approach increases the likelihood of relevant buyers investing the resources to fully engage. This is why rare art and collectibles often sell at auction and three-bedroom houses rarely do.
- Importance of fit. If you were to choose a spouse, would you rather spend quality time getting to know them or just a few scripted hours together? If you are retaining a significant component of the business post-closing, or if fit is extremely important, then chemistry is likely a top priority. A negotiated process with just a small number of prospective buyers enables you to maximize high-quality time getting to know the buyers.
- Market conditions. It's easy to sell a business in a strong market. What separates good investment bankers from mediocre practitioners is their ability to close in a weak market. When conditions are poor, you typically want to approach a limited number of buyers in a high-quality fashion.
- Confidentiality. Mathematically, casting a wide net increases the chance of your employees, competitors, and suppliers finding out – with consequent risks. For some sellers and in some circumstances, confidentiality is of low importance. For example, businesses in extractive industries (e.g. mining) or in bankruptcy may not worry about word getting out. However, we often find sellers are petrified about management and the competition finding out. They often worry about the risks if the deal fails to close.
- Universe of buyers. I advise sellers to market widely when there is a large universe of potentially relevant buyers, and it's unclear who would value the business the most. Similarly, if you have a very limited universe of truly relevant buyers, you need to focus on the quality of each interaction over quantity. There is sometimes a single natural buyer for a given business. In that situation, you spend all of your time and attention building the relationship and understanding the human factor of your counterpart to gain every insight and edge you can get.
- Complexity of deal. In some cases, buyers need a lot of time to engage. If the deal is not straightforward, or if it's a highly nuanced business, the

buyer will be required to invest significant time in assessing the opportunity. A targeted effort is generally required to get the buyer's attention and commitment. Conversely, there's less downside to going wide for a plain vanilla opportunity that buyers can quickly and easily assess.

- Seller resources. If the seller has limited availability or resources, there's no real choice other than approaching a limited set of buyers because the broader the outreach, the greater the burden.
- Speed to closing. The consequence of casting a wide net is that it requires additional resources and time. A large, formal process has been described as *herding cats*: It's a challenge to simultaneously command the focused attention of a large number of prospective buyers. To accommodate as many buyers as possible, exceptions and extensions are frequently granted.
- It's essential that no stone goes unturned. According to Filippell, the worst nightmare of many is a call from a buyer after the deal closes saying that they "would have been seriously interested in the business and would have paid a price significantly higher than the seller received from the successful buyer" (Filippell 2010, p. 153). Conducting a broad auction with as many bidders as possible is the only way to minimize the likelihood of overlooking a relevant buyer.

The reality is that after you've exhausted your highest-conviction prospects, there is a diminishing value in reaching out to additional buyers. The incremental probability of success for your next best option is very low. Filippell explains that "the 90–10 rule applies: there is a 90% chance that one of the selected 10 buyers will be best. In this situation, the seller has to ask if it is worth the risk of blowing confidentiality by broadening the auction to the other 90 buyers when there is only a 10% chance of an improved offer" (Filippell 2010, p. 153). Consequently, for the majority of transactions, I end up recommending a limited process with around 15 to 25 of the highest probability buyers based on deep insights.

SELECTING THE RIGHT BUYERS TO APPROACH

Regardless of the number of buyers approached or the exact sales process used (competitive process, negotiation), identifying and prioritizing the highest-probability buyers remains the same. Identifying who will perceive the most value from your business and have the financial means to pay for it is critical. You also need to do some introspection and prioritize the characteristics that are important to you, as there are often implications regarding the specific buyers that should be approached. There's no point in wasting time with buyers that could easily have been excluded with some reflection.

A significant amount of research is required to understand a potential buyer's strategy, motivations, and financial wherewithal. While time-intensive, this is a high-payoff activity, as it ultimately allows you to focus your time and attention on high-conviction buyers.

This identification process is often a collaborative process between you and your investment banker, as it ensures everyone's collective expertise is harnessed. Given your hyperspecialized knowledge of your business and industry, there's a decent chance you either already know or know of the buyer. Your M&A advisor will ask about previous inquiries from competitors and other buyer groups as well as any prior efforts to sell.

WHO BROUGHT WHO?

Many owners want to distinguish who brought a prospective buyer, often with the objective of receiving some kind of discount. Any good investment banker who is going to obtain for you an outsized outcome will not care about this distinction. Moreover, you don't want to create misaligned incentives where your advisor wants to steer you away from specific options in order to receive their full compensation.

Remember, in most transactions, identifying and contacting potentially interested parties is a commodity that can easily be performed by any competent advisor. Unlike a broker, the primary value of an advisor is to structure and operate a competitive process to negotiate the best possible offer and to help you objectively select the best fit regardless of who initially originated the specific buyer. Remember, the advisor will end up conducting virtually the same amount of work regardless of who found them.

Through experience, investment bankers should have an intuition regarding likely interested buyers. They will often make strategic calls to the *right* connectors within that industry (often industry-specific M&A attorneys, headhunters, etc.) to confidentially get their thoughts and recommendations. Additionally, database subscriptions and other research tools help identify the most comprehensive universe possible, ensuring less obvious names are also considered. While it's quick and easy to reuse old buyer lists from prior transactions (common among many industry-specialist M&A advisors), I strongly recommend that a fresh list is built from scratch to address your specific preferences and business characteristics.

KEEP AN OPEN MIND

I can't stress enough the importance of keeping an open mind regarding who to contact. Many sellers are absolutely certain they know who will end up acquiring their business. From my experience, and from discussions with other leading M&A advisors, I can say this perfect buyer is rarely the winner. In fact, two-thirds of the time, the ultimate buyer is unknown to the seller. Just because someone seems to be the ideal buyer doesn't mean they will be willing to outbid everyone else. Just like it's impossible to know whether a business plan on paper will work until you test it out in reality, you only really know a prospective buyer's true interest when you review it with them. Many other factors behind the scenes impact an individual buyer's appetite, such as ownership changes, strategy shifts, preoccupation with other deals or integrating them, an earnings miss, or the unavailability of capital. These shifts can happen quickly, taking a perceived favorite out of the running at the last moment.

I've also found that sellers often hold simplistic or incorrect preconceptions about the trustworthiness, intentions, and culture of competitors, or they have notions about broad categories of buyers that are simplistic or incorrect. These peculiarities mean that even for expert M&A advisors who do this for a living, predicting the winner is almost impossible.

Identifying Relevant Buyers

You need to think expansively, and sometimes out of the box, for businesses that can benefit from your operations, assets, and brand. While these are frequently direct or indirect competitors, they can also be suppliers, customers, or even companies from totally different industries that could profit from customer access or your unique know-how. Work to develop a perspective regarding how specific companies could benefit from your business. Here are some common motivations:

- New products that complement existing lines of business.
- Ability to improve their market share or dominance.
- Benefit from your brand reputation.
- Access to new customer segments.
- Expand to new geographic markets.
- Insights on how to operate more efficiently or reduce costs.
- Opportunity to use your unique/special capabilities.

When researching, emphasis should be placed on those with strategic and cultural compatibility. While this is impossible to determine with certainty, their website, investor presentations, analyst reports, earnings calls, and news articles can all provide relevant color. Your M&A advisor should develop an educated perspective on why each buyer should be highly interested in order to craft the most effective initial sales pitch.

Also important is picking bidders of the appropriate size. John Warrillow shares a rule of thumb that strategic acquirers not owned by private equity (PE) tend to be between 5–20 times your current revenues. On the low end, a buyer generally needs to be sufficiently large to have the cash to consummate a deal with enough buffer that if the transaction fails, it won't destroy their entire enterprise. At the other end of the spectrum, large multinational companies have a finite capacity to make acquisitions, and there needs to be sufficient scale to move the needle of the buyer's overall financial performance.

Prioritize and Focus

All potential buyers should be prioritized by attractiveness. If you can't do that, insufficient research has been done to form an educated opinion. On our team, we prioritize all prospective buyers into tiers based on our findings and level of conviction and allocate our time and efforts accordingly:

- Group 1: Absolutely interested. This group includes strategic buyers actively spending time and resources to originate your specific kind of business. It also encompasses prospective buyers who have previously reached out to you in a targeted fashion (i.e. they understand your business model well). Most of the bespoke efforts will be focused on this group.
- Group 2: Should be interested. These parties have a buy box, and your company fits squarely within their investment criteria, and they have had prior investments in closely related businesses.
- Group 3: Might be interested. For this group of buyers, your profile generally fits their investment criteria, but they've made no prior investments within the general sector (a lot of financial investors claim to be interested in every industry and the kitchen sink). This category could also include those that would fit in Group 1 or 2 but there is some uncertainty regarding their ability to pay.
- Group 4: Long shots. These are buyers where you have little insight into whether the deal might be a good fit. You won't even bother to contact them unless your initial outreach yields little interest, and this is your last-ditch effort.

CONTACTING THE RIGHT INDIVIDUALS

Your M&A advisor will focus on identifying the right individuals to approach within each targeted organization. Reaching PE funds is simple, as they are actively seeking opportunities and publicly list their contact information. For PE-owned strategics, the ideal approach is to find and contact the PE partner running the deal, who generally also sits on its board.

Most large strategics are highly decentralized, with thousands of employees, making it nearly impossible to understand from the outside. According to Dennis Roberts, "the best way to approach a public company almost always is by directly contacting a division or operational executive with sufficient authority and clout to consider the opportunity and subsequently lobby for it within the company" (Roberts 2009, p. 33). I find that most active owners have had prior industry interactions with relevant individuals and often best understand the nuances of any internal politics.

To the extent that the right individual cannot be determined or reached, the following titles are typically contacted (generally in this order):

- Head of corporate development or M&A
- CFO
- CEO/President
- Board members
- Other senior managers

In the worst-case scenario, we engage with whoever we can reach within the organization until we find a foothold to help navigate their internal organizational structure and bureaucracy. It is important to get multiple points of contact (e-mail, phone, LinkedIn) for reaching individuals, as many times they don't check a particular format.

For your highest-conviction targets, your advisor will be relentless in contacting them until they definitively determine that they have reached the right person and the buyer is not interested.

LUXURY OF BEING INTENTIONAL

To the extent you have a small, targeted list of potential buyers, you have the luxury of dedicating the time to take the absolute best shot on goal possible. This approach will feel familiar if you have a B2B business involving large transactions. You likely put significant effort into understanding your clients at a deep level to obtain every possible edge. This level of time and attention will provide valuable insights that can be capitalized upon, such as:

- What are their priorities?
- What motivates them?
- What are they most proud of?
- What hobbies or affinities can help build rapport?
- Who influences their decisions?
- What do they find to be most persuasive?

TOP 3 TAKEAWAYS

- Buyers hate auctions and need to feel they have a realistic chance of prevailing, so it's very unlikely that your business will ever go to a formal auction. Instead, your advisor should help you determine how wide a process is suitable for your particular business sale.
- The specific dynamics of your business and circumstances generally determine the relative advantages and disadvantages of how wide to go. There's definitely a trade-off between the quantity and quality of interactions.
- Buyers should be prioritized based on potential. Ranking prospective buyers should be a collaborative effort between you and your advisor, each with a unique vantage point.

CHAPTER 18

Keeping the Secret

Stephen and Melanie (not their real names) entered my office and glanced around nervously. "Is this area secure?" Melanie asked. "We don't want anyone to know that we are thinking about selling," Stephen added. "Loose lips sink ships!" I assured them that my office was secure, but I did make a point to shut the door extra tight.

Sellers are often petrified of word getting out about their sale. They feel that irreparable damage could occur if the deal fails to occur. Fundamentally, there are two kinds of secrets owners try to keep – first, the very fact that they are selling, and second, sensitive internal information that could be damaging if it falls into the wrong hands. To put you at ease, by and large, it is extremely rare for there to be a release of your sensitive data as a result of a merger and acquisition (M&A) process. That kind of leak is easy to trace and would expose the buyer to significant legal liability. The most common leaks generally involve your status as a seller.

If news of your effort to sell becomes public, this disclosure can be destabilizing to your business. You can rest assured that your competitors will try to capitalize upon it. Moreover, the associated risks provide prospective buyers with additional leverage.

News of a sale impacts each stakeholder differently. Customers are concerned about what a sale would mean to pricing and service levels. Certain kinds of users may also worry whether the company will continue to honor long-term warranty and service commitments. Suppliers get anxious about a transaction's impact on their sales volumes and the timeliness of payment. Employees are worried about how their jobs will be impacted or whether they will even have a job. No one likes change, particularly when it's completely out of their control. This fear can impact their job performance during a critical period. Uncertainty around the company's future can also induce many employees to start looking around. While some owners feel guilty – as if they are betraying their employees by keeping a secret from them – telling the broader organization is a mistake. The downsides are real.

PREVENTING LEAKS

To maintain confidentiality, sellers leverage a web of interlocking tactics. While each of these techniques by itself provides limited protection, combined, they minimize the chances of extensive damage occurring. Among them:

- Insist on a blinded nondisclosure agreement (NDA). The buyer signs an agreement with the investment bank on behalf of the seller before its name or any associated details are disclosed. However, let's be honest: NDAs are extremely difficult to enforce – they essentially serve as a moral commitment for the recipient to keep the information secret.
- Use a code name. To help cloak the seller's identity, all involved team and advisor members should refer to the company by a code name rather than its actual name. Always.
- Hide the bankers. Visits to the company by the bankers should be limited. Seeing the same strangers multiple times can elicit suspicion among your staff. When they do visit, reference them as prospective insurance agents or commercial bankers looking to gain your business. They should conveniently forget to bring their business cards or other identifying information.
- Deploy strategic quiet periods. The timing of going to market may be delayed until after major trade shows or conferences where various stakeholders are likely to gather around the watering hole. With alcohol involved, gossip can spread like wildfire.
- Stage the release of sensitive information. Release sensitive information gradually. For example, the disclosure of some information may only occur after the buyer is invited to a management meeting. Some items, such as the names of your largest customers, may be withheld until weeks before closing, particularly if it's an industry competitor.
- Take care with e-mails and mail. To minimize the risk of IT accidentally finding out, have all communication sent to your personal e-mail address. Similarly, proper protocol should be agreed upon with your bankers. For example, the sender should call the recipient before faxing anything to the seller's office. If physical information is mailed to a prospective buyer, place it inside double envelopes with "Confidential" boldly marked on each to minimize the chances that a mail clerk inadvertently opens it.

- Deputize your inner circle. Team members who know about the transaction should keep their ears open for any relevant leaks. Any rumors should immediately be reported to you so you can contain them from further spreading.
- Speed is advantageous. Mathematically, the longer you are actively marketing the business, the higher the probability of leaks getting out.

CONSIDERATIONS FOR INTERESTED STRATEGIC BUYERS

While it's unlikely that buyers will steal your secret information, there's generally heightened risk with strategic buyers. After all, they can potentially directly use your own information against you. The ideal solution is to determine what information is absolutely needed for them to analyze the business and present an offer. You may present anonymized data or summaries to help them understand the fundamentals of your business without disclosing sensitive details. The release of specific information is then delayed until certain milestones occur, which will make you feel more comfortable about the certainty of closing.

Judgment should be used regarding which strategic buyers to approach. If you have personal experience with their unsavory tactics and wouldn't trust them if your life depended on it, then the best course is to skip them altogether. For those with a reputation for having sharp elbows, I recommend delaying reaching out to them until toward the end of the process when the seller is close to converging on a deal with another buyer. They will be informed that the business is being sold, and they need to come back with a strong offer. Given the time sensitivity, I generally provide price guidance, adding a 10–20% premium above the current highest bidder.

NOT A MATTER OF IF BUT WHEN

Buyers are not in the business of intentionally leaking information – their professional reputations depend upon their discretion. They tend to take their commitments seriously and generally will keep your information secret well beyond the expiration of your NDA. Despite all that, from my experience, rumors of a potential transaction nearly always circulate by the time closing comes around. Remember the children's game Telephone, where a message gets whispered – and exaggerated and

(Continued)

(Continued)

distorted – as it goes down the line? Rumors can be more damaging because half-truths and misconceptions can cast the sale in a much worse light than the actual truth.

These happen nonetheless for a variety of reasons. Probably the most common are internal slip-ups where something was overheard or innocent comments by family who were not explicitly explained the importance and responsibility of confidentiality. The seeds of rumors also frequently emerge from employee suspicions. For example, suspicions can arise from urgent, out-of-the-ordinary requests. Similarly, buyers and their advisors will also frequently review the LinkedIn profiles of your team. In isolation, this is not a big deal, but when all of a sudden a manager sees that a dozen PE investors all looked at their profile, they are likely to assume something is going on.

Buyers are supported by an ecosystem of advisors who are further removed from confidentiality obligations and are frequently less tight-lipped with information. They don't intend to break confidentiality, but things can slip. Buyers can also inadvertently reveal your identity as part of their diligence efforts. For example, they may call up industry contacts and describe your business with sufficient specificity that an astute individual could put two and two together and guess who you are.

HANDLING LEAKS

Juicy information travels quickly; once the cat's out of the bag, good luck getting it back in. Unfortunately, ignoring it is generally not a good strategy as it risks festering further and potentially creating panic within the organization. If you're approached directly about a rumor, you can either: (i) side-step by deflecting and shifting the conversation on to something else, or (ii) use sarcasm or vague semantics, such as:

- We receive calls daily about acquiring the business. . . . Why do you want to buy it?
- We're always for sale . . . no one can pay my price.
- I wish – I could improve my handicap!
- I'd be wealthy if I had a nickel for every time I heard that rumor.

Prepare and practice these responses beforehand so you can quickly and nonchalantly respond.

If a leak does occur, the first step is to assess the scope of damage to determine your best response – is it just a few people, or did the newspaper publish an article? To the extent that just a few employees know, Filippell advises, "It is best to talk individually with each of the enlightened people. Senior management should impress upon them their responsibility to downplay this incident and keep everything quiet, a mix of 'responsibility, obligation, and fear of consequences.' It seems to work best if the people believe that if the leak spreads, they will be the ones deemed responsible" (Filippell 2011, p. 83).

Under the worst-case scenario, where the rumor is a raging wildfire within your industry, you must strategically communicate with the entire organization. You can either come clean and be entirely candid, or you can attempt to hide the transaction in plain sight by explaining you are exploring raising capital to expand the business.

I recommend speaking with groups in waves based on their seniority. Notify them of the sale, calmly address their questions (including what you know and don't know), and request their support in trying to reassure their subordinates. You should then join them in their meetings with their direct reports, if possible. Pay particular attention to ensuring that the messages are consistent across meetings.

TELLING EMPLOYEES

Most sellers want to err on the side of telling no one about a potential sale. Obviously, the more who know, the greater the chances of leaks, but there needs to be a balance as there's significant value to having strong leaders participating in the sales process. The management team is a critical element of what is being sold to a buyer, particularly for financial buyers who don't have preexisting infrastructure and will rely upon the team to operate the business and potentially consolidate the industry. They are your best marketers, and their involvement is often what hooks a buyer emotionally.

Worse, if they are not engaged in the process, the buyer often perceives them as ineffective or less valuable to the organization. Conversely, since you are likely to be doing all of the early communications, excluding the management team overstates your criticality to the business (i.e. emphasizing greater key-person risk). This often results in you being asked to stay longer with the business post-closing, with potentially less cash up front.

There's also a practical consideration as well: The workload in a transaction is massive, and it's a lot easier if you can share the burden with competent team members who have relevant context. The broader your bench strength, the faster you can respond. Outside advisors can assist to a point, but unfortunately, they don't have the institutional knowledge regarding what exists and where to find it.

Determine who needs to be involved to get the deal done. At the very least, that's the CEO/President and CFO (or your most senior accounting team member). It's impossible for data requests to be fulfilled without them figuring things out, particularly when you'll be asking them to urgently prioritize random requests over their day-to-day responsibilities. Because of their unique position, CFOs take a disproportionate brunt of the burden in a transaction. The involvement of other senior managers is largely situational and may depend upon how well they come across to potential buyers. You may delay telling the remaining leaders on a need-to-know basis until the letter of intent (LOI) is signed or later. The remaining rank-and-file employees should be informed after the ink dries on the closing documents. There might be some hurt feelings that you hid the transaction, but it's the prudent thing for both you and the broader business.

ALIGNING INCENTIVES WITH CRITICAL TEAM MEMBERS

So, how do you induce your senior management team to enthusiastically assist? Money. Success bonuses compensate these individuals for the significant amount of additional time and energy above and beyond their daily responsibilities. Many requests will be urgent and need to be prioritized over their personal commitments. In fact, vacations should be canceled between the management meetings and the final closing date. Having a financial package in place minimizes the financial uncertainty associated with a transaction and makes it a positive event for these managers to anticipate and celebrate. Finally, keeping them happy minimizes the chances of their departure during the sales process, which can be highly destabilizing to the transaction. Leaders who also happen to be minority shareholders are generally not eligible since they already have more than enough incentive.

How much should the success bonus be? The appropriate amount is contextual. It needs to be meaningful to incentivize behavior, but you don't want to dangle an amount so large that it counterproductively induces the person to walk away and retire early, particularly if they are late in their career.

From my experience, the success bonus should range from three to five years' salary for a CEO, around a year's salary for the CFO, and 3 to

12 months for the other roles involved. It should go without saying that the payout is contingent upon maintaining confidentiality. Some of this payment may be deferred (generally a year, but sometimes corresponding to your expected earnout period) to maximize retention.

If one is not already in place, you may also consider providing an employment agreement to minimize their concerns about losing their livelihood immediately after closing. Regardless, this may be necessary in order to induce them to sign the noncompetition/nonsolicitation agreements generally expected by buyers. Emphasize to senior leaders that the sales process is an excellent opportunity for them to showcase their capabilities to their potential new bosses, helping them to position themselves for future success.

Failure to take these precautions can result in sabotage, particularly when ownership is passive. Feelings of bitterness and jealousy often emerge when leaders understand the large sums of money the owners will make. I've been in a situation where a disincentivized CEO essentially told a prospective buyer there's nowhere to go but down from here. It's nearly impossible to recover from that.

TOP 3 TAKEAWAYS

- Maintaining confidentiality is critical to a deal's success. Interlocking tactics are used to minimize the probability of leaks and the severity of consequences, but in the end, leaks happen.
- While the natural tendency is to want to tell no one about a sale, it's generally advisable to incorporate your critical leaders early on in the process. They will be invaluable in helping you gather information and can often serve as your best internal champions.
- Critical employees should be incentivized with a transaction bonus. This not only helps align incentives to enthusiastically embrace a transaction but also helps get signed the noncompetition/nonsolicitation agreements that most buyers will require.

CHAPTER 19

It's a Process

"Okay, what's next?" It's a question I'm often asked by clients. While I can give a general idea of how things will unfold, unpredictability is the name of the game. Anything and everything can happen in the course of the deal. Clients have died midway through. Get a divorce. Decide to bring on family members. The only thing I can guarantee is that selling your business will be a process.

Selling a business is like a funnel where prospective buyers exclude themselves at each stage. A buyer must be sufficiently interested to move along to the next step (Figure 19.1).

Depending on the number of buyers on your target list, it can take your investment banking team between a day and a week to complete an exhaustive initial outreach. This generally involves sending an e-mail with the teaser and nondisclosure agreement (NDA) attached and then doing a follow-up phone call acknowledging receipt. While a newsletter-style blast (e.g. Mailchimp) is faster, I find it far more effective – and a better reflection of our sophistication and professionalism – to customize outreach to each recipient. If possible, I try to explain in detail why this opportunity would be a good fit for each potential buyer, given their current operations or past investments.

Some of the best buyer types, such as publicly traded strategics, are notoriously slow through the sales process. Given the importance of synchronizing bids to maximize competitiveness, I tend to approach these slower groups a few weeks before the rest so they have a head start.

Serious buyers tend to get back to you quickly. Response times can range from a day to a week. Unfortunately, a large number of buyers have the bad habit of not providing any response when they are not interested,

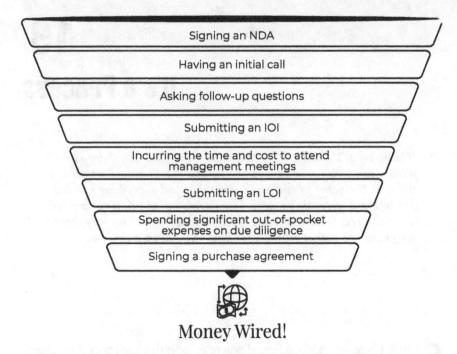

Money Wired!

FIGURE 18.1   Typical go-to-market process through final closing.

which leaves open the possibility that they failed to receive the message in the first place. Particularly for the highest-probability targets, outreach efforts should persist until it is confirmed that the right decision-maker has been reached and they have explicitly communicated that they are *not* interested.

This is where investment bankers present a huge advantage; not only can they approach buyers confidentially, but they are also incentivized to be aggressive, so no one thinks anything of this persistence. This is an important but underrated psychological advantage. If a seller exhibits that same persistence, they risk appearing desperate, likely turning off some potentially relevant buyers.

The number of interested recipients depends on the quality of your original buyers' list and the marketability of your business. For highly targeted buyer lists, 75% or more will be interested in proceeding, and for processes with broad outreach, this percentage can be less than 25%. While some curious buyers want to see a confidential information memorandum

(CIM) purely for the purpose of gaining market and industry intelligence, most professional buyers will choose not to sign NDAs unless they are legitimately interested. This is because they have plenty of more exciting things to do with their lives, and in the eyes of their lawyers, each presents potential legal liability. Don't be surprised if your banker is contacted by unknown buyers who were forwarded the teaser by a targeted recipient – to the extent they meet your buyer criteria, I encourage you to graciously welcome their interest.

NAVIGATING THE NDA

If there's interest, you can expect buyers to suggest changes to your proposed NDA electronically, often known as a *redlined* or *marked-up* version. Don't take offense to this. They have compliance and legal departments that need to prove that they're adding value. Sometimes, the markups are just cosmetic and can be quickly signed "as is" by both parties. Conversely, their changes may not be acceptable, and it may take up to a week to get on the same page, often due to scheduling challenges. Try to understand their underlying concern, and if it's reasonable, see if you can accommodate a solution. I have never encountered an impasse regarding an NDA that could not be satisfactorily addressed. This is your first negotiation with a prospective buyer, so you and your advisors want to convey being reasonable and open to listening and being persuaded.

This also is a great preview of the future negotiations you're likely to encounter with the counterparty. If buyers demand changes without a logical reason on your industry-standard NDA, you can bet your last dollar that they will be a pain when it comes time to negotiate hundreds of pages of legal documents. When confronted with a buyer who nitpicks, I like to assertively push back and hold strong on something to set the right tone for potential future negotiations. It's important to implicitly convey that you have options and are selling on *your* terms.

The volume of these marked-up agreements can be significant. While you can send along each marked-up version to your attorneys to review and respond individually, this can get expensive. With feedback from their attorneys, most clients will provide their investment bankers with general guidance regarding the scope they are comfortable with, leaving the bankers leeway in quickly converging on an acceptable solution.

INITIAL CONVERSATIONS

Once the buyer has signed the NDA, they are sent a CIM shortly thereafter. While, historically, these were physically bound and mailed overnight, today, they are typically sent electronically. To the extent it's relevant to the particular sales process, they are also sent a *process letter* explaining the expected timeline and requested elements in the indication of interest (IOI).

After reviewing the materials, an interested buyer schedules a call (either via video or telephone) with the seller's mergers and acquisitions (M&A) advisor. These calls generally last an hour and are an opportunity for prospective buyers to ask questions. It's an excellent sign if a buyer takes the initiative to set up this call and has thoughtful questions. I find it's valuable to be patient and allow the buyer room to take the initiative so I can gauge their true level of desire. Consequently, I typically wait seven to ten days before following up to ask the recipient their initial reaction and if they have any questions.

The questions asked during this introductory call, and any follow-up calls, tend to cover similar issues. While your investment banker should be able to answer the vast majority of questions, there are likely some they aren't initially equipped to fully answer and will need to follow up afterward. Over time, the most relevant questions will be covered so your M&A advisor will become more and more equipped as they get to know your business in great detail. An FAQ document can speed up the process by addressing common queries. The simple act of creating this document provides the opportunity for you to craft and refine the optimal answer, particularly for the more challenging questions.

These initial calls can also be a great way to gain additional intelligence about a buyer's priorities so that future messaging can be shaped accordingly – during these discussions, the banker may also inquire about other topics such as prior experience or efforts with similar deals, their strategic plans and priorities, and financial wherewithal. All of this information provides relevant data points in order to prioritize focus and efforts accordingly.

Many buyers also frequently request to meet the seller. I almost always oppose this as it undermines the sales process and generally sends the wrong signal. Remember, a major value-add of the process is to shield you from conversations until it's clear that the buyer is in the same ballpark regarding valuation and structure. Establishing reasonable boundaries with logical rationales sets the right tone as an assertive and credible seller and reinforces the fact that you are controlling the sales process.

Within the sales process, this initial go-to-market phase is the least time-intensive period for you; the vast majority of the efforts will be performed by your investment banker. Use this relative *lull* to focus 100% of your efforts to maximize business performance because things will soon get a lot crazier.

UNDERSTANDING QUESTIONS BEHIND THE QUESTION

Once management meetings occur, you will be interacting with prospective buyers directly. You shouldn't take all questions at face value. Many, if not most, have a *question behind the question*. These questions typically mask a deeper concern about something. Whenever possible, the true issue should be identified and addressed. While these can be highly contextual, Figure 19.2 shows a few examples.

Question BEHIND THE Question

WHAT THEY ASK	WHAT THEY MEAN
Why are you selling now?	Are you trying to jump from a sinking ship?
What is your involvement in the business?	Should we accept your proposed salary addback? Are you critical to the success of the business?
What's behind your large margin increases? Why are they above industry averages?	Is your current financial performance sustainable?
Which employees are 1099 vs. W2?	Are you compliant with labor laws? How much should I reduce EBITDA to account for correct classification?
How many buyers are you engaging with?	Is it worth my time to dig into this opportunity? Do I have a reasonable opportunity of being the winning bidder?

FIGURE 19.2 Illustrative questions behind the question.

(Continued)

(Continued)

While it seems inefficient for buyers to ask questions indirectly, this generally elicits the least suspicion. Consequently, a seemingly innocent question increases the chances of you being candid and letting an inconsistency or unfavorable information slip. For example, these questions may be an attempt to ferret out information (such as your willingness to consider less money). It also provides the buyer with plausible deniability for sensitive questions that have the potential to insult the seller. Remember, similar questions are often purposefully asked in slightly different ways to ensure the answers are compatible. On the other hand, there are some questions where buyers are intentionally direct and straight to the point.

HOW TO FIELD QUESTIONS REGARDING YOUR MOTIVATION TO SELL

Every private equity (PE) buyer lives in fear of making a bad purchase, so in each interaction, they are constantly probing for red flags. Looking in from the outside, it's impossible for the buyer to have your level of familiarity with the business. They will never know the true strength of your customer relationships or the capabilities of your staff and their levels of job satisfaction.

A universal question in M&A deals is: "Why are you selling?" Buyers are primarily concerned that you know about some underlying negative factor inducing you to sell, such as the business has peaked. This suspicion tends to be greater for younger sellers further from retirement.

At the same time, some responses will disqualify you for certain buyers. For example, many consolidators of professional services businesses want sellers who want to continue to grow over the long term rather than retire. Regardless of your retirement plans, it's vital that you convey your willingness to assist in transitioning the business – I find this is best framed as "This is my baby. I want to see it thrive." You need to credibly convince them that while you would like to exit, you believe the business to be strong. The right response is contextual to the circumstances of you and your business.

Don't get caught off guard by this question – practice and role-play this response numerous times before any buyer meetings. Be careful that the reason you give is consistent and that your rationale is logical. If a buyer starts to fret that your story doesn't fit the facts, you can bet they'll keep asking more and more questions – and possibly reconsider their interest altogether.

DEFLECTING QUESTIONS ABOUT YOUR ASKING PRICE

Middle-market businesses rarely present an asking price because doing so is a no-win scenario. Any price mentioned will functionally serve as a ceiling, with buyers focusing on the minimum necessary to strike a deal. And if the number is too high, you may scare off buyers before a competitive environment has developed.

That said, nearly all buyers will ask for an asking price or pricing guidance, frequently in the last moments of a meeting. This is a sensitive question because buyers are essentially trying to determine whether it's worth their time and resources to pursue the opportunity. If they feel the probability of success is low, they will likely be discouraged and not participate. Particularly in a competitive process, one of the primary objectives in answering this question is keeping the buyer encouraged about their chances and *in the game*. More offers are better, as they provide additional options.

I find it best to try and sidestep pricing questions and to emphasize that my client is reasonable and will entertain all fair offers. I also try to highlight that my client highly values factors other than price, such as chemistry and fit, with a brief rationale regarding why I think they would be compatible.

If pushed, I will respond with "I don't know," highlighting the nuances of their business and the relative unavailability of relevant comps. Sometimes, the buyer relentlessly presses further. If so, I will generally respond that I expect a price range between $X and $Y (where those numbers are a little aggressive) based on my market observations, but it's ultimately for the market to determine.

Be aware that buyers may try and pose this question directly to you as a seller at some point, often when your advisors have stepped away. Under no circumstances should you respond – there is no upside, and they can often glean valuable insights from your body language and phrasing. Tell them you leave valuation discussions to your banker.

MANAGING FOLLOW-UP REQUESTS

Buyers often come back with follow-up questions and other requests. Detailed, intelligent follow-up questions are a great sign as they indicate that the buyer is expending their limited time and resources to thoroughly review the opportunity.

These questions can range from clarifications of information in your CIM, requests for more detailed underlying data, or new information not presented in the CIM. Some requests will be reasonable and easily available, while others are not. Not all requests need to be satisfied, but ideally, you try to understand the rationale behind the request and see if you can provide some proxy information or other high-level data that can address the *gist* of their question. For example, you'll frequently be asked for data regarding your largest customers. Rather than provide them with this information, you can disclose an anonymized summary of key information with the promise that they can access the full data set once the process is further along.

HANDLING REJECTION

Rejection is a fundamental aspect of any sales effort. As a successful business owner, you have undoubtedly overcome significant obstacles and rejection. That doesn't ease the potential sting, particularly when prior interactions were seemingly promising. However, this is a gift. It's a lot easier to string you along with an indefinite *maybe*. Similar to Silicon Valley's mantra of "failing fast," it's most valuable to gain clarity on where you stand quickly so you can move along, focusing your time and energy on those with the highest probability of success.

The majority of buyers who choose to pass provide a brief explanation for why it's not a good fit. At this stage, the reasons tend to involve the business's fundamentals and its compatibility with the buyer (i.e. declines in margin, too much customer concentration, doesn't fit within their investment criteria). Multiple buyers providing a consistent reason provides relevant market insight and is likely to be a preview of what other buyers will be sensitive to. Remember, most financial buyers underwrite their investments similarly, and they often use the same advisors.

TOP 3 TAKEAWAYS

- Signing an NDA represents the first negotiation (of hopefully many) with a prospective buyer. It is important that this interaction sets the right tone – that you are a reasonable and accommodating seller who is also assertively running a process on your terms.
- The overwhelming majority of early conversations will occur through your M&A advisor in order to minimize the burden on you. You will typically be spared any meetings until it has been determined that the buyer is in the ballpark regarding both price and terms (generally after an IOI has been received).
- Develop and practice a logical story for the inevitable question regarding why you want to sell *now*. There's also little upside in discussing your pricing expectations. Direct all questions regarding pricing to your advisors.

CHAPTER 20

Seeing Where You Stand

Karen and her partner Steve (not their real names) called me almost daily about the sale of their cosmetic company. I could hear the anxiety in their voices as they asked if there were any updates. Sometimes, I did have some information, but more often than not, the best I could say was that things were moving along in the background. As unsatisfactory an answer as that is, it's the typical reality once you put your business on the market.

After going to market, you'll endure an anxiety-inducing period of silence. During this period – which lasts a few weeks to a couple of months – you will wait for preliminary offers and see where the various buyers stand. This tends to be a particularly nerve-racking time for sellers as they impatiently wait to see if anyone is going to show up to their party. Before this point, some casual references or perspectives on value may be shared, but this will be the first time concrete numbers are presented in writing.

Most formal processes have a deadline imposed by the seller's investment bankers. All of the buyers are concerned that sending their offers early will be used to induce other higher offers. Consequently, most send their offers in the late afternoon of the due date, resulting in an agonizing wait for that first e-mail. In most processes, you'll have at least a couple of prospective buyers who will request a few more days. I tend to accommodate it as long as it's requested in advance with a reasonable excuse. (There's no upside in being so much of a stickler that legitimate offers are disqualified.)

The primary purpose of an indication of interest (IOI or term sheet) is to validate that the buyer and seller are in the same ballpark. This important milestone serves as a gateway for prospective buyers to be invited to engage with the seller and its management team. IOIs can be a formal signed document or just a short e-mail with some bullet points. What's important is the buyer provides a clear offer that can be easily assessed and compared with other options. Because buyers have had limited information and no interactions with management yet, it's typical for these offers to present general frameworks and ranges. Your mergers and acquisitions (M&A) advisor will frequently have follow-up communications with the buyers to clarify aspects that may be unclear.

ALL OFFERS ARE VALUABLE

All offers, even underwhelming ones, should be encouraged. In the best case, they serve as the foundation for a successful transaction. In the worst case, the elements of a weak offer can be leveraged to help improve other offers. It's highly unusual that a bidder immediately presents their best and final offer – from my experience, nearly all bids have room for improvement. No matter how unacceptable an offer is, nearly all have some provision that can be used to help negotiate up the more competitive ones. For example, to provide leverage in getting other offers to increase the amount of cash up-front, I may mention that an all-cash offer has already been presented (there's no obligation to share that it happens to be a low offer). Regardless of an offer's competitiveness, I express gratitude for every bidder's time and effort. If it's a lowball offer that's well out of the realm, I thank them for their interest and honestly convey where it stands relative to other offers.

SELECTING WHO TO INVITE

After receiving the IOIs, you will sit with your investment bankers to review the offers and determine who should be invited to proceed to the next phase. Your advisor will attempt to prioritize and recommend specific buyers based on your preferences (Figure 20.1). Typically, the M&A advisor will create a summary chart comparing each offer across a number of relevant factors, such as:

- Enterprise value.
- Consideration (i.e. breakdown of earnouts, seller notes, etc.).
- Up-front cash received.

IOI Matrix Example

	![BC Capital]	XYZ	123
Enterprise Value	$40mm	$38.5–44mm	$32mm
Assumed EBITDA	$4.2mm	$3.5–4mm	$4mm
Valuation Multiple	9.5X	11X	8X
Cash Up-front	$24mm	$17.5–23mm	$32mm
Equity Reinvested	$8mm (20%)	$6mm (15%)	N/A
Earnout at 12% Growth	$8mm all paid in year 3	$15mm paid 1/3 over 3 years	N/A
Transition Expectations	3-year contract	1yr + 1yr consulting	6 months consulting
Buyer Effort	**High:** Senior leadership flew out and team has proactively been asking detailed questions	**Medium:** Buyer is involved with another deal; only cursory questions asked to date	**Low:** No involvement other than single junior team tember
Perceived Cultural Fit	Medium	Medium	High
Buyer Financial Strength	$2bn PE fund	$500mm PE fund	Unclear how they will fund given high debt levels

FIGURE 20.1 Illustrative side-by-side comparison of various presented offers.

- Ownership percentage retained.
- Financial wherewithal.
- Buyer effort exhibited.
- Fit.
- Other factors.

Your confidence in an offer should be directly proportional to the amount of time and effort the buyer invested into assessing the opportunity. Since an IOI is nonbinding, and any professional buyer can customize their standardized template in 30 minutes, you need to assess various other factors. Here are some factors to consider that reflect a buyer's true interest and commitment levels:

- Amount of time spent.
- Depth and quality of questions.
- Initiative shown in scheduling meetings and following up.
- Level and quantity of senior involvement.

- Support or approval from their investment committee.
- Spending out-of-pocket money on third-party advisors.
- Subjective assessment of their level of *desire*.

To keep the discussions manageable, I recommend the top four to six bidders are invited to meet you. In a highly competitive process where many offers are close, it may be challenging to make this selection. When one or two offers come in dramatically higher than the others, you may be reluctant to waste time with the others. However, I personally recommend inviting an extra "throwaway bidder" for the first meeting to practice.

I also recommend considering different kinds of buyers and structures to get a better sense of what might be the best fit for you. Some clients end up selecting vastly different structures than they initially anticipated once the pricing implications get factored in.

MANAGEMENT MEETINGS

Management meetings are typically batched to fill up a couple of intense weeks. They normally involve a four-hour meeting with some additional time for lunch or dinner afterward. To avoid arousing suspicions among employees, these gatherings are often held away from the seller's place of business, such as your investment banker's or attorney's offices.

Given the meeting's tight time frame, I am a big proponent of anticipating and addressing any potential issues or delays ahead of time. For example, check that your audiovisual equipment is working and that the whiteboard has markers. Arrange the room to showcase your business – to better engage your visitors and provide valuable context, set up relevant product samples, catalogs, and photos. To prevent food servers from interrupting at awkward moments or jeopardizing confidentiality, provide water, coffee, and a buffet-style meal (or snacks).

Some buyers may request to meet via video call. I highly discourage this for a couple of reasons. First, it's nearly impossible to develop rapport and assess fit via videoconference. And second, videoconferencing involves very little effort on their part to participate. I prioritize buyers who invest time and energy because it indicates momentum – and it's harder for them to walk away.

The meeting will typically have eight to ten attendees in total – two to three from the buyer, two from the banker's team, and three to five from the seller. You, along with any managers who are aware of the sales process, will attend. Each manager will prepare a short presentation and must know their department or division cold in order to answer challenging questions.

At this point, the buyer's junior analysts will have already reviewed the opportunity in detail and will have previously asked detailed questions of your investment banker. Consequently, the discussions will naturally be high-level in nature. This may be the first time some of the buyer's senior decision-makers meaningfully engage with the opportunity, and their time will be focused on covering qualitative areas that require their judgment, such as your strategy and vision, the business's competitive environment, your motivations, and their assessment of your trustworthiness and fit. To the extent that detailed questions arise, those are typically addressed in follow-up conversations. Beware that buyers frequently ask similar questions framed differently; the intent is to corroborate other statements in the confidential information memorandum (CIM) or in prior conversations.

This is your show, so your investment banker will largely remain silent unless something that can be taken out of context needs to be clarified or reframed or to lob you a softball question to help you remember an important point. Throughout the meeting, they will carefully observe your counterpart's reactions and body language.

PRACTICE MAKES PERFECT

I've said it before, but I'll say it again: You only get one shot at a first impression. You want each manager's presentation to contribute to communicating your intended takeaways in a coherent fashion. Most managers are not public speaking experts, so practice as much as you think is necessary and then practice a couple more times. Beware that certain technical roles (CFO and head of engineering come to mind) have a tendency to get lost in the details.

While this is going to be contextual for every business, here are some themes that make sense to emphasize in any discussion:

- Highlight your bench strength – the company operates well without you.
- Express a sense of optimism regarding the company's future outlook.
- Explain your detailed plans for how you will achieve your goals.

Like a lawyer preparing a client for cross-examination, your banker will help you rehearse by asking challenging questions that are likely

(Continued)

(Continued)

to come up. Anticipating and preparing for these questions is important – the exercise might not be fun, but you want to be sure your team does not get caught flat-footed. As much as possible, try to avoid situations where your managers need to improvise on their feet.

Your advisor will also provide insight regarding how a buyer will likely interpret your answers and suggest the most constructive alternatives. Through practice and familiarity, each presentation will be easier and stronger than the one before. Consequently, meetings are generally sequenced in reverse order of offer attractiveness so the wrinkles can be ironed out in the early meetings. Because most buyers realize this, it's common to insinuate to the last scheduled buyer that an additional meeting or two remains.

Get into the Right Frame of Mind

The primary goal of management meetings is to humanize the investment opportunity and showcase elements that are impossible to convey through a document. To help build an emotional connection, get acquainted and build rapport with the buyers. Counterintuitively, these meetings tend to primarily involve the buyer selling themselves and all the *unique* "value-add" they offer their portfolio companies. Try to listen carefully to what they emphasize so you can reframe future points in the most compelling way.

Dennis Roberts writes, "The seller's demeanor in this first meeting should be open, honest, and very friendly, but it also should be relatively reserved. Any overt attempt by the seller to sell his company risks being interpreted as anxiousness, while signaling to the buyer that he may as well stop selling himself (e.g. the seller seems maybe a little too desperate or needy)" (Roberts 2009, p. 212). You want to be perceived as a peer and that you're engaging in a two-way interview. The worst-case situation is treating the buyer as a superior, because it insinuates a weak negotiating position.

Own Your Story

As the owner, it's fully expected that you completely understand and own all of the functions of your business. You don't need to be an expert on all the details, but you do need to show you *know enough to be dangerous* to effectively manage your respective managers. After all, they all work for you. Deflecting responsibility for requested materials on your investment bankers, accountants, or team members casts doubt on your leadership capabilities and leads the buyer to question their accuracy. If you cannot confidently stand behind the information you share, why would the buyer?

SITE VISITS

If your physical facilities are relevant to your business' value, then a site visit frequently occurs immediately before or afterward. If visits from outsiders are common in your business, try to make the visit consistent and seem like another one of those. If not, you can either use a cover story (prospective sales reps) or push to host the tour after hours.

During a visit, a buyer will mentally take note of various elements:

- Are the facilities clean and organized?
- Is the business busy or slow?
- Do the employees seem happy?
- Are you running a tight ship? Conversely, are you overstaffed?
- Are the employees A-players?
- What is the culture and atmosphere of the business?

ADHERING TO THE PROCESS

The seller's goal is to proactively and intentionally control the process. At its core, every sales process is designed to maximize competition or the implicit threat of it. Competition requires that all of the offers are synchronized. As a seller, you want to have all of your options available at the same time so you can make a fully informed decision about what's best. Otherwise, you may be put in a position of having to accept an offer or decline it, hoping that something better will come along (i.e. take a bird in hand versus two in the bush).

Part of the art of M&A is how to slow down overeager buyers while managing the other buyers to ensure they keep to the schedule. While many of these eager buyers will complain and insinuate they will lose interest, legitimate ones understand it's within your right to give sufficient time to hear the other offers.

The pacing of the process is designed to your advantage. In *Mergers & Acquisitions*, Roberts advises, "In every transaction, there will be a time to go slow and a time to move fast. In general, though, the early stages tend to be best handled at a slow pace, and only the later stages [post-LOI] at a 'sense of urgency' pace" (Roberts 2009, p. 218).

Be prepared that if left to their own devices, some buyers will attempt to bypass the process to get an inside track on the deal, often called an *end run*. Specifically, they use a friendly demeanor to convince you that a simple solution can easily be agreed to without advisors who frequently "get in the way." Do not fall for this ploy. End runs undermine the credibility and effectiveness of your advisors and negate the whole process, which is designed specifically to maximize value.

While it might be tempting, remember that it is highly unlikely you will obtain a better outcome than your professional advisors who do this for a living. You hired them for a reason. The good news is these amateurish attempts reveal that the buyer has a high degree of interest. They would not attempt such tactics if they were indifferent about the opportunity.

Similarly, all follow-up communications after the management meeting should occur through a single channel: either the banker (recommended) or the CEO or CFO. Having buyers call individual managers is disruptive and carries an additional risk of them inadvertently going off script or worse.

A deadline to submit letters of intent (LOIs) is typically set two to three weeks after the management meetings have finished. If there is legitimate buyer interest, they will normally request additional information to complete their internal processes to obtain formal approval to submit an LOI. Consequently, your bankers will be in nearly daily contact with the buyers' junior team members, addressing these follow-up requests. While uncelebrated, this responsiveness is important to success. There may also be some discussions with the buyer's senior leaders where they solicit the banker's perspective regarding the seller's preferences between different options.

TOP 3 TAKEAWAYS

- Receiving IOIs is the first opportunity to truly see where you stand. Your advisors will interpret, normalize, and prioritize the various offers and will assist you in selecting the top four to six bidders to invite for management meetings.
- An offer is only as valuable as the rigor of the underwriting and analysis that went into analyzing the potential and risks of an acquisition because it's nonbinding. Many buyers treat signing an LOI as a free option – heads I win, tails you lose.
- Management meetings are critical in developing emotional buy-in by a buyer's senior decision-makers. It is important to plan ahead and rehearse as many challenging questions as possible. You want to come across as a peer who is also interviewing the other side.

CHAPTER 21

Purchase Price and Terms

The one question I can guarantee that every client will ask is when they are going to get paid. It's natural to want to see the cold, hard cash at the end of the sale. I remember one client who got up and paced my office as I explained that he probably wasn't going to receive the amount of money he was expecting . . . at least not right away.

You've probably sold a piece of property, and you almost certainly received a wire transfer or check for the full amount at the closing table. Business transactions are different. Unlike what you've experienced in a real-estate sale, it's rare for a middle-market seller to receive 100% of the purchase price in cash at closing. While cash is nearly always a major component of the proceeds, it generally represents 60–80% of the stated purchase price. The remainder is paid for by different types of *consideration* or alternative kinds of payment.

You would think determining the *true* purchase price would be straightforward. Everyone can easily agree on the value of cash. However, anything else is open to interpretation and highly subjective. Without a third-party, arms-length transaction validating its true value, buyers have the liberty to frame it however they want.

Filippell shares a fun quip that sums up the reality of subjective valuations: "Daddy, I sold my frog for $10,000! I swapped him for a pair of $5,000 goldfish" (Filippell 2011, p. 51). Consequently, you'll often hear deal guys joke, "You set the price, and I'll set the terms." Because of its apparent simplicity and comparability, most everyone focuses on the headline valuation, referred to as the enterprise value. However, they should focus on the actual value of the various kinds of consideration they will receive.

ENTERPRISE VALUE

The enterprise value presents the *gross* value of the entire business independent of any debt or cash the company keeps – the amount received at closing is net of whatever debt may exist.

Because of the leeway in calculating this number, buyers frame it in a way most likely to impress you. While most buyers try to be reasonable, others will use imaginative semantics to distort the reality of the seller's economics. Here are some common games I see:

- Treating money earned in the future the same as cash today.
- Taking credit for anticipated future appreciation of the seller's reinvested equity.
- Valuing equity subordinated to debt is the same as a debt-free business.
- Showing credit for earnouts that are unlikely to ever be achieved.
- Proposing seller financing at significantly below market rates.
- Making offers based upon to-be-determined pro forma numbers whose calculation is a black box.
- Imposing significant contingencies and clawbacks.
- Proposing a formula that results in an artificially high level of working capital (functional discount).

DIFFERENT FORMS OF PAYMENT

Buyers are typically more willing to stretch the total potential purchase price in exchange for greater non-cash consideration. This is a classic risk–return trade-off. Many clients are adamant about receiving an all-cash offer until they realize the valuation will be correspondingly lower.

Aside from minimizing a buyer's required investment, these other forms of payment are used by buyers to allocate risks and to better align interests with the seller to maximize the chances of a successful transition (Figure 21.1). Consequently, buyers view some of them as substitutes for each other.

While cash is typically preferred, a compelling advantage of other kinds of payments is the ability to defer taxation if structured properly. As they say, the devil is in the details. Non-cash consideration has plenty of room for details that are hard to understand, particularly from the outside.

Let's delve into a few of the most common forms within middle-market deals.

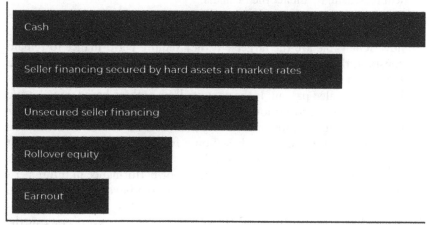

Cash

Seller financing secured by hard assets at market rates

Unsecured seller financing

Rollover equity

Earnout

LEAST CERTAIN   MOST CERTAIN

FIGURE 21.1   Relative value of different kinds of consideration.

EARNOUTS

Earnouts are contingent payments made to the seller in the future if certain performance metrics or conditions are met. Earnouts are a mechanism to shift some of the operating risk to the seller. They are particularly useful for bridging valuation gaps. A buyer may be skeptical about the seller's promises of future performance gains or because of a volatile history. Buyers view earnouts as a useful tool to force sellers to put their money where their mouth is. Moreover, they are frequently self-funding if the desired performance occurs.

While they can be tied to nearly anything (such as the retention of a key client), earnouts are most commonly associated with certain revenue or EBITDA (earnings before interest, taxes, depreciation, and amortization) targets. The range of achievability can be massive. Earnouts can have a super-low bar and be viewed as nearly guaranteed, or they can be all but impossible to hit. You, as a seller, are in the best position to accurately estimate the likelihood of achieving them.

Here are the most important elements of an earnout:

- Term. What is the duration of the earnout? Does the payout occur in one lump sum payment or in multiple smaller payouts? Most earnouts are one to three years long and proportionally pay out each year. I recommend against longer earnouts as it's difficult for sellers to accurately forecast that far out. Moreover, factors outside the seller's control and foresight will increasingly impact the business.

- Target. What metrics and/or conditions trigger whether the payout is owed? This is perhaps the most important element. The key question is how achievable are the targets? If they require performance to remain constant, the likelihood of payout is much higher than if they require a significant level of growth.
- Binary vs. scaled payout. Is the payout all-or-nothing based upon hitting a metric, or is it proportionate to what is achieved relative to the target? Binary payouts create distorted incentives and should generally be avoided. Most earnouts are based on a formula allowing partial credit (albeit some have a minimum floor).
- Offsetting. Can the seller make up for poor performance in future periods? This is favorable to sellers, and often, the buyer permits it if you ask for it.
- Capped or unlimited upside. Is there a maximum payout, or can the seller potentially earn an unlimited amount?
- Other conditions. Are there any other prerequisites that must be met to be eligible? For example, the agreement may require certain margins to be maintained.
- Fine print. What happens if the buyer defaults? What kind of provisions are in place to protect the seller?

Earnouts are generally only appropriate when the seller intends to remain running the business and can influence future performance. Remember that post-closing, the buyer owns the business and has operational discretion to make decisions that can negatively impact the entity's earnings.

While the most pressing worry is outright manipulation, the reality is that other legitimate decisions made to improve future profitability may drag on today's earnings – things like investing to improve IT systems, hiring additional or more qualified corporate managers, or launching marketing campaigns.

The further down the financial statements, the greater the potential for the financials to be impacted. Top-line metrics are harder to manipulate and are immune to cost allocation decisions and other potentially distorting factors. Consequently, when earnouts are used, earnings are the benchmark only about 10% of the time, according to the American Bar Association's Private Target Mergers & Acquisitions Deal Points Study (Pearlman and Paterno 2023). Most earnouts are tied to revenue.

A note on the potential risks of earnouts: Many lawyers joke that "earnouts are an invitation for future litigation." Every joke contains an element of truth. If a seller files a lawsuit post-transaction, it almost always involves the earnout provision.

After closing, buyer's remorse may cause new owners to *look* for future opportunities to even the score. Given that possession is nine-tenths of the law, buyers are in an advantageous position regarding the earnout's payment. That said, I have rarely encountered this in my transaction history, and I believe most risk of nonpayment can be mitigated through good legal drafting. Specifically, ambiguity is a recipe for disaster. All of the measurements should be explicitly defined up front in the legal documents.

SELLER FINANCING

Seller financing is essentially a loan that the seller offers the buyer, allowing payment to be deferred until a future date. Of primary importance is its likelihood of being repaid. Depending on the amount of overall debt incurred by the buyer and the note's seniority, these loans can range from being equivalent to an AAA-rated bond to a speculative junk bond that has a real risk of losing principal.

Given that range of risk and to fully understand what you're signing up for, it's important to carefully analyze the specific loan terms relative to the deal's overall financial risk. Here are some of the common elements to assess and compare relative to market norms:

- Term. What is the loan's term? These are commonly three to seven years in length.
- Interest rate. How does the interest rate compare to market rates? Most of the time, the offered rate is below market. For simplicity's sake, these tend to use fixed versus floating interest rates.
- Amortization. How much of the principal is repaid each year, if any? These loans tend to have limited amortization. Many are structured as interest-only loans with a balloon payment at the end of the term.
- Seniority. Is the loan in a first-lien position secured by collateral? These tend to be unsecured or secured in a subordinated position to other lenders. If so, it's important to understand the amount of senior debt on the business.
- Fine print. What happens if the buyer defaults? What kind of provisions are in place to protect you?

In general, these notes are made at below-market rates and terms – otherwise, the buyer would have just borrowed from a third-party lender. Given your familiarity and comfort with the business, you may perceive less risk and be willing to accept slightly less attractive terms. For many sellers, this option presents a compelling alternative to some fixed-income investments you would otherwise make with your sale proceeds. Seller notes are a particularly relevant tool to help induce buyers to make an acquisition at an acceptable price in tough market environments, where lending is tight and interest rates are high.

ROLLOVER EQUITY

Buyers can pay for a portion of the purchase price by offering sellers stock, often called *rollover equity*. Depending on the structure, sellers will either continue to retain a portion of the equity in their current company or receive equity in a new holding company. Regardless of the structure, the Internal Revenue Service (IRS) should treat this rollover equity as a nontaxable event.

I functionally view this as if the seller received all of the proceeds in cash and then turned around and reinvested a portion into the new company's stock. Because the buyers use debt to pay for a portion of the transaction price, sellers can often maintain a relatively high percentage of ownership in the post-transaction business with a modest dollar amount of rollover equity.

Rollover equity allows the seller to participate in future upside and can turn out to be highly valuable. It's not uncommon for sellers to earn more in their second sale than in their initial transaction. Private equity (PE) firms are in the business of maximizing returns, and while results differ across investors and investments, their net annual returns for middle-market deals have historically averaged 15–20% (better than public market alternatives).

When you sell your business, your wealth advisor will likely reinvest the proceeds in a portfolio of investments. Most sophisticated investors proactively seek opportunities in PE and allocate a meaningful amount of their portfolios to it due to attractive returns and lower perceived risk relative to the public markets. This rollover equity can be viewed as investing in a highly concentrated substitute for that investment category. Just like you would vet a prospective fund manager before investing, you should do the same with the buyer and develop your own assessment regarding their capabilities and likelihood of success.

What You're Signing Up for

If you receive rollover equity as part of your sale, understand what you're signing up for. Lenders typically put in place covenants requiring that cash flow is used to pay down debt principal before distributions can be made, other than those to cover taxes. Regardless, most buyers will use excess cash to reinvest in the business or make acquisitions.

From a PE investor's vantage point, their number one priority is to boost the business's adjusted EBITDA at the time of its eventual sale in order to maximize the exit value. Consequently, they are relatively unconcerned about spending money on consultants and other one-time initiatives (e.g. implementing an enterprise resource planning [ERP] system) that can be treated as addbacks in a later transaction.

Most PE firms will also charge their portfolio companies various fees on an ongoing basis. These are typically set as a percentage of EBITDA with a minimum floor (the norm is 3–5%, with an annual minimum of $300,000–$500,000). On top of that, some also charge fees for supporting specific transactions, refinancings, or other individual consulting projects.

Consequently, other than tax distributions, you should not assume any real payouts until the business is ultimately sold. If performance is strong and there are few opportunities to reinvest, these funds sometimes structure a debt recapitalization to make a large special distribution. However, I would not rely on this occurring. While PE investments average five years in length, the amount of time can vary significantly across companies. It's important to make sure you are aligned with the buyer on expectations.

MINORITY SHAREHOLDERS: ALONG FOR THE RIDE

Minority shareholders need to assume that they will not be able to exit until the majority owners do. Nearly all operating agreements provide restrictions or outright prohibitions on selling to outsiders. Even without any restrictions, shares in private companies are not marketable, as few investors are eager to become a minority partner with practical strangers. The only realistic exit option is selling your interest to other shareholders. While you can sometimes get lucky and encounter someone eager to increase their ownership percentage, if you really need to get out, a substantial discount is likely the only way to induce buyers to acquire your shares. If you can negotiate it, the ideal scenario is to have a *put* option, allowing you the right to require the new owners to purchase your shares at a predetermined formula.

(Continued)

> *(Continued)*
>
> Minority shareholder rights are limited and are typically focused on ensuring that the majority owner cannot unilaterally make changes that are disadvantageous to you, such as:
>
> - Providing you access to information (viewing the quarterly consolidated financials at a minimum, ideally enabling you to review the books and records).
> - Guaranteeing certain levels of distributions (generally tax distributions).
> - Requiring consent of disinterested shareholders to approve any related party transactions.
> - Mandating shareholder consent to incur debt or increase the number of shares (i.e. diluting you).
> - Approving major actions (annual budgets, sale of business, etc.).
>
> While most PE investments permit just the first few items, the ability to negotiate more substantial rights depends on your level of negotiating leverage.

Publicly Traded Acquirers

While relatively rare for middle-market transactions, it's possible a publicly traded acquirer will offer to use some of their stock as a form of payment for your business. Be aware that most of the time, these deals involve restricted stock that must be held for a minimum of six months. Fortune 500 stocks tend to have relatively stable values. On the other hand, the price of smaller public companies with low trading volumes may not reflect their true value. Of greater concern, selling a large block of stock can risk tanking its share price.

Making an Informed Decision

Because there are no formal universal definitions, buyers can vaguely refer to *equity* and mean a wide range of things. And unfortunately, many use this ambiguity to take advantage of unsophisticated sellers. Bankers often pay for themselves many times over just by navigating this complexity. Here are some questions for sellers to ask:

- Will my equity be on a *pari passu* (Latin for "equal footing") basis with the buyer's equity (i.e. will we have exactly the same equity)?
- If not, you need to deep dive into the exact mechanics of the investors' interests. What does the distribution waterfall look like under different financial scenarios?
- What exit rights do I have?
- What is your strategy? What returns do you project, and over what time period? How long do you anticipate holding this investment?
- Will I have a board seat or board observer role?
- What happens if the business needs to raise additional cash?
- Are additional capital calls anticipated?
- What is the plan for cash generated by the company?
- How much debt will be incurred by the business, and what are its terms?

NORMALIZING AND COMPARING OFFERS

It's highly likely you will receive offers from various buyers that look different from each other. To determine the best financial deal, it's important to look past the nominal valuation conveyed by the buyer and focus on the nature of the offered consideration. It's vital to attempt to compare each element on a cash-equivalent basis. Otherwise, you will be comparing apples, oranges, and bananas.

This is as much art as science because there's considerable judgment required to develop a perspective regarding the anticipated payout, its likelihood of collection, and the timing. While your banker will assist you with these efforts, you need to be deeply involved because valuation is both subjective and deeply personal. Two intelligent people can disagree about which option is best based on a number of factors, such as:

- Need for money now.
- Risk tolerance.
- Outlook for the business.
- Alternative investment options available.
- Expectation of valuations in the future.
- Confidence in the new owners.

The goal of this exercise is to convert each type of consideration offered into its current cash value. Your banker will first normalize the offers by applying a consistent set of numbers and assumptions across them (Figure 21.2). For example, you shouldn't assume a 10% growth rate to analyze one offer and a 15% rate for another. The resulting future payout can then be calculated and a discount applied to estimate its value today. This is often referred to as the *time value of money* (money received today is more valuable than money received in the future since you could have invested it and earned a return during the period). Rather than spending a lot of time calculating the exact discount rate, I recommend using 10–15% per year.

Let's apply this approach to a hypothetical earnout. Start by determining your *realistic* future performance expectations and use them to calculate your ultimate payout. Let's assume this 10% annual growth rate will result in an expected lump sum payout of $10 million in year three. We then discount it back to reflect the fact that it will take three years to receive that money. I'll spare you the mathematical formulas – you can find discount rate calculators online. Assuming a 10% discount rate, this would have a current present cash value of ~$7.5 million.

Conversely, there may be situations where no discount is expected. For example, sometimes sellers have the opportunity to match a lender's term sheet. Given that the seller financing would represent a market interest rate and terms, we would assume full cash value.

FORM OF CONSIDERATION	OFFER 1		OFFER 2	
	Nominal Value	Cash Value	Nominal Value	Cash Value
Cash	$20.000	$20.000	$20.000	$20.000
Earnout	$50.000	$30.000	$40.000	$38.000
Secured Note @ 7%	–	–	$5.000	$5.000
Unsecured Seller Note @ 7%	$5.000	$3.000	–	–
Purchase Price Paid as Compensation	$5.000	$2.000	–	–
Total Pre-tax Consideration	**$80,000**	**$55,000**	**$65,000**	**$63,000**

FIGURE 21.2   Illustrative comparison of two competing offers.

TOP 3 TAKEAWAYS

- Unlike real-estate transactions, sellers rarely receive 100% cash up-front. While most people focus on the headline enterprise value, you need to pay particular attention to the value of the different forms of payment received, many of which have significant subjectivity.
- Buyers are most willing to stretch the total purchase price in exchange for greater non-cash consideration. Some common forms include earn-outs, seller financing, and rollover equity. They view these other forms of payment as a better way to align interests to ensure a successful transition. The devil is in the details.
- It is important to normalize offers received on a consistent cash-equivalent basis. You should be highly involved in developing a perspective, as the true value is often highly personal.

CHAPTER 22

Negotiating and Signing the Letter of Intent

Damien (not his real name) looked at the letter of intent. "It's getting real," he said softly. I nodded. Until the LOI is signed, there can seem to be unlimited options. Once a client has the LOI, it is, as Damien said, "getting real." I've seen clients be excited at this point, and I've seen clients suddenly get cold feet. I've even seen them go back and forth between the two states of mind within minutes.

The letter of intent (LOI) is the filtering mechanism that selects a single buyer from the various interested parties. While either party maintains the right to choose not to proceed, if everything checks out, there is generally a moral commitment to honor the terms. So, it's essential to be in full agreement with *all* of the LOI terms before signing it. Attempting to change agreed-upon terms during the confirmatory due diligence phase without a legitimate rationale reflects negatively on the seller's judgment and integrity (not the impression you want to leave a potential business partner you are courting).

Ultimately, this document is just an agreement in principle and serves as the foundation to craft the purchase agreement and other formal legal documents. These legal documents collectively reflect hundreds of pages, so many details must be filled in. The devil really is in the details.

THE LEVERAGE SHIFTS WITH THE STROKE OF A PEN

Never in the history of deal-making has a buyer voluntarily improved their offer after encountering conditions more favorable than initially expected.

However, rest assured they will be looking for concessions if they encounter something negative during due diligence. In other words, the LOI represents the *maximum* potential price and terms the seller can ever hope to receive.

As the sales process progresses, the seller's negotiating position is strong. After all, several buyers are eagerly competing. The seller can use every opportunity to improve price and terms. These dynamics reverse once the LOI is signed with a single buyer. This is because LOIs almost always require exclusivity from the seller, prohibiting them from having further conversations for a period of time (typically 45 to 90 days) with other potentially interested parties (more on that later) – and this presents a huge opportunity cost.

While it is possible to reject any concessions a buyer may request and remarket the business once the exclusivity period has expired, this is generally a very unfavorable situation as the seller is likely to face scrutiny from the same potential buyers for a second time. This time, however, they know that the "winning" bidder got a look behind the curtain and found something they didn't like – and they will generally assume the company is *damaged goods*. Moreover, given these other interested parties were not selected the first time, they are unlikely to offer nearly as generous terms. As a result, it is not uncommon after a failed LOI for a seller to remove the company from the market for 12–18 months to reset expectations and achieve a clean slate for a future sale attempt.

THE POWER OF PROACTIVE HONESTY

Just as no person is perfect, no business is flawless. One hundred percent have at least one blemish. While it goes against the instinct of many sellers, it's *critical* to fully disclose these potential negative items before entering into an exclusive agreement. As a seller, you have the unfair advantage of determining when and how to convey them to minimize their impact. Ideally, the disclosure occurred nonchalantly earlier in the sales process, but if not, it should be presented to the various buyers while you still have leverage, and competition prevents them from taking advantage. Before signing, I generally require the winning bidder to affirm in writing that they have reviewed all of the provided information and that their offer incorporates those facts – I reinforce that changes based upon information that was previously known will not be tolerated.

Honesty is the best policy because, in the end, full disclosure is unavoidable. In his book *The Messy Marketplace*, Brent Beshore writes: "Like going on a first date, then dating, then being engaged, and ultimately married, a company's hidden quirks, dark secrets, and weaknesses eventually come out" (Beshore 2018, p. 91). Moreover, the final legal documents will require you to stand behind all your claims made throughout the sales process.

Praying that the buyer will not spot the issue is foolish. All buyers hire sophisticated advisors who are incentivized to be conservative and uncover issues. It's not a matter of if but *when* they find that problematic issue. This proactive honesty helps build trust and respect with the buyer, which may be needed later in the process. And look at the bright side: To the extent irreconcilable differences exist, it's far better to discover them early and quickly move along to your next best option.

KEY ELEMENTS OF AN LOI

While every buyer has their own format for drafting an LOI, they typically run four to seven pages on the buyer's formal letterhead and cover the 10 to 15 most important terms of a transaction. Nearly all will contain the following:

- Exclusivity.
- Structure (stock vs. asset purchase).
- Valuation.
- Form of payment.
- Treatment of working capital.
- Handling real estate and other noncore assets.
- Key assumptions.
- Intentions for management.

Exclusivity

Only a handful of provisions within an LOI are binding, and exclusivity is one of them. Without exclusivity, few buyers would be willing to take the risk of investing the necessary out-of-pocket expenses on third-party professionals to consummate the deal when a competitor could just scoop it up at the last second. Exclusivity provisions expect you to cease all communications with other potential buyers.

"Exclusivity is an enormous concession that the seller should make with great care," Mark Filippell writes. "In a marital context, exclusivity is much like being engaged. The difference is that in M&A, there is a strong legal force behind the engagement, such that the seller is forbidden by law to even talk to other suitors. And there is no out for a Las Vegas bachelor party!" (Filippell 2011, p. 198).

This obligation should be treated seriously. Failure to do so may put you at risk of a lawsuit where you'll be responsible for reimbursing the buyer for all of their out-of-pocket expenses and potentially their anticipated profits as well.

The length of exclusivity is directly related to the expected closing date, as buyers intend to close before this exclusivity expires. Most buyers request 90 days for exclusivity. From my experience, this is frequently reduced to 60 or even 45 days (however, be careful about what you ask for because most middle-market sellers are not equipped to respond and proceed at a 45-day pace).

Preventing Retrade   Because of the risk of being held hostage in exclusivity (particularly for a long period), I am adamant about including language that allows my client an early out if the buyer exhibits bad-faith behavior. One approach is to provide the buyer with a short window of exclusivity for them to quickly conduct their confirmatory diligence. While we generally end up with 30 days, the shorter, the better because every extra day makes it much harder to reapproach the second- and third-place bidders. To continue to receive extensions, various milestones must be reached, such as affirming the purchase price or resolving specific outstanding contentious issues. Similarly, "affirmative response clauses" require the buyer to affirm in writing that they do not contemplate any material changes to the LOI's deal terms – exclusivity ends automatically if this representation is not made. Because buyers could potentially be exposed to damages for making a misrepresentation, it provides the seller leverage to walk away and cut bait. I find demanding this protective language strongly signals to prospective buyers that you will not tolerate games.

Structure (Stock vs. Asset Purchase)

In a stock purchase, the buyer purchases the seller's shares – and functionally steps into their shoes. The business experiences no change, just new owners. On the other hand, asset purchases involve the buyer forming a new holding company that then acquires the business's assets, as well as any liabilities that they select. Any other remaining obligations will remain with the original corporate entity, which the seller will continue to maintain responsibility for.

Depending on the industry and its corporate structure, some sellers incur significantly less taxes via a stock sale. On the other hand, I've seen plenty of deals where there's virtually no difference. What really matters is how much you get to keep after taxes.

Optimizing your after-tax proceeds is highly contextual and definitely beyond the scope of this book. It's critical to work with your tax advisors to understand your specific circumstances and the implications *before* going to market, so you provide initial guidance that's to your advantage. Similarly, before signing an LOI, I recommend having that advisor carefully review the proposed structure and confirm that it complies with your desired tax planning.

Conversely, buyers prefer asset sales because of the limited liability and the associated tax advantages to them – specifically, they can amortize their goodwill. The value of these tax savings can result in a functionally reduced purchase price in the buyer's eyes.

While asset purchases are the most common structure for middle-market transactions, you do see stock purchases, particularly in businesses with a large number of vital contracts, such as in healthcare. This is because each one of these agreements would then need to be re-executed – not only is this a time-consuming pain, but also there's the risk the new contracts will be on less favorable terms.

Valuation

For nearly every seller I've met, this is the first section they flip to. After all, the bottom line is what it's all about. I'm not going to rehash all of the details on the topic from Chapter 21 other than to re-emphasize that valuation is nearly irrelevant without deeply understanding the form of payment.

Rather than list a dollar value, some buyers will quote a multiple of EBITDA (earnings before interest, taxes, depreciation, and amortization) or revenue. I strongly prefer that an actual price be listed because it leaves much less room for ambiguity – you don't want to argue about the proper base to multiply by later in the process. Moreover, this framework allows the buyer to nickel and dime for every penny of difference, creating a more contentious confirmatory due diligence process. From my perspective, if nothing materially changes, I expect the price to remain the same (i.e. if we are within 5%, the initial offer should be honored).

Form of Payment

The LOI will describe the various forms of payment (e.g. seller notes, earn-outs, rollover equity) that the buyer is offering. Please see Chapter 21 for the importance of understanding the details to develop your perspective on the offer's true present value.

Consulting agreements for ongoing services are common and are only fair to compensate the sellers for their valuable time. That said, some buyers will offer consulting agreements at above-market rates or for services not performed as part of the sales price. These tend to be taxed at higher ordinary tax rates and often have other contingencies that make them unattractive relative to other kinds of consideration. If at all possible, I would advise pushing to convert these to an earnout or seller note.

Make sure to fully understand the buyer's proposed capital structure (i.e. how much debt they are using). This allows you to make a fully informed decision regarding the value of the equity you are receiving and will also help you understand whether there might be any hidden financing risks to further ask about. It's important to delve into the details and understand the true level of uncertainty involved. For example, a financing contingency requiring a high level of debt and/or below-market interest rates is considerably riskier than one predicated upon a conservative structure.

Treatment of Working Capital

Upon purchase, the buyer expects to receive all of the operating assets required to sustain continued operations without needing to infuse additional cash into the business. While machinery and other required equipment are expected to be included, many sellers incorrectly assume that they should get to keep their inventory and receivables, which they were responsible for generating. However, this would require the buyer to pump additional cash into the business to fund its commitments. Unfortunately, a buyer is not going to pay you a multiple of your earnings and allow you to keep the ordinary and necessary balance sheet. When you return a rental car, you are expected to drop it off with a full tank of gas. Similarly, middle-market buyers expect a sufficient level of working capital to continue to finance the business's daily operations.

At its most basic, working capital is defined as current assets minus current liabilities. However, reasonable people can disagree on the correct amount because there are multiple areas for subjectivity. This is particularly complicated for businesses that experience seasonality.

The LOI should describe the expected level of working capital, even if it's just a high-level framework. Many buyers will leave it vague, such as,

"The business will have working capital consistent with historical averages." I highly recommend calculating the implications of various kinds of working capital methodologies (e.g. 6-month average or 12-month average) and pushing to insert specificity for a method that is most advantageous to you. Your CFO needs to be at the center of this process as they will uniquely understand the implications within the context of your business.

While the sellers usually to keep the cash in the business, if there's insufficient working capital, your net proceeds at closing will be reduced dollar for dollar in order to meet the target.

Handling Real Estate and Other Noncore Assets

All valuation methodologies essentially assume that the business pays a market-rate lease for its real estate without owning it. That said, it's not uncommon for sellers to own their real estate, either through the business or a related entity. To that extent, the LOI will mention the buyer's intent for the property. While some strategics will be interested in buying the underlying real estate, most buyers prefer to lease it. The most common scenario is requesting a three- to five-year lease with the right to multiple renewal extensions – these have annual rent escalators that tend to be 2–4% or the consumer price index (CPI). For many owners, continuing to own the property provides them with an excellent source of passive income.

There is likely going to be some subjectivity regarding what is the appropriate market rate. All other things considered, it's in your interest to charge a higher lease rate because the multiple you receive when you sell the real estate is likely to be substantially higher than the EBITDA multiple from the sale of the business.

Similarly, assets not needed to operate the business – such as excessive inventory, unrelated real estate, or aircraft – are generally excluded from a transaction and either retained by the owners or paid for above and beyond the purchase price.

Key Assumptions

Prospective buyers typically reference the key assumptions that underlie their offer. For example, they may reference that certain financial statements previously provided to them are assumed to be accurate and form the basis of their valuation. Don't be surprised if they reference the projections that you have provided. Beware that buyers often include this to lay the groundwork for justifying negative price adjustments when it's revealed that your performance is falling short.

On a related note, they may bring up other areas of concern, such as a pending lawsuit, which need to be addressed for them to get comfortable. All of these caveats should be taken into consideration when determining the buyer's likelihood of closing.

Intentions for Management

Buyers want to make sure they are receiving the business' full value. Fundamentally, their goal is to seamlessly transfer ownership without losing the value of the company's important customer, employee, and supplier relationships.

Consequently, to sell for full value, you will be expected to assist in transitioning the business for a minimum period of 12–18 months. This can be as long as three to five years if the business is unique and/or highly dependent upon you. In *Mergers & Acquisitions Playbook*, Filippell writes, "the thinner the seller's management team, the longer [you] will have to stay if [you do] not want to accept a haircut to the purchase price linked to the uncertainty of a management transition" (Filippell 2011, p. 5).

Warrillow explains, "The more flexible you seem before signing an LOI, the more offers you are likely to attract. In an ironic twist, by encouraging more offers, your flexibility puts you in a better position to dictate the role you want to play post-exit. The opposite is not true. If you are too rigid and appear unwilling to help the new owner integrate what they are considering acquiring, you are likely to turn off a lot of buyers. As a result, you'll likely undermine your negotiating leverage" (Warrillow 2021, p. 170).

To the extent the seller does want to transition to retirement, they will typically continue running the business while assisting in identifying and hiring a replacement, followed by a part-time role focused on special projects, and finally, with a consulting role on an as-needed basis.

You should expect the buyer to require you to sign an agreement with noncompete and nonsolicitation clauses for five years or more. These restrict your ability to establish a competing firm as well as prevent you from hiring any employees in any kind of business during the period. Similarly, don't be surprised if they mandate your managers sign similar restrictions, even if they don't own the business.

PROCESS

Like indications of interest (IOIs), LOIs all tend to arrive on the evening of the deadline to minimize the chances of their offers being shopped around. In the days after receipt, you will sit with your bankers, who should present to you a table comparing the various offers on a consistent basis, which was discussed in Chapter 20. You'll provide feedback and guidance regarding what your advisor should prioritize in their negotiations.

LOIs are infrequently accepted as is. If you did, most buyers would worry that they offered too much. Moreover, it's virtually impossible for your attorney not to have some recommended changes to improve clarity. From my experience, there's almost always some room to improve their *best and final* offers further. It's only the realistic magnitude that's in question. The number of offers close to the top and their dispersion will dictate how your bankers focus their negotiating efforts.

In the week or two following their submission, there are typically numerous rounds of simultaneous negotiations with the various bidders to clarify and improve terms. Warrillow writes, "To get an acquirer to increase their offer, you have to find the middle ground between expressing gratitude for a firm bid – they've probably already done a lot of work to get to that point – and nudging them gently to do better. The more offers you have, the harder you can push" (Warrillow 2021, p. 177).

While it might be tempting to rush to get the LOI signed and start the closing process, this is the time to be patient and use time to your advantage. In *Mergers & Acquisitions*, Dennis Roberts writes, "inexperienced buyers may tire too early of offers and counteroffers and remove themselves [prematurely] from the auction" (Roberts 2009, p. 206). To strike the best deal, it's not uncommon for there to be upwards of half a dozen exchanges. Moreover, in parallel, you will likely be making quiet reference calls regarding the buyer's reputation.

FORCING CLARITY

To the extent that the offers contain discrepancies in their key assumptions (e.g. one assumes a certain level of EBITDA, while the other assumes a higher level), I recommend a deep dive into the source of the differences and addressing them while competitive tensions remain strong.

If your attorneys are not already engaged, this is the time for them to get involved. They should carefully review the document from a legal perspective and will inevitably point out ambiguities that will need to be resolved at some point. Given that they will be the ones ultimately drafting and negotiating the subsequent formal legal documents, I believe they should take the lead in pushing for as much clarity *in writing* as possible.

Many buyers push vague offers with room for interpretation, using a *we'll figure it out* attitude. However, it's almost always more advantageous for sellers to err on the side of inserting as many of the finer details as possible while the leverage remains on your side. Whenever there is something open to interpretation, assume that it will be interpreted against you. I've seen many buyers have convenient lapses of memory once they gain the leverage. Removing ambiguities also helps to minimize *misunderstandings* that may trip up the deal further along, such as:

- Referencing a multiple without being specific regarding the associated earnings number (some addbacks may not be accepted, last year's vs. last 12 months vs. a multiyear average EBITDA).
- Mechanics and terms of an earnout.
- Working capital levels to be left in the business.
- Terms of noncompetes, particularly if they will be applied to the owner's family members.

Before signing the final LOI, I recommend sitting with the buyer and reviewing the LOI together in "plain English" to unearth any differing interpretations. If you have a highly competitive transaction, sellers can even require that virtually all of the details of the purchase agreement be resolved before signing. Buyers are provided a seller-favorable purchase agreement draft, and buyers need to mark it up with any required changes as part of their offer.

LIKELIHOOD OF CLOSING

One big factor to keep in mind as you compare offers: the odds of a bidder crossing the finish line. Across all buyers, it's important to understand their level of commitment and *desire* for doing the deal – is this a "must have" or a "nice to have"? Beware of selecting a lukewarm buyer. A highly engaged buyer has a dramatically higher chance of closing on favorable terms.

Recall from Chapter 20 that the credibility of an offer and the likelihood that a buyer will follow through is directly proportional to the time and rigor that went into reviewing the opportunity. Remember that drafting an offer can take professional buyers half an hour using a template. While many buyers view an LOI as a moral commitment to transact, others can view deals as a *free option*. They only start digging in once they've locked up a deal. Statistically, they tend to close on a low proportion of deals (sometimes single-digit percentages). Only after they win exclusivity do they use internal resources to review in depth. If they are pleasantly surprised, they will then engage third-party professionals to review. If not, they will choose to walk away despite the damage it inflicts on you.

Buyers who were frequently in contact and asked deep, intelligent follow-up questions did their homework. Most likely, they will have spotted and asked questions regarding your *warts*. This is excellent as it not only reflects a genuine interest level but also provides the seller the comfort that the buyer's offer fully reflects this negative information. Your banker will also analyze usage data from the virtual data room (VDR) to gauge each buyer's amount of engagement.

Buyers should disclose the level of internal review and approval that the LOI has received. Your buyer counterpart will almost always need formal approval from their investment committee. If not, you should demand it before signing an LOI. This group is formed by their most senior partners or board members. Their role is to make sure that every transaction goes through the same level of systematic rigor and to prioritize the highest-quality deals.

Consequently, their role is to be objective and unemotional about the investments they approve. Because most groups acquire only one out of 100 deals they initially review, they tend to assume a conservative stance and operate under the mantra that you earn all of the money in the deals you don't make.

They are greatly influenced by the seniority of the sponsor and other supporters and their level of enthusiasm for the deal. Therefore, it's important to assess the quantity of time senior decision-makers have committed to the process and the amount of initiative they have exhibited. Beware if your only contact with the buyer has been with relatively junior team members – for deals that buyers are seriously interested in, I would expect senior decision-makers to physically come out and meet with you and to be highly engaged in the negotiations and process through the signing of the LOI. Similarly, if it's clear the senior decision-maker does not understand your business model, that's a huge red flag. No investment committee is going to approve an investment that the partner can't fully and passionately defend.

A buyer's strong *desire* for wanting the asset is a huge advantage. During the final LOI negotiations, keep an eye on a buyer's sentiment and level of engagement. Persistence and creativity from a buyer in their counteroffers is a great sign that they are highly interested.

FINANCIAL WHEREWITHAL

A buyer's excitement and commitment to doing a deal are irrelevant if they can't pay for it. The deal needs 100% of the funding to close – 99% won't cut it. Many offers have financing contingencies – it's important to understand the expected level of debt and terms relative to the current market realities to assess the associated risk levels.

You also need to get comfortable that the equity capital is available and secure. For some kinds of buyers, like private equity (PE) funds with available committed capital, this will be a nonissue. However, this is a factor when considering less institutional PE investors (such as independent sponsors and search funds) as well as many smaller strategics. Your banker should thoroughly review the buyer's current debt levels to determine their likelihood of successfully obtaining financing. To the extent that third parties will be investing in the transaction, I highly recommend pushing to speak directly with them to assess their commitment level and the likelihood of funding.

FACTORING IN FIT

In the book *Sell Well*, the authors write, "the business owner's urgency, fervor and enthusiasm for the sale can create blinders that mask flaws and red flags that almost everyone else in the room can see" (Robichaud et al. 2017, p. 37). Listen openly to feedback from your team, advisors, and spouse and take the time to introspect.

Compatibility is contextual based on your personality. You know yourself and should take stock regarding what is important to you and the environment where you thrive the most. If you are a successful middle-market seller, you are likely going to be financially independent post-transaction. Life's too short to be in bed with someone you don't trust. Despite being trained as a lawyer, I am a firm believer that a good buyer is better than a good contract – an unscrupulous counterparty is going to find a way to screw you one way or the other.

Rather than focusing on someone's personality and how much you would enjoy having a beer together, I recommend focusing on whether you trust them, whether you feel they are transparent, whether you respect them, and whether they can add value. The goal is not to find a new friend. It's to find someone that you feel you'll be successful with. Often, the ones who build the best rapport with sellers are just smooth talkers.

MAKING A FULLY INFORMED DECISION

You only want to go through the sales process once. It's worth your while to spend the time and energy to truly understand what you're getting into while you still have various options available to you. Here are some questions to ask buyers before officially signing: We've covered some of these in Chapter 7, but it is good to review them one more time.

- Of the last five LOIs that you signed, how many closed?
- What was the reason for these deals failing to close?
- Can you introduce me to the owners of the last three transactions you closed on? (Specifically, ask them whether the buyer tried to inappropriately change any aspects of the deal.)
- How long does your confirmatory due diligence last?
- How much on-site access is required?
- Who will I be working with and reporting to? What is their management style?
- Describe your culture.

MAKING THE FINAL CALL

Rather than selecting the highest offer, I highly recommend selecting the top buyer or two with the best fit and then trying to use the other offers to jockey up their price and terms. You'll often find that they will match the highest offer or come close. Once the offers can be pushed no more, you'll ultimately have a hard decision to make. Go with your gut.

For most owners the signing of the LOI is when the fact that the company is being sold starts feeling real. While signing the LOI is an important milestone, the road to closing the transaction is long and hazardous.

KEEP LOSING BIDDERS WARM

Once you sign the LOI, you are required to stop all communication with other buyers. Given that there were likely frequent discussions prior to the signing of the LOI, it's difficult to suddenly cut off communications and not have that prospective buyer assume that you selected another winning bidder. To maximize our options, I generally avoid letting the second and third buyers know we went with someone else. I often explain up front that the seller needs a month or so to handle some personal matters before committing themselves 100% to completing the transaction.

If discussions with the original buyer fall apart within the first few weeks, I should be able to return, with the second-place bidder not knowing any better. Any further out, and the buyer has likely moved on and is focusing their time on other opportunities. In these circumstances, I need to be candid and communicate that we proceeded with another bidder who was unable to close, but the seller would be open to re-engaging with them. At a certain point, the best option may be to take the company off the market and revisit in the future.

TOP 3 TAKEAWAYS

- The LOI documents the 10 to 15 most important terms of a transaction. It will serve as the foundation for the hundreds of pages of legal documentation needed to close. LOIs are infrequently signed "as is," with the seller typically heavily negotiating various aspects. It's nearly always to the seller's advantage to push for specificity.
- All leverage shifts from the seller to the buyer once an LOI is signed. Consequently, it's critical to proactively disclose all warts beforehand while you still have competition from other interested bidders. The LOI sets the maximum you can hope to receive. You should not proceed unless you are comfortable with all of its terms "as is."
- Given that only 50% of signed LOIs successfully close on average, it is vital to assess and prioritize a buyer's likelihood of closing just as much as valuation and other financial considerations.

CHAPTER **23**

Playing Defense

One of the things I warn my clients about is that once the ink is dry on the LOI, don't assume the work is over. You don't want to pop the champagne quite yet. In reality, your hard work has just begun. The LOI means your relationship with the buyer has officially transitioned from the honeymoon phase. The pivot is an abrupt one. The buyer team generally morphs from friendly to scrutinizing.

An author sums up sellers' misconceptions well: "From a psychological standpoint, the seller's biggest challenge is not to relax after the LOI is signed. The first-time seller will be tempted to believe that the deal is done and that all that has to be completed is the paperwork. However, experienced sellers realize that millions of dollars can shift sides between the signing of the LOI and the closing of the sale, if the closing happens at all" (Filippell 2011, p. 216).

Only one in two signed letters of intent (LOIs) actually close, with this probability highly dependent upon the buyer's integrity (the absolute highest buyer close rates are around 80%). Unfortunately, this process has no upside; the best-case scenario is an uneventful due diligence based on your prior preparation. Your LOI sets the maximum you can hope to achieve. Any changes are almost always going to be a one-way street less favorable to you. Mathematically, the longer you extend the process, the higher the probability that something negative will occur. Time kills deals, so speed is to your advantage.

PREPARE YOURSELF EMOTIONALLY AND PSYCHOLOGICALLY

There's no way around it: For the next 60 to 90 days, this process will be an emotional roller coaster. A tremendous amount of stamina is required during this stressful period. To the extent you can prepare yourself for what is

going to occur, you improve the chances you'll handle it well. And don't forget to manage expectations for your family and team ahead of time as well. Filippell writes, "The sale process is one time when compartmentalization is an absolute necessity. The seller and its management team must put the sale process out of their minds while they perform day-to-day management responsibilities. Likewise, they must learn to put everyday issues aside when dealing with the sale. To do otherwise will not only result in unrelenting pressure but also increase the chances of an embarrassing slip-up in front of employees, customers, suppliers or competitors" (Filippell 2011, p. 228).

Many sellers are caught off guard once they sign an LOI. The prior tone of a courtship now shifts toward a scrutinizing stance. Some sellers interpret this as a lack of trust from the buyer. While easier said than done, you shouldn't take this personally as it's universal to the process, regardless of buyer.

CONFIRMATORY DUE DILIGENCE

A buyer and their advisors can review your business in detail for years and will never have the same level of comfort and insight that you have as its owner. Their big worry is there's some major hidden liability. Remember, a buyer is asked to marry a seller based on limited information. Until this point, their perspective is informed entirely by a handful of highly choreographed interactions and sources, such as your website, confidential information memorandum (CIM), a handful of calls, and a single agenda-packed management meeting.

Most buyers dedicated all of their prior diligence efforts on analyzing the business' fundamentals, its strategic context, and risks to determine valuation and their corresponding bid. Significant time and effort are also focused on structuring and arranging necessary financing. Throughout this process, the buyer is operating under the assumption that all of the provided information is true.

After the LOI is signed, the buyer conducts confirmatory due diligence to independently verify these critical assumptions. This due diligence is a natural extension of the efforts that the buyer performed internally when preparing their LOI. The only difference is now with closing within sight, real money comes into play. So, despite the buyer having done their homework to prepare the LOI, the buyer's team will sharpen their pencils for even greater scrutiny. Additionally, the seller often restricts access to certain information and resources until the LOI is signed. Of surprise to sellers, many buyers want to meet with key customers and employees before closing.

Not only will the level of detail be far greater than the prior phases, but also the buyer and their advisory team will ask for precise explanations and the corresponding supporting information. Wherever weakness or inconsistencies emerge, they are going to dig in deep until they are 100% comfortable.

Behind the scenes, your buyer counterparty is periodically updating their investment committee on the process and key takeaways, always trying to ensure their continued support. Any material changes to the deal will need to get additional approvals from this group. Moreover, in parallel, they are working with their lenders and other capital sources to fulfill their requirements.

Most buyers sequence their efforts and will not start drafting the legal documents until the buyer is comfortable with everything discovered and there is broad agreement on any necessary adjustments to the purchase price or terms. This is a hedging tactic as they don't want to incur unnecessary costs documenting a deal that won't happen. It's an excellent sign when the lawyers show up to start drafting documents.

Whenever possible, I try to push the buyers to accelerate this drafting process because time is of the essence, and it provides the seller additional leverage. Getting the buyer to spend money works to your advantage – it further cements the buyer's commitment and makes it harder for them to walk away. Conversely, if they delay bringing in advisors, it's a red flag that they are lukewarm on the transaction.

GET READY FOR YOUR FINANCIAL AND LEGAL CLOSEUP

You will undergo the financial and legal equivalent of a colonoscopy. While a comprehensive and accurate virtual data room (VDR) will provide a significant head start, rest assured that additional seemingly irrelevant and nebulous follow-up requests will be made. LOIs provide buyers with virtually unlimited access to any item requested, and most anything is considered fair game. The buyer is investing a lot of money and has a right to understand every aspect of the acquisition. If it provides any comfort (unlikely, I know), consider this: You'd do the same before you made a similarly large purchase.

Similar to applying for bank financing (and because the buyer is likely using some kind of financing themselves), certain standardized information is absolutely necessary based on internal criteria and protocols. Without it, they cannot proceed. As a seller, you can simplify the buyer's job and speed up the process by providing them with all the requested information and the corresponding backup documentation or reference sources. You should aspire to serve accurate, real-time information on a silver platter.

The buyer will request an overwhelming flood of data. This is a particularly challenging exercise for smaller middle-market firms because they are often understaffed with disorganized IT and accounting systems. Most entrepreneurs succeed by trusting their guts and have grown accustomed to making decisions with little data. Unfortunately, this makes it tough for outsiders to understand and get comfortable with the true state of affairs.

Similarly, they will request contracts and other documents that may be decades old. If you're like most middle-market businesses, finding them is not a simple exercise. Given the nature of the various questions, your CFO will be by far the most burdened team member. While your bankers and lawyers can often assist, as outsiders, there's only so much they can do without intimate knowledge of the business and what exists. This is one of the key reasons why it's valuable to have more team members aware of the transaction, as they can help share the workload.

Many sellers don't understand why this level of diligence is needed, especially if the deal is structured as an asset purchase. The answer is under certain circumstances, the legal concept of successor liability allows creditors to pursue their claim against the buyer. Because most acquirers have deeper pockets than you, they rightfully worry that their deep pockets make them an even bigger target.

THIRD-PARTY ADVISORS JUMP IN THE MIX

Until the LOI, most buyers will not have spent any money on third-party professionals. If they did, it was very limited in scope. They tried to do as much as they could themselves. The seller will now hire an array of specialist advisors who will validate their findings and who serve as CYA for the buyers ("You don't get fired for buying IBM"). Here are some of the groups that will likely be involved:

- Accountants will conduct a quality of earnings (QofE) analysis. This involves a thorough analysis of your financial statements and addbacks tied to your bank statements and tax returns. It may also provide an assessment of other related matters to determining sustainable financial performance, such as customer longevity, churn, and contracts.
- Attorneys will review your contracts, any pending litigation, and other potential areas of legal or regulatory risk. They will also conduct lien searches to discover any unpaid amounts that need to be resolved before closing.
- IT consultants will review your systems, cybersecurity protections, and any prior breaches.
- HR consultants will review your staff records and files to check for proper classification and compliance.

- Insurance advisors will review your level of insurance coverage to ensure its adequacy.
- For regulated industries, you'll often have compliance consultants who review a sampling of transactions to ensure they comply with all regulations.
- For businesses handling hazardous substances, environmental consultants may review the property for contamination.

As you can imagine, all of these advisors are very expensive. One hundred percent of them are incentivized toward uncovering red flags that either warrant the buyer walking away or justify a purchase price reduction. Even with the best-intentioned buyers, you need to assume that anything that can be used against you *will* be used to improve the price or terms for their client. Advisors view this as an opportunity to prove their value to the clients ("By hiring us, you saved money").

Advisors are a necessary evil. The process will not move forward without them. So, treat them respectfully and try to be as collaborative and accommodating as possible. You will likely have to repeat many of the same topics you previously covered with the investment team – and do so across different advisors. Not only is this natural as these other professionals gain the necessary context to get up to speed, but it's also an attempt to corroborate the consistency of your responses.

Brent Beshore observes that "without exception, the seller will think the buyer is asking stupid, insulting, or out-of-bounds questions. Buyers . . . will think the seller is withholding information, too sensitive, and slow to respond. On both sides, there will be 'aww, screw it' moments. It's important to keep your head, be rational and be slow to anger" (Beshore 2018, p. 93). Be patient to a fault – frustration and pushing back may be interpreted as defensiveness and having something to hide.

TIMELINE MATTERS

The diligence period is expected to coincide with the amount of exclusivity granted in the LOI. Because it's customary (and often mandated in the LOI) to automatically extend the exclusivity period if both parties are negotiating in good faith, the buyer often takes their time, as there's always *some* additional item that can be requested in a follow-up.

I find it valuable to project manage both parties to ensure that everything is on track to close as scheduled and to hold the buyers accountable. The best way to do this is to initially develop and mutually agree upon a timeline for various milestones and then have frequent (generally weekly or biweekly) calls to ensure that everything is on track and to address any issues that may arise.

During this entire period, the buyer is extremely sensitive to your real-time financial performance. If you are at or ahead of budget, no problem. However, any slippage in performance during the closing process will likely force the buyer to extend their due diligence to ensure that this is a temporary blip and not a trend that will continue after the transaction closes.

Sellers are also frequently at fault for delays because they are slow to provide the requested information. Unfortunately, poorly prepared sellers that take forever to compile information get into a costly spiral – they are so slow in providing the requested information that the buyer then waits for the subsequent month's financials and the process drags along forever. It's common to hear of transactions that took over a year to close after signing the LOI. The longer the period, the higher the probability that a slip-up occurs and performance misses budget.

This policy won't make you popular with your team, but vacations need to be canceled during this critical period. Waiting for a certain person to return from a trip to provide requested information adds unnecessary risk. Hopefully, the allure of a big payday will help lessen the sting.

Beware that buyers often try to use this to their advantage: Knowing that time disadvantages the seller, many buyers purposefully draw out due diligence. They know that the more time, money, and energy you invest in a transaction, the more psychologically committed you will be to closing, making it harder to walk away even in the face of *retrading* (reductions in price and terms, often justified by minor issues and discrepancies).

FEND OFF RETRADING

Theoretically, the price and terms should not change after the LOI is signed. However, a meaningful minority of buyers will try and capitalize on their leverage (the hassle and risk associated with you walking away and revisiting the market) and your fatigue by looking for immaterial discrepancies to justify pushing for changes at the last minute. I've even seen unscrupulous buyers brag about their antics to reduce the purchase price at the closing table. These, unfortunately, are the same individuals who told you certain elements did not need to be covered prior to signing the LOI and then will come back asking for changes because things were different than they thought. I consider this unethical retrading.

However, many times, price adjustments are legitimate. The buyer's offer was predicated on the fact that all potentially relevant information needed to form a perspective on value was provided and accurate. If the business' performance materially changes or something negative is discovered that was not previously revealed, a price change is likely to occur.

Jonathan Brabrand points out that 75% of deals end up failing due to a "seller-related development, revelation or discovery." He explains: "When a negative surprise leads a buyer to believe a business is riskier than they had thought and the sellers offer no offsetting concessions, buyers will often walk away from a deal" (Brabrand 2020, pp. 170–171).

Particularly because sellers can often respond emotionally to proposed changes, it's vital that your advisors *honestly* explain how alternative buyers would react to the same circumstances and recommend a sensible compromise. You've come a long way and spent a lot of money to get here – the goal is to find a mutually agreeable way to close.

NEVER SURPRISE THE BUYER

During this critical window, your business will encounter some issue or matter that is problematic – being named in a lawsuit, writing off receivables due to a customer bankruptcy, whatever. It's critical that you proactively share this negative news *immediately* after you hear about it. It's generally better to communicate what you do and don't know rather than wait until you have all the details. This trust element is critical because once your credibility is lost, it's almost impossible to gain back.

Counterintuitively, being upfront with issues makes you appear more authentic (you're an open book) and helps deepen the reservoir of trust needed to get through some of the more intense negotiations that often occur as closing approaches. Remember, the buyer is not just analyzing the content of the issue but also filters the news through the vantage point of trust and transparency. Did you intentionally withhold relevant information that they feel you should have disclosed earlier? Nearly any negative development can be managed, but surprises can potentially kill deals because they erode trust, which is a prerequisite for closing the transaction.

All provided information should be thoroughly reviewed to ensure that it reconciles with other information and is consistent with previous statements made to the buyer. To the extent you do encounter something that contradicts a previous statement, even if it's small and immaterial, it's critical that you proactively communicate to the buyer that you were mistaken or miscommunicated in your prior statements. Like a surprise, inconsistencies jeopardize trust.

NAVIGATE MISUNDERSTANDINGS

Communication is key during this phase of the sale process. The stakes are high, and everyone is stressed and on high alert, so it's easy for tensions to flare up. Even if you crafted the *perfect* LOI, you will inevitably encounter some challenging situations where you and the buyer have different expectations. For example, new circumstances will emerge that were unanticipated in the LOI with no framework for how to handle them.

The best approach is to acknowledge the matter and try to be reasonable in determining an appropriate solution. I would use this as your guiding framework: How would the offers have differed if this information had been known before signing the LOI? Be aware that the strength of your negotiating position also heavily influences how these matters can be handled. If push comes to shove, your most powerful card is to choose not to sell and take the company off the market.

RESOLVE ANY OWNERSHIP ISSUES EARLY

Few things derail a transaction faster than an internal dispute arising right ahead of closing. Roberts writes, "Promises of compensation or a share in the proceeds from the sale of a business . . . constitute a sleeper issue that, if inadequately addressed, can prove disastrous. Offhand remarks made or not made by owners can prove no less disastrous if minority shareholders and/ or key employees misinterpreted or imagined promises of greater compensation or greater shares in the proceeds pending the sale of the firm" (Roberts 2009, p. 47).

From my experience, a transaction's large sums of money are a magnet for drama. Ex-wives, former partners, and everything in between can come out of the woodwork. And those curveballs generally get thrown right before closing while the individual feels emboldened with leverage – they know there's a limited window for a buyer to remain interested, extorting you to pay up. Try to anticipate and resolve any ambiguities as early as possible.

Ultimately, in the purchase agreement, you will need to represent that there are no other relevant claims. To the extent that disgruntled parties do come forward after a sale announcement, you will *personally* be liable to reimburse the company for any claims made.

TOP 3 TAKEAWAYS

- Confirmatory due diligence is intended to independently verify all of the information that formed the basis of a buyer's offer and valuation. The tone of the relationship will change from courtship to scrutinizing in what many describe as a financial and legal colonoscopy.
- The buyer will bring in an army of third-party advisors whose job is to err on the side of conservatism. It's generally best to give them what they request because defensiveness may be interpreted as having something to hide. Maintaining speed is to your advantage.
- Successfully closing is predicated upon trust. Consequently, it is essential to never surprise the buyer. To the extent a negative development occurs, err on the side of communicating it immediately. Failure to do so may cause them to question your honesty and transparency.

CHAPTER 24

Legal Documentation
and Critical Elements

"More contracts to review?" Alexandra looked at the stack in front of her. "I'm afraid so," I said. For newcomers to middle-market transactions, the sheer volume of legal documents often comes as a surprise. For the transaction to be consummated, every detail must be fully documented. The legal documents easily total more than 50,000 words across 100 or more pages. Given the contextual nature of most deals and the lack of universal definitions for many items, this means that there are hundreds or even thousands of potential micronegotiations.

Each legal agreement serves a specific purpose within the broader transaction. Here is a list of common legal documents you'll see within just a single transaction:

- Purchase agreement to effectuate the transaction. We'll deep dive into this in the next section.
- Escrow agreement to cover the mechanics and conditions of any escrows.
- Noncompetition agreements to restrict the owners from competing for a period of time.
- Employment or consulting agreement if the owner(s) will continue working post-closing.
- Leases for any related-party real estate.
- Financing agreements for any associated seller financing.
- Shareholder resolutions authorizing the execution of the agreement.
- Operating agreement to cover how the entity will be governed if the owner will own equity alongside the buyer.

- Transition services agreement if the seller's entity will continue providing services for a temporary period until the buyer can make alternative arrangements. This is most common when the deal is rushed, and there's not enough time to arrange for all of the loose ends prior to closing.

Your attorney will guide you to select the best approach given your specific circumstances, so I am going to skip covering mergers and acquisitions (M&A) law (if you are interested, I've listed excellent resources in the Bibliography). However, I do want to share a general overview of the primary document – the purchase agreement – and how the process unfolds.

PURCHASE AGREEMENT

The purchase agreement (often referred to as an asset purchase agreement or stock purchase agreement, depending on the deal's structure) is the one universal document found in every sale. The agreed-upon terms in the letter of intent (LOI) will be reflected in this document, along with all the corresponding details. A large portion of the document revolves around the allocation of risk between the buyer and seller under various circumstances. Aside from validating that the document accurately reflects the agreed-upon deal terms, here are some of the key elements to focus your attention on.

Reps, Warranties, and Indemnification

While the buyer has spent significant time scrutinizing the business, it's impossible for them to know as much about it as you do. Consequently, sellers are required to make representations (often referred to as *reps*) and warranties to the buyer regarding the condition of the business. This reaffirms all of the claims made by the seller and their advisors within the confidential information memorandum (CIM), management presentations, and information stored within the virtual data room (VDR). To the extent that there is a discrepancy, you could be held responsible for indemnifying the buyer for damages associated with the misrepresentation.

This section will have three or four dozen subsections, each making statements of fact about various aspects of your business. Your lawyer will spend an overwhelming percentage of their time debating just three areas:

- What are the definitions of "materiality" and "knowledge"? Specifically, if your managers know about something or you should have known after doing reasonable inquiry, are you responsible?
- How long are you liable for any inaccuracies?
- What is your total potential financial liability?

If the statement is not completely accurate, the lawyers modify the language to make it correct or create a corresponding disclosure schedule listing all relevant exceptions. These schedules can also be used to document files that were previously shared with the buyer. Collectively, all of these disclosure schedules can total dozens or even hundreds of pages.

The most important rule to remember is that you can't be held liable for things you disclose. Some clients jokingly refer to this process as the "confessional." Therefore, it's important that you carefully review the accuracy of each of the reps and their corresponding disclosure schedules in great detail with your senior management team and lawyer. You need to think carefully because seemingly minor events from years back may be relevant and need to be disclosed. The buyer will carefully review each of the disclosed items on the schedules, which frequently leads to follow-up questions.

A REAL-LIFE REPRESENTATION

"To Seller's Knowledge, each of Seller's employees or independent contractors is authorized to work in the jurisdiction where he or she provides services to Seller. Other than as indicated on Schedule 4(f)(ii), each independent contractor of Seller has executed the standard independent contractor agreement."

To the extent that the seller has any applicable individuals who have *not* signed the standard agreement, they would need to be listed on Schedule 4(f)(ii).

Indemnification – Paying for Breaches

Indemnification requires the seller to reimburse the buyer for damages resulting from an associated misrepresentation. In every transaction, some minor unforeseen expenses emerge. To disincentivize buyers from nickel-and-diming, indemnification is typically subject to a deductible. Creative insurance professionals designed a policy that covers potential liability associated with certain breaches, called rep and warranty insurance. I find this is a great solution to maximize the seller's cash at closing (since they enable much smaller escrows) and allows them to feel off the hook. However, these policies cover unknown liabilities and typically exclude any major known issues. The price tends to be around 2–4% of the policy limit, and the cost is customarily split between the buyer and the seller. For this to be available and make economic sense, transactions generally need to involve at least $50 million.

Escrows

To protect themselves from potential shortfalls or liabilities, the buyer typically withholds a portion of the purchase price (called an escrow) and deposits it in a separately managed account held by a third party (generally a bank or law firm). This is similar to the earnest money a lawyer holds when you make an offer on a home. Once the conditions are met, the money is released to the seller. Each escrow typically operates independently. Here are the most usual kinds:

- Working capital escrow. Covers any shortfalls in the amount of working capital delivered at closing relative to what was promised. Generally, 90 days post-closing, there's a reconciliation process to ensure a sufficient amount was provided. This escrow typically represents 1–2% of purchase price.
- Indemnification escrow. Covers any indemnification payment the seller may owe due to liabilities associated with the representations and warranties (see Indemnification section). It typically is released in increments over 12–24 months and ranges between 5–10% of the purchase price – this amount is significantly reduced if the parties utilize representations and warranty insurance.
- Liability-specific escrow. While relatively uncommon, this covers specific contingent liabilities or risks that were identified and will remain the responsibility of the seller (e.g. litigation, discharging loan encumbrances). The amount and timing depend on the specific matter at hand.

Simultaneous vs. Deferred Closing

In a simultaneous signing and closing, closing and funding occur at the time of signature. Alternatively, a deferred closing involves signing the documents with closing sometime in the future once specific conditions have been met. Before moving forward, buyers frequently require approvals or consents from various third parties (e.g. regulators, landlords, major customers, employees) who are unaware of the transaction. A deferred closing allows the seller to publicly disclose the deal while having the confidence of a binding agreement. Nevertheless, there's always a small element of risk since the seller may fail to meet the closing requirements or something may occur that significantly reduces the value of the business (considered a material adverse event). According to the American Bar Association's Private Target Mergers & Acquisitions Deal Point Study (Pearlman and Paterno 2023), more than 80% of middle-market transactions use a deferred closing.

Getting the Calculations Right

Lawyers are experts at contracts but are generally not privy to the implications of certain definitions and the context of how they might impact you financially. This leaves a potential gap if the bankers, accountants, and CFO are not in sync. Buyers frequently take advantage of this vulnerability, and millions of dollars are easily at stake. The CFO is generally responsible for administering the agreement post-closing, so it's essential that they are fully versed on the *details* of the agreement.

While calculating future earnouts can be problematic, working capital is almost always challenging. This is because it's a moving target that fluctuates daily, and we're always looking at it in the rearview mirror – financials are not completed until a couple of weeks after the month's end. The exact methodology and what is included or excluded in the net working capital target can have a real financial impact. Some areas with major implications include:

- Cash or accrual basis of accounting.
- Difference between month-end and year-end accruals: Many companies only record bonuses in December rather than on a monthly basis.
- Impact of any EBITDA (earnings before interest, taxes, depreciation, and amortization) adjustments or pro forma adjustments on the balance sheet.
- Treatment of old or obsolete inventory.
- Handling aged and nonoperating related accounts receivables and payables.

To minimize the chances of games or surprises, I typically require that the agreement stipulate that the methodology must remain consistent whenever measuring something over time. Otherwise, the buyer has the opportunity to intentionally tilt the playing field by changing definitions or the measurement process.

HOW THE PROCESS UNFOLDS

Around halfway through the exclusivity period, your attorney should receive an initial draft of the purchase agreement. While some stray outstanding diligence issues may remain, there's typically a shift to a closing mentality, with the lawyers now taking the lead. It's customary for the buyer to present an initial draft for the various agreements. It's important to note the party creating the first draft has an implicit advantage because it's easy to bury seemingly *unimportant* language that can be meaningful within your specific context. Of course, your attorney will carefully review and provide *redline* comments to their proposed language, but there's a limit to how much they can adjust before your counterparty starts saying your counsel is nitpicking and being unreasonable.

Legal ethics prevent the buyer's lawyers from communicating directly with you – everything must occur through your counsel. Your attorney will forward you the received drafts along with an *issues list* that they will prepare, which identifies in "plain English" all of the concerning areas, along with recommendations for how to handle the associated issues.

Based on your feedback, your attorney will redline or mark up the draft. Rather than negotiating through e-mail, I highly recommend that both attorneys speak – walking through the various issues and their rationales for their positions and trying to collaboratively resolve them. Otherwise, it's easy for one side to insert something and the other to remove it through multiple iterations. Impasses on issues are to be expected. This is when it's important for you and your banker to periodically reconvene and hash business issues out. In parallel with all of these efforts, the buyer's operations team will likely work with you to develop an integration and communications strategy.

MANAGING YOUR MINDSET AND STAMINA

If the scrutinizing tone of the confirmatory due diligence came as a shock, be ready for an even more adversarial experience. There are hundreds of details to negotiate within a short time, and transactional attorneys, by design, focus on the downside. The overwhelming majority of these details involve allocating risk in circumstances that are *extremely* unlikely to occur. Unfortunately, these negotiations are generally a zero-sum game where reducing risk for one party inevitably ends up with greater uncertainty for the other. Buyers always want more certainty and protection, while sellers want the freedom to walk away without strings attached (Figure 24.1).

Ultimately, there is no *winner*. The goal is to find a middle ground that both parties are willing to accept. This is highly influenced by the relative negotiating leverage between them. From my experience, both parties will leave these negotiations feeling slightly disappointed. Impasses will likely occur various times across multiple issues, and you may start feeling the buyer is being unreasonable. Many sellers will want to walk away. Conversely, others start caving in on various points out of fear of losing the deal or wanting to just get this over with. That outcome is equally

FACTOR	SELLER PREFERENCE	BUYER PREFERENCE
Rep strength	Weak	Strong
Definition of "material"	Limited & specific	Broad
Definition of "knowledge"	Limited to actual knowledge	Wide encompassing definition
Survival of representations	Short	Long

FIGURE 24.1   Typical seller and buyer positions for key elements of a purchase agreement.

unattractive because buyers who smell blood in the water will find ways to take advantage.

The last few weeks are generally the most nerve-racking because it's difficult for a novice to differentiate deal brinkmanship from a true near-death experience. However, the collective time, money, and commitment sunk by both parties creates a powerful momentum that generally forces a solution.

Take a disciplined, systematic approach to addressing your differences with the buyer, and weigh their relative economic value. That said, there will be some circumstances where the buyer will not budge, and you'll have to make a call. Always compare these terms and the final transaction value to your realistic alternatives if you don't close.

If you're like most sellers, you will be overwhelmed trying to review and digest the volume of documents while juggling the remaining diligence requests and continuing to operate the business. Unfortunately, much of this can only be done by you and cannot be outsourced to others. You will inevitably feel fatigued, stressed, and anxious, but you are almost there. Stay strong!

YOU ARE THE ULTIMATE DECISION-MAKER

The sale process involves multiple outside advisors, each with their own set of incentives and objectives. In particular, lawyers often want to take the most conservative position possible to protect their clients. Combined with their hourly billing structure, there can be the tendency to endlessly fight over relatively minor issues. Continually challenge your advisors to frame hotly contested negotiations from a cost–benefit standpoint, discussing both the likelihood and magnitude of various theoretical risks.

Similarly, ask your attorney to explain what is reasonable and customary given the circumstances. Various legal surveys track the frequency of legal clauses within M&A deals. Attorneys frequently start with an unrealistic negotiating position with the goal of eventually compromising somewhere in the middle. Have them explain the realistic likelihood of achieving those requests and the broader intended outcome. Otherwise, through the various rounds of negotiations, many sellers feel that they are giving in on every issue. I've unfortunately seen some threaten to walk away because they perceived the negotiations as completely one-sided – unsurprisingly, many of the buyers felt the same way.

Remember, this is your deal. Your advisors work for you, not the other way around. Don't be afraid to make the final decisions – you've successfully built your business by taking calculated risks, and only you have the full context regarding your business' vulnerabilities and, ultimately, your risk tolerance. Tell your advisors what you want so they can get you the best possible result on your terms. Ultimately, you will be held responsible for everything within these agreements, so it's vital that you take the time to understand what you are committing to.

TOP 3 TAKEAWAYS

- The purchase agreement represents the core of various legal documents needed to effectuate a transaction. Given its length, expect numerous micronegotiations over the finer details. Most of these will involve the allocation of risk under various improbable circumstances.
- The calculation and mechanics of working capital and any required adjustments are frequently one of the most challenging topics. Involving your CFO and accounting advisors in these discussions is vital as they are best positioned to understand the implications of various approaches.
- The sales process is an exhausting emotional roller coaster. You may find yourself wanting to walk away. Before doing so, make sure to compare the outcome against your likely alternatives. You are the final decision-maker and will need to make difficult judgment calls.

CHAPTER 25

Closing Craziness

Sandy slumped in his chair. "I guess it's really happening." I told him the finish line was in sight, but not to completely let down his guard. I explained that in the days leading up to closing, there would be a rush of last-minute issues to resolve. I told him that, unfortunately, some items are purposefully designed to occur immediately before closing. For example, the absolute most accurate estimate for the level of working capital being delivered at closing can only happen right before. He nodded. "I'm ready for this to be done." He paused. "When will I get my money?"

The buyer's attorneys prepare a checklist of all outstanding items that must be resolved and executed to officially close the transaction. This will serve as a project management tool that both sides can use in their daily calls. The most stressful items on the checklist tend to be obtaining consents or approvals from various third parties, who are generally in no hurry. To expedite the process, call in every favor you can. Similarly, based on prior lien searches, the buyer will generally require that you pay off and obtain a *discharge letter* from the corresponding creditor proving that there's no outstanding liability. Most clients are surprised to discover the number of outstanding liens they had no clue about. Some are long-forgotten holdovers, while others are small balances from minor suppliers who sell on credit.

The buyer will also prepare and share a "flow of funds" document that delineates exactly where each penny of the purchase price is going, along with the associated bank account information for each recipient. Triple-check its accuracy! Notify your bank to expect a large wire transfer so they can prepare accordingly. Otherwise, there's the risk that the unusually large receipt gets flagged – and is then stuck in the bank's bureaucracy for days.

The actual closing day tends to be hectic as there are always a few remaining matters, and everyone's nerves are frayed. It's not uncommon to have one or two minor holdout items. It's the buyer's option to choose to waive these items. From my experience, they generally agree, so long as the outstanding issues are small and low risk. Dennis Roberts observes, "There is always something that comes up at the last minute that seems like a deal-killer but usually isn't. Unless something drastic comes up at the last minute, the sheer momentum of emotional commitment (the parties never admit it, but it is powerful and always there) will carry the day." He jokingly describes the sentiment as "sheer boredom interspersed by moments of pure terror" (Roberts 2009, p. 252).

Modern agreements can be signed by each party separately. Both you and the buyer will sign all of the documents, and your lawyer will hold them in escrow until all of the signatures have been obtained. At that point, all completed documents will be circulated, and the wire transfers will be authorized. All that remains is an agonizing wait to see the money hit your bank account. I've had clients call me a dozen times in a single hour to see if I've received anything.

While you'll inevitably celebrate, if you're like most sellers, you'll go straight home to catch up on some sleep. Once the dust settles after a few weeks or months, it's customary to schedule a closing dinner with everyone involved to celebrate, commiserate, and thank them for all of their hard work and help.

POST-CLOSING TRANSITIONS

You've built a successful business, and you want to see it succeed. Moreover, you likely have a strong financial incentive to ensure that the transition occurs smoothly and successfully. As a result, the immediate aftermath is generally no less hectic than the period before. This is because many transitional activities and communications must occur within 24 to 48 business hours after closing.

The change can be stressful for your staff and suppliers. To the extent you continue to run operations and maintain some stake in the business, the transaction can often be played down and framed as a nonevent. Specifically, it can be referred to as *recapitalization,* where you bring on board another investor to help fuel the business's future growth. It's ideal to have representatives of the buyer participate alongside you in these meetings. To get the most bang possible from the first impression, coordinate who is going to say what and the major themes to emphasize.

Fear travels quickly, so you need to proactively manage the message and alleviate the concerns of your various stakeholders. Having a specific communication game plan beforehand will minimize anxiety and improve the chances of things running smoothly. For each of your stakeholders, I recommend crafting a bulleted fact sheet summarizing the main talking points you want to convey. Each of them will view the transaction through the lens of what it means for them. Consistency in messaging is important because word will eventually reach other groups. Most of the time, there should be no need to sugarcoat things: A buyer pursued your business because it's successful, viable, and growing.

Breaking the News to Employees

Employees will understandably have anxiety. They'll wonder whether their jobs are at risk. Your messaging should be upbeat. Thank your employees for all their hard work, loyalty, and support, share some fond memories of your time, and wrap up with a brief explanation of why you decided to sell. If a new CEO is taking over, introduce the new boss, who takes it from there.

The buyer should emphasize the positive aspects that attracted them to the company and stress that the team is a crucial component of the company's success. Future growth potential should be emphasized. Lean on your senior managers to allay fears and provide their reports with a time and venue to ask questions and feel heard. It's crucial for them to acknowledge the uncertainty and worry while avoiding making promises that could lead to future regrets.

Notifying Major Customers and Suppliers

You and your team should create a prioritized list of customers and suppliers to reach out to based on their importance and potential risk. Visit the most important clients and vendors in person and make a phone call to the others. It's impossible for you to handle all of these discussions yourself, so you should delegate the communication to your other trusted senior executives. The lowest-priority stakeholders can be informed by their respective sales representatives or with a mass e-mail, with an offer to speak if desired. Regardless, proactively reaching out is important as some customers may feel slighted if they don't get the courtesy of being informed.

The general message should emphasize the plan to continue business as usual. Emphasize the importance of the relationship and the desire to further build upon it. To keep everyone on script, provide your team with a bulleted fact sheet.

RELEASE OF ESCROWS

Typically, 90 days post-closing, a true-up calculation is performed where any discrepancies in working capital are fully resolved. This provides sufficient time for the buyer to fully analyze the true state of working capital after taking control of the business. The escrow is used to fund any deficiencies in the amount of working capital delivered at closing relative to the agreed-upon target. Anything remaining gets released back to the seller. Conversely, if the amount delivered was more than anticipated, the entire escrow gets released back to the seller, plus the buyer will pay dollar-for-dollar for any excess above the target.

The potential for disputes arises when the new ownership takes over the accounting post-closing and claims to have discovered items improperly recorded on the balance sheet. The purchase agreement typically lays out the exact procedure for resolving these disputes.

Similarly, indemnification escrows are typically released in stages over time. For example, it's common for 50% to be released after 12 months and the remaining 50% to be released after two years. The logic is that this period should provide the buyer with sufficient time to fully inspect the business and file any relevant claims for inaccuracies.

TOP 3 TAKEAWAYS

- Closing is chaotic. While holdout items may seem like the deal is going to die, the sheer momentum of emotional commitment means it's likely to be successfully resolved.
- Post-closing, your involvement in communicating and various handoffs will be critical in ensuring a seamless transition.
- Escrows will be released over the coming 3 to 24 months, as provided in the initial purchase agreement.

CHAPTER 26

Managing Your Emotions and Psychology

I caught up with one of my clients about a year after the sale. "How's it going?" He smiled and said that the first six months were amazing. He and his wife took some "once-in-a-lifetime" trips. He improved his golf score. They visited friends and family in a new RV. "Sounds great," I said. "Yeah." He paused. "If I'm being completely honest, not having the business isn't quite as much fun as I thought it would be. It's been harder than I expected." I told him that was a common experience for founder/owners who devoted the better part of their lives to a company, only to hand it over after a sale.

Selling your business is a psychological process as much as a financial one. It's similar to becoming a parent in that you never really know what you're getting into until you experience it. And while you may normally have ice running through your veins, staying calm grows more difficult when life-changing amounts of money are at stake – likely a sum that's an order of magnitude larger than any other you've ever been personally involved with.

Brent Beshore offers a bit of insight into the emotional roller coaster. "A transaction is going to be an emotionally challenging and draining process. Expect nothing less," he writes in *The Messy Marketplace*. "I've never heard of a deal going 'smoothly.' You will have moments of doubt, feelings of losing control, and misaligned expectations. You will get confusing and conflicting advice. The pace will be too fast, except when it's too slow. You will encounter expected and unpredictable experiences. There is no perfect buyer, no perfect lawyer, no perfect [investment banker], and no perfect seller, you included" (Beshore 2018, pp. 9–10).

SELF-SABOTAGE IS REAL

While some business owners want to exit no matter what, most have the luxury of choosing not to sell. While this is good in providing you with a strong hand at the negotiating table, it also creates room for a seller to change their mind or to self-sabotage. Over the course of a transaction, I observe one out of two clients exhibiting behaviors inconsistent with their objectives. While I try to prepare them for the moment, they still frequently defy advice that is logical and unbiased. Generally, this happens when emotions get the best of them.

The inner workings of the human brain remain a medical mystery, and I'm no psychologist, but I believe that once the transition begins to feel real, the seller gets scared and subconsciously finds reasons not to do the deal. The status quo always feels safer and more comforting than the unknown sales process and future.

FIND SUPPORT

Self-care is crucial during this trying process. Don't forget to get as much sleep and exercise as possible. Maintaining healthy habits will be a challenge, but doing so often helps you keep your sanity. Another piece of hard-won advice: Try to communicate. This process is much easier if you can speak with others rather than hold it all in. Lean on your advisors and board if you have one. Otherwise, engage with a close circle of trusted advisors and tap into their common sense.

Also, you cannot underestimate the importance of having a supportive life partner. When times get tough, they can cheer you along and remind you why you're doing this in the first place.

PREPARE FOR LIFE POST-TRANSACTION

A sale is viewed as the rewarding conclusion of a successful entrepreneurial journey. And given the odds, it truly is a remarkable achievement. However, the entrepreneur's life must continue beyond an exit. The Type A personality common among entrepreneurs and owners results in similar emotional reactions and predictable patterns. It's vital to go into this process with eyes wide open so you can prepare yourself psychologically ahead of time. When you are armed with a game plan, this event presents not just a life-changing financial windfall but also an exciting opportunity to design your future life based on your unique dreams, preferences, and circumstances.

EXPERTISE DOESN'T ELIMINATE EMOTIONS

I've been through the wringer as a seller myself. I had over a decade of relevant experience when I exited my first major private equity (PE) investment. The transaction was relatively plain vanilla, but the business had a limited universe of relevant buyers, making the outreach particularly long and arduous. This was all amplified by the fact that the results would be life-changing for my family and me. I was a basket case. Thankfully, I recognized that a third-party advisor would be able to negotiate far more effectively. They also served as my shrink and counseled me throughout the process.

Expect Changes

After you're out of your company, the pace of your life quickly decelerates from 100 miles per hour to a virtual standstill (Figure 26.1). Whenever a transition occurs, best practice is to have a clean exit from the prior leader to fully empower the incoming one. This means that you go from being the center of all the action and attention to being totally out of the loop. Particularly when you see the business moving along and succeeding without you, it can feel like getting rejected by your own child or getting fired. Only after the fact do my clients realize how much their egos crave people needing them in order to feel important and valued.

ARRIVAL PARADOX

Many sellers experience mixed emotions during and after the sale process, with a common set of patterns. Harvard professor Tal Ben-Shahar coined the term "arrival paradox" to describe the reality that an accomplishment never makes us as happy as we had anticipated.

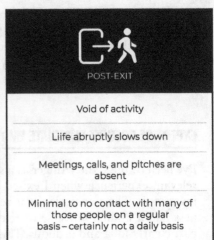

PRE-EXIT	POST-EXIT
Center of a swirl of activity	Void of activity
Life operates at 100 miles per hour	Liife abruptly slows down
Days are filled with meetings, calls, and pitches	Meetings, calls, and pitches are absent
Plentiful social contact with employees, customers, vendors, and industry peers	Minimal to no contact with many of those people on a regular basis – certainly not a daily basis

FIGURE 26.1   Comparison of life pre- and post-exit.
Reprinted with the permission of the Yale School of Management from
What's Next: The Entrepreneur's Epilogue and the Paradox of Success by
Jeanne Odendaal, Rick Eigenbrod, A. J. Wasserstein, Mark Agnew, and
Brian O'Connor.

This is best known and documented among Olympic medalists, who
often experience post-glory malaise or depression. After they achieve their
overarching life objective, they realize that they have likely achieved the biggest accomplishment they ever will – and it's only downhill from there.

Business owners frequently experience something similar after selling.
After dedicating so much of themselves to the business, as if it were a child,
it's common to experience a certain level of distress when it's gone.
A.J. Wasserstein explains, "Before the exit, the entrepreneur's life is filled
with structure and meaning; they wake each day with a clear mission as a
CEO: lead, build value, grow, and drive operational and customer service
excellence. After the exit, there is a sense of being adrift" (Odendaal
et al. 2020, p. 3).

Psychologists have observed that this void often causes sellers to experience symptoms of mourning as they lose a sense of identity, meaning, and
structure. In other words, you've won, but you've also lost some vital parts
of your being; aspects that are crucial to your happiness and mental health.

Finding a New Identity

As CEO, you automatically sit at the center of your business's universe.
Bankers, suppliers, and service providers jockey for time on your calendar.

You are admired and respected in the community. Your sacrifices and hyper-focus on building the business often came at the expense of other facets of your life. Consequently, your sense of identity is frequently wrapped up in the business and your role as CEO.

Once the business is sold, much of this attention evaporates. It's difficult to go from king of your universe to irrelevant, but that's essentially what happens. Moreover, it isn't easy to define yourself without the business as context. Even addressing that most innocent conversation starter – "What do you do?" – can turn awkward. Returning to your old life is impossible; that prior *you* is gone. Remember that guy who kept showing up to college parties because he just couldn't move on? Clinging to the past is not productive and only delays arriving at a new, exciting future.

Searching for Meaning

Your life as an owner also gives you purpose. Running a company can feel like an intoxicating adventure. Being responsible for supporting your employees' families often provides a sense of purpose. Moreover, the team's camaraderie and shared mission create a bond. When the company is *winning*, success is addicting. The social circles of owners also tend to be intertwined with their work activities.

This is lost with the sale of the business, leaving owners without a forcing mechanism to stretch and accomplish goals.

Lack of Structure

Work revolves around consistent daily, weekly, and seasonal rituals that can help to mark the passing of time. Without this structure, days bleed onto each other. All of these activities to look forward to are now gone. If there's no workweek, Saturday has no significance. To fill the void, it's not uncommon to start injecting yourself into your spouse's routines and areas of responsibility – unsurprisingly, this can cause friction.

NEXT TASK – YOUR PERSONAL TRANSFORMATION

Unless they have prepared beforehand, sellers go through a predictable transition process. Initially, after closing, there will be a sense of euphoria, celebration, and relief. The newly free owner binges on travel, golf, and other leisure activities to catch up on everything they missed while building and selling the business. Contentment will be through the roof.

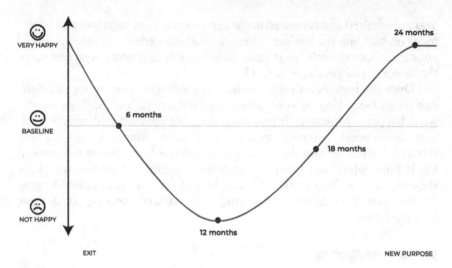

FIGURE 26.2 Typical emotional arc of a selling founder owner.
Reprinted with the permission of the Yale School of Management from
What's Next: The Entrepreneur's Epilogue and the Paradox of Success by
Jeanne Odendaal, Rick Eigenbrod, A. J. Wasserstein, Mark Agnew, and
Brian O'Connor.

But there is only so much leisure you can enjoy, only so many tennis
matches you can play – eventually, hard-charging owners become bored.
Leisure derives its value when it's balanced by work and effort. After a few
months, the new reality sets in, and sellers often start feeling lonely and
empty (Figure 26.2). This rudderless feeling pushes the seller to a low point
of happiness. Ultimately, owners reinvent themselves, and happiness rebounds
as they are reinvigorated by a new life.

DEALING WITH REGRET

At some point after the sale – often during some of these inevitable emotional
low points – a seller will feel some seller's remorse and question whether they
made the right choice. Some will wish for their old lives back. Others may
feel guilty about what happened to their employees. And others will feel the
new owners are ruining everything that was special about the company.
     Writes Beshore: "This is the point at which you'll need to remember
why you sold, the benefits of selling (financial and otherwise), and why you
chose the buyer you did" (Beshore 2018, p. 99). He suggests maintaining a
notebook during the process, documenting your objectives, decisions, and

their underlying rationales. When you're frustrated, you can walk through your earlier reasoning, which helps put current irritations in context.

Remorse is generally minimized when a seller feels they had a *good* exit. In his book *Finish Big*, Bo Burlingham shares common denominators among those who escape post-sale bitterness. These include feeling treated fairly and compensated appropriately, experiencing a feeling of accomplishment and peace, creating a new life outside of business, and pride that the business will survive without you.

DEVELOP A GAME PLAN

Because they're all in, dedicating everything they've got to ensure the business succeeds, few owners take the time to truly contemplate what life will be like after a sale. Most typically only think about being freed from the grinding daily duties of managing employees, making payroll, and the other burdensome responsibilities that come with leading a business.

While those responsibilities can be exhausting, they also gave you identity, meaning, and structure. Now that those things are gone, you need a plan to fill this void. This transition offers you an incredible and beautiful gift – the opportunity to apply your entrepreneurial talents and drive to reinvent yourself. The options are limitless, so the biggest challenge is to figure out what you want to do. Some key questions can help unearth this:

- What are the situations in which I am at my very best?
- What were my childhood dreams?
- What have I contributed to the world so far in my life?
- What do I still have to contribute to the world?
- What is my true identity?

Your plan will be highly personal. A spiritual leader or a life coach can be an excellent resource in helping you navigate this journey. From my experience, most sellers don't want to return to the stress of 80-hour work weeks – nor do they want to be 100% retired. Finding something in between is ideal, if challenging. Many sellers reorient their focus toward giving back, both financially and with their time.

MANAGING YOUR NEW WEALTH

After selling a successful middle-market company, you're likely financially independent. In some cases, your children and grandchildren are set, too. The objective now changes from becoming wealthy to *staying* wealthy.

This involves not only investing well but also controlling your spending. As one of my clients pointed out, being rich is expensive because all the toys must be maintained and protected. Wasserstein warns, "When every day feels like a blowout vacation, that becomes the norm, and it is no longer unique or special but can feel like a gilded treadmill, on which a bigger toy and more elaborate experiences are needed to achieve the next adrenaline rush. This cycle of consumption can be tricky and expensive. It is easy to fall into that trap of excess" (Odendaal et al. 2020, p. 16). And remember, this not only impacts you but also your entire family. You know how hard you had to work for your new wealth. Easy, quick wealth is disorienting and can be a curse to your children.

On the other end of the spectrum, the lack of a monthly salary can cause some people to assume a scarcity mindset, making them conservative and worried about running out of money – regardless of its amount.

FIND THE RIGHT ADVISORS

If you haven't already engaged one, you need to find a competent wealth advisor whom you trust to manage your money. They will provide relevant advice, serve as your psychologist to weather tough markets, and can assist with various other related areas, such as estate planning. Having a third-party advisor also greatly minimizes the burden on your spouse and family in case something were to happen to you. They are a source of stability that your loved ones can rely on. Here are the questions to ask when selecting the best advisor for you:

- Who is your typical client?
- How do you operate? Who will I be interacting with?
- What other services do you offer? How do you charge for them?
- Do you owe a fiduciary duty to me? Are you legally committed to always putting my interests first?
- Describe your investment approach and philosophy.
- Explain to me why you are recommending this specific allocation.
- Can I speak to a handful of your current clients?

BECOMING AN INVESTOR? TREAD CAUTIOUSLY

Many former business owners will decide to make direct PE investments. Take your time and err on the side of caution – take 12 months to acclimate before any major purchases or investments. As long as you go with eyes wide open about the illiquidity and risk, the strategy often makes a lot of sense. That said, being successful in running your specific business is a completely different skill set than becoming an effective PE investor.

TOP 3 TAKEAWAYS

- Selling your business is highly stressful and will test you psychologically. Many owners attempt to self-sabotage the deal at some point. Find and lean on support during this nerve-racking time.
- The type A personality among most business owners results in similar emotional reactions and predictable patterns. Your life will change, and most sellers experience, at some point, mixed emotions as they confront their loss of identity, meaning, and structure derived from work.
- This is an exciting opportunity to reinvent yourself. Proactively develop a game plan for what you want to do afterward as early as possible.

Postscript

We began with congratulations, and we end with congratulations. If you've read this far, you are serious about learning the ins and outs of selling your middle-market business with *confidence*. While nothing in life is guaranteed, I feel certain that if you pay attention to the principles I've outlined, assemble a strong and reliable team, and prepare yourself for what will be a difficult and stressful time, you will end your career as an entrepreneur with well-deserved pride in a job well done.

Entrepreneurs are the backbone of the American economy, and it is always an inspiration to hear their stories. It's truly an honor to work with them. Their drive and creative energy never cease to amaze me. It's one of the reasons I love my job and receive so much joy and fulfillment, helping them to obtain full value from their life's work. My North Star is to represent every client as if it were my family's business – using every tactic at our disposal to fight for every last penny.

You've worked hard. This is the final leg of the journey. May it be more rewarding than your wildest dreams.

I hope you received value from this book, and I wish you the best in your journey to sell and beyond. To the extent that you ever have questions or would like to share your experiences, please feel free to reach out directly to me: dmccombie@mccombiegroup.com. I'd love to hear from you.

Acknowledgments

I t's lot easier to read a book than to write one, but writing this book has been one of the most fulfilling efforts of my professional life. It allowed me to offer what I know in the hopes that I can make the process of selling a middle-market businesses as understandable and as straightforward as possible.

No one writes a book like this without the help of many others. Just as selling requires a team, so does producing a successful book. I'd like to acknowledge the assistance and sacrifice of those who have helped me along the way.

First and foremost, thank you to my wife and family for their patience and understanding during this monumental exercise. I wouldn't have even attempted it without your support. Similarly, to the entire McCombie Group team. You picked up a tremendous amount of slack while I dedicated the necessary time to write this book and I am grateful. I must also thank Kirby Rosplock for encouraging me to become an author as well as my Young Presidents' Organization (YPO) Forum who have pushed me to play big and have held me accountable.

From an editorial standpoint, I'd also like to express my deep gratitude to Woodeene Koenig-Bricker, Jeff Ostrowski, and Julie Kerr. This level of work quality could not have happened without you.

I'd also like to thank the numerous subject-matter experts who reviewed this book and provided relevant insights and feedback. These include Eddy Arriola, Ramiro Ortiz, John Chung, Emily Gresham, Ari Shedlock, Columba Alcantara, Michael Rodriguez, and Finn Graeff. You were truly instrumental in making my vision a reality.

And finally, to all my clients, past, present, and future. You have helped me as much as I have tried to help you.

About the Author

David W. McCombie III is founder and CEO of McCombie Group, an M&A advisory firm that helps mid-market owners sell their life's work at the best possible price and terms. He has personally negotiated billions in deals and has been recognized for setting record valuations. Unique among advisors, he has also successfully led various private equity investments himself.

An ongoing contributor to Forbes, he frequently shares his insights regarding deal-making. He is also an active member of the Young Presidents' Organization (YPO) and serves as Chair of its Investment Banking network. Prior to founding McCombie Group, he worked at McKinsey & Company and Citigroup Global Banking.

David graduated from Harvard Law School where he focused on M&A and negotiation, and also completed extensive finance coursework at Harvard Business School. His thesis, "Hispanic Private Equity – A Cultural Approach to Achieving Superior Investment Returns" was published in the Harvard Latino Law Review. He graduated Phi Beta Kappa from the University of Miami.

A naturally curious person, David finds joy in reading across topics and learning something from everyone he meets. He also loves boating on Biscayne Bay with his wife and two daughters.

Glossary

Every industry has its own specific jargon that can feel intimidating to outsiders. Here is a guide to common terms used in selling a middle-market company.

Addbacks   adjustments to the reported level of EBITDA to reflect the true economics that a buyer can expect to receive as an owner of the business post-transaction.

Add-on acquisition   a business that will be acquired and integrated into a platform company, most typically funded by private equity. While they are most usually smaller than the acquirer, they do not have to be.

Assign   the ability to transfer ownership or contractual rights to a new owner.

Auction   formally describes a competitive sales process where prospective buyers bid on an asset, with the highest offer winning. In the middle market, the term auction also describes a more informal process that provides the seller the leeway to further negotiate the various offers and the discretion to select whatever option it believes is best.

Closing   point in time when cash is wired, and title officially transfers from the seller to the buyer.

Collateral   an item of value pledged as security against the repayment of debt.

Committed capital   a pool of capital available to fund acquisitions that is contractually committed to a private equity fund.

Confidential information memorandum (CIM)   this is the primary document shared after a nondisclosure agreement (NDA) is signed that presents the business in sufficient detail that a prospective buyer could make an informed indication of interest (IOI). Often also referred to as the pitchbook, offering memorandum, or "the book."

Consideration   a form of payment that can be used to purchase a business. While cash is generally the most preferred form, other types include earnouts, seller notes, and rollover equity.

Due diligence   a comprehensive, independent investigation and verification of a business by a prospective buyer to gain sufficient comfort to proceed with the transaction.

Earnout   additional future payments to the seller based upon the company meeting or exceeding some predefined criteria.

EBITDA (earnings before interest, taxes, depreciation, and amortization)   calculated by taking net income and adding back any expenses associated with interest, taxes, depreciation, or amortization. This represents the pretax earnings of the business and is used as an imperfect proxy for cash flow.

Enterprise value the headline number everyone notes; this is the gross value of an entire business independent of any debt or cash the company keeps.

Equity ownership interest in a business entitling you to a corresponding portion of any distributions.

Escrow a separately managed account held by a third party in order to cover potential obligations, such as working capital, indemnification, or specific liabilities.

Family office the private investment arm of ultra-high-worth individuals, some of whom will consider making direct private equity investments.

Financial buyer buyers that make acquisitions as a way of generating financial returns on their investment.

Going concern while the formal accounting definition describes a business that can meet its financial obligations as they come due, it is generally used to describe a company that can continue indefinitely, independently of its owners.

Holdback a portion of the purchase price that is deferred until specific conditions have been met. These amounts are typically placed in escrow.

Indemnification requires the seller to reimburse the buyer or any other party for damages resulting from their actions, such as a misrepresentation.

Independent sponsor private equity investors that do not have a guaranteed source of capital and need to raise the necessary money on an individual, deal-by-deal basis.

Indication of interest (IOI) a preliminary nonbinding offer that indicates a general valuation range and terms that a buyer is willing to offer. It generally precedes the submission of a letter of intent and provides a seller comfort that they are in the same ballpark before investing time engaging with potential buyers.

Letter of intent (LOI) a nonbinding offer that details an offer's structure and terms with great specificity. This generally requires exclusivity from the seller, prohibiting them from engaging or negotiating with other prospective buyers for a stipulated amount of time.

Middle market medium-sized businesses between large publicly traded enterprises and small businesses. While there is a range of interpretations, I define this as companies with revenues between $10 million and $1 billion.

Multiple a multiplier applied against some financial or business metric (industry standard is EBITDA) used to calculate the value of a business. This provides a consistent metric that allows for comparison on a more apples-to-apples basis.

Nondisclosure agreement (NDA) a legal agreement that protects any sensitive, confidential information you share with a buyer. Often also known as a confidentiality agreement.

Off-market a deal opportunity occurring outside of a competitive process. This is typically associated with a less attractive price and terms to sellers.

Operating agreement legal document for recording the ownership of a corporate entity and outlining how decisions will be made and the rights and responsibilities of each respective owner.

Platform company   a business with sufficient financial scale to support the systems, technology, and managerial talent necessary to successfully acquire and integrate many small acquisitions at scale.

Portfolio company   used to describe a company that a financial investor owns or has an ownership stake in.

Preferred equity   equity with some debt-like protections, providing preference ahead of the common equity in a downside scenario. Structured equity is also frequently used.

Private equity (PE)   an investor acquiring private businesses with the objective of generating investment returns through distributions and/or capital appreciation. Often referred to as a financial buyer.

Purchase agreement   a final, binding legal agreement that describes the terms and conditions of transferring the business's equity or assets from the seller to the buyer.

Quality of earnings (QofE)   a rigorous independent financial review that attempts to substantiate the underlying financials, addbacks, and other adjustments in order to reflect the true, normalized earnings that a buyer can expect to receive post-transaction. This frequently involves analyzing the financial statements and addbacks and reconciling them to bank statements and tax returns.

Representations and warranties (reps and warranties)   assertions made by the seller in the purchase agreement regarding the true condition of the business.

Retrade   when one party attempts to renegotiate the purchase price or terms of the deal after they have been agreed upon in the letter of intent without a justifiable material misrepresentation.

Rollover   equity that a seller retains in the business alongside a new buyer.

Rollup   a consolidation strategy where a platform business acquires various other competitive or adjacent companies with the objective of increasing the collective valuation. Sometimes also referred to as a buy-and-build strategy.

Schedules   disclosures that accompany a purchase agreement listing relevant files that have been shared with the buyer or exceptions to specific representations and warranties.

Search fund   an investment structure where an entrepreneur raises capital from investors in order to search for, acquire, and operate a single business.

Seller note   financing offered by the seller to help the buyer fund a portion of the total purchase price.

Strategic buyer   a corporate acquirer within your sector that views an acquisition as a strategic business move, with the primary motivation of building up their competitive position (versus trying to achieve a financial return on investment on their capital).

Synergy   additional incremental value is obtained when two businesses are combined. This is typically associated with cost savings from eliminating duplicative overhead, greater collective efficiencies, or the ability to cross-sell additional products and services.

Teaser   a one-page document that can be widely shared among prospective buyers, presenting the highlights of your business and the investment opportunity without revealing your identity.

Unsecured loan   a loan based upon a business's cash flows, with no underlying collateral protection.

Virtual data room (VDR)   a repository where detailed backup information about the business is stored and shared in a digital format.

Working capital   formally defined as current assets (e.g. inventory, accounts receivables) minus current liabilities (e.g. accounts payable), this is the amount of capital needed to operate the business without requiring the buyer to inject additional money into the business. This is important because a defined amount must be delivered to the buyer at closing, or the purchase price will typically be adjusted accordingly.

Bibliography

Agrawal, A., Cooper, T., Lian, Q. and Wang, Q. (2023). Does hiring M&A advisors matter for private sellers? *Quarterly Journal of Finance*. https://pdxscholar.library.pdx.edu/busadmin_fac/299/ (accessed April 17 2024).

Beshore, B. (n.d.). *Do Diligence: Navigating the Due Diligence Process to a Deal*. Permanent Equity. https://www.permanentequity.com/diligence (accessed April 6 2024).

Beshore, B. (n.d.). *Welcome to Finding Middle Ground: Demystifying Deal Structure*. Permanent Equity. https://www.permanentequity.com/deal-structure-and-terms/intro (accessed April 6 2024).

Beshore, B. (2018). *The Messy Marketplace: Selling Your Business in a World of Imperfect Buyers*. Boring Books.

Brabrand, J. (2020). *The $100 Million Exit*. New Degree Press.

Bruner, R. (2004). *Applied Mergers & Acquisitions*. Hoboken, NJ: Wiley

Burlingham, B. (2014). *Finish Big*. New York: Penguin.

Cohen, H. (2003). *Negotiate This! By Caring, But Not T-H-A-T Much*. Warner Business Books.

Everett, C. (2023). *Private Capital Markets Report*. Los Angeles County: Pepperdine University. https://digitalcommons.pepperdine.edu/cgi/viewcontent.cgi?article=1015&context=gsbm_pcm_pcmr (accessed April 6 2024).

Filippell, M.A. (2011). *Mergers & Acquisitions Playbook: Lessons from the Middle-Market Trenches*. Hoboken, NJ: Wiley.

Frankel, M. (January 30 2023). First Conversion to LOI Session 3. *M&A Science Podcast*. https://www.mascience.com/podcast/first-conversation-to-loi-session-3 (accessed April 6 2024).

Freund, J.C. (1992). *Smart Negotiating: How to Make Good Deals in the Real World*. New York: Simon & Schuster.

GF Data M&A Report. (November 2023).

Gompers, P.A., Kaplan, S.N. and Mukharlyamov, V. (2014). What do private equity firms (say they) do? *SSRN Electronic Journal*. http://dx.doi.org/10.2139/ssrn.2447605 (accessed April 6 2024).

Marks, H. (2018). *Mastering the Market Cycle: Getting the Odds on Your Side*. New York: Harper Business.

Marks, K.H., Slee, R.T., Blees, C.W. and Nall, M.R. (2012). *Middle Market M&A: Handbook for Investment Banking and Business Consulting*. Hoboken, NJ: Wiley.

McDonald, M.B. (2016). *The Value of Middle Market Investment Bankers*. Fairfield, CN: Fairfield University.

Odendaal, J., Eigenbrod, R., Wasserstein, A.J., Agnew, M. and O'Connor, B. (2020). *What's Next: The Entrepreneur's Epilogue and the Paradox of Success*. New Haven: Yale School of Management.

Orosz, J. (2022). *The Exit Strategy Handbook: A Complete Guide to Preparing Your Business for Sale*. Morgan & Westfield.

Pearlman, J. and Paterno, T. (2023). Announcing the ABA's 2023 Private Target Mergers & Acquisitions Deal Points Study. American Bar Association. https://www.americanbar.org/groups/business_law/resources/business-law-today/2023-december/announcing-aba-2023-private-target-ma-deal-points-study/ (accessed April 6 2024).

Phillips, M. (January 26 2016). How accurate are estimated private company valuations? Pitchbook blog. https://pitchbook.com/blog/how-accurate-are-estimated-private-company-valuations#:~:text=For%20most%20professionals%2C%20a%2015,outside%20of%20that%2015%25%20threshold (accessed April 6 2024).

Reed Lajoux, A. (2019). *The Art of M&A: A Merger, Acquisition, and Buyout Guide*, 5e. New York: McGraw Hill.

Roberts, D.J. (2009). *Mergers & Acquisitions: An Insider's Guide to the Purchase and Sale of Middle Market Business Interests*. Hoboken, NJ: Wiley.

Robichaud, R., Kubasek, P. and High, W. (2017). *Sell Well: Understanding the M&A Process and Avoiding the Most Common Mistakes of Selling a Business*. CreateSpace Independent Publishing Platform.

Sakovska, T. (2022). *The Private Equity Toolkit: A Step-By-Step Guide to Getting Deals Done from Sourcing to Exit*. Hoboken, NJ: Wiley.

Seiler Tucker, M. and Lechter, S. (2021). *Exit Rich: The 6 P Method to Sell Your Business for Huge Profit*. Austin, TX: Greenleaf Book Group.

Simon, J. (2021). *Search Funds & Entrepreneurial Acquisitions: The Roadmap for Buying a Business and Leading It to the Next Level*. Victoria, BC: Tellwell Talent.

U.S. Securities and Exchange Commission. (September 14 2017). Investor Bulletin: Financial Professionals' Use of Professional Honors – Awards, Rankings, and Designations. https://www.sec.gov/oiea/investor-alerts-and-bulletins/ib_professionalhonors#:~:text=While%20in%20some%20cases%20this,abilities%20of%20the%20financial%20professional (accessed April 6 2024).

Tepper, M. (2014). *Walk Away Wealthy: The Entrepreneur's Exit-planning Playbook*. Austin, TX: Greenleaf Book Group.

Warrillow, J. (2021). *The Art of Selling Your Business: Winning Strategies & Secret Hacks for Exiting on Top*. Austin, TX: Greenleaf Book Group.

Index